Borders & Borderlands
as Resources in the Horn of Africa

EASTERN AFRICA SERIES

* forthcoming

Borders & Borderlands
as Resources in the Horn of Africa

Edited by

DEREJE FEYISSA
& MARKUS VIRGIL HOEHNE

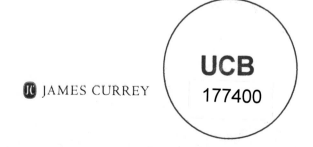

James Currey
www.jamescurrey.com
is an imprint of Boydell & Brewer Ltd
PO Box 9, Woodbridge, Suffolk IP12 3DF, UK
and of Boydell & Brewer Inc.
668 Mt Hope Avenue, Rochester, NY 14620, USA
www.boydellandbrewer.com

British Library Cataloguing in Publication Data
Borders and borderlands as resources in the Horn of Africa.
-- (Eastern Africa series)
1. Borderlands--Horn of Africa. 2. Horn of Africa--
Boundaries.
I. Series II. Feyissa, Dereje. III. Hoehne, Markus Virgil.
963-dc22

ISBN 978-1-84701-018-6 (James Currey Hardcover)

Typeset in 10/11 pt Baskerville
by Long House Publishing Services, Cumbria, UK
Printed and bound in Great Britain by
by CPI Antony Rowe, Chippenham, Wiltshire

Contents

Contents

Maps, Tables & Charts

Preface

Anthropology, contemporary history, political science, and related disciplines are close to politics and, therefore, close to morality. This is not to imply that much of politics is shaped by morals. Such an assumption would surely lead us astray if we tried to use it to explain what actually happens. What I mean is that moral and normative appeals abound in political discourse, where morals are used as a discursive resource. This discourse is about 'legitimacy', 'corruption', 'failed' states, etc., and it judges states and other forms of organization by comparing their actual forms and outputs with a normative idea about what states or other organizations and institutions should be good for: the common good, justice, security, and so on. Functional thinking persists here. States and organizations are assumed to fulfil a function for the benefit of all of their citizens or members; and if these functionalist assumptions are contradicted by actual observation, they become subject to the two dominant forms of framing or reframing that are applied to social phenomena in our times, namely, juridification and medicalization. Issues such as oppression and poverty – until recently treated in terms of politics – become juridified as human rights issues or they become medicalized as social pathologies. Things are measured against standards of law or standards of health or other such standards. The Weberian ideal-type of statehood also comes into play here. A normative element clearly shines through in all variants of these discourses. And it is good that this is so. It is good that there are people who think about how the world ought to be.

The explanatory power of the many moralizing variants of social science, however, is low. Often moral assumptions and empirical observations are woven into a dense web, and that is not helpful for analytical purposes. Analysis is about taking things apart, not about combining them. In addition to engaging in politics – and that is what social scientists do when they become public intellectuals and give TV interviews – we should care about keeping alive a perspective in social science that abstains from value judgements and tries to describe the forces on the ground in their actual interplay. The realities described are not always beautiful, and that is why social scientists who abstain from such judgments and try to model the decisions of all actors, including both those we like and those we dislike, are often branded as cynics by others.

The contributors to this book examine the effects that borders have on real people on the ground, and the ways in which these people use borders in pursuing their own interests. Like cell membranes, state borders are semi-permeable. Cells are selective in what they let in and what they keep out. And some micro-organisms overcome these mechanisms of selectivity and succeed in intruding. Even at this cellular level, different 'actors' have different 'interests', although these terms sound a bit metaphorical, as we are dealing with entities that are not assumed to have consciousness.

The focus of this book is on local people in the borderlands, and even among these there are many differences. Some use state borders as resources; they instrumentalize them in developing political or economic strategies. State boundaries can only become a resource for some people at the exclusion of others. Obviously there would be no price differences for goods on each side of a border, and therefore no gain for smugglers, if everyone found it easy to smuggle. If that were the case, price differences would even out and smuggling would disappear. And there are many other examples of ways in which different people are affected by and use borders differently. Local herdsmen may be able to cross the border, while soldiers in uniform cannot do so – and so on. Different skills, interests, opportunities, rules, expectations, and bodies of knowledge allow things (including social constructs such as borders) to be or to become resources for some and not for others.

This differentiating perspective on various categories of people reflects the research interests (identity and difference) of the 'Integration and Conflict' programme of the Max Planck Institute for Social Anthropology, which I have the privilege to direct. It is in the framework of this programme that both editors of this volume have carried out their doctoral studies and postdoctoral projects. It was also the venue for the colloquium in which most of the other contributions to this volume originated.

To train young scholars is a by-product of a research institute. The main institutional aim is to gain knowledge. Sometimes, fortune lets the two combine. Then one learns from one's juniors. Another reward is to be able, from time to time, to be proud of one's products. Few people can boast of a Markus and a Dereje.

Günther Schlee
Halle/Saale

Editors' Preface

It all began back in 2005, when we shared an office at the Max Planck Institute for Social Anthropology in Halle/Saale, Germany, and occasionally chatted about current affairs in the Horn of Africa. We both had done research in border areas and among borderlanders, and were astonished by the high degree of resonance between our field materials. Together with our common friend, Tobias Hagmann, we contemplated the idea of holding a conference on borders in the Horn of Africa. Regrettably, Hagmann's participation came to an abrupt end due to other academic obligations. We would like to thank him for his fruitful engagement with our ideas as well as the continued moral support we received from him throughout the production process. Günther Schlee, the Director of the Max Planck Institute for Social Anthropology and Head of the Department I (Integration and Conflict), generously approved our plans.

Despite the fact that we circulated a call for papers expressing an explicit interest in state borders as *resources*, many of the abstracts we received approached borders as constraints rather than resources. Nevertheless, we received enough relevant responses to put together a conference in Halle/Saale from 6 to 8 September 2006 under the title, 'Divided They Stand: The Affordances of State Borders in the Horn of Africa'. It featured a good mixture of younger scholars, many of them from the region, and senior figures such as John Markakis and our most vivid and resourceful discussant, Christopher Clapham. Despite strong empirical case studies and the determined interventions of the organizers, a skeptical and normative undertone remained with regard to viewing borders as resources. Not all participants followed us in the 'post-conference' phase of further developing our approach on how borderlanders make the best of being divided. For this reason, we have included some new contributions that were not originally part of the conference, but that better fit the theme of the volume.

Editors' Preface

During the process of putting together this volume, a number of friends and colleagues were helpful. We wish to thank all the conference participants for lively discussions. John Markakis in particular helped us to sharpen our argumentation through his well-founded critical remarks. Günther Schlee, Luca Ciabarri, Markus Schlecker, Hussein A. Mahmoud, and Christopher Clapham commented on our conceptual framework at various stages in the development of the manuscript. The editors presented earlier versions of their introductory chapter at two conferences of the African Borderlands Research Network (ABORNE), in Edinburgh and Bayreuth, respectively. We profited from comments of the wider 'border and borderlands community' there. John Galaty and Michael Bollig engaged with all contributions as external reviewers and provided constructive criticism. Douglas Johnson and Lynn Taylor of James Currey Publishers offered the necessary guidance and advice for completing the work. Last but certainly not least, we wish to thank our families for patiently putting up with all the overtime hours we had to invest in the preparation of this volume.

Dereje Feyissa & Markus Virgil Hoehne
Halle/Saale

Notes on Contributors

Cedric Barnes studied for his BA and MA in African (Area) Studies at the School of Oriental and African Studies (SOAS), University of London. He undertook research in the Faculty of History at Trinity College, University of Cambridge, for a PhD entitled 'The Ethiopian State and its Somali Periphery, 1888-1948' (awarded in 2000). From 2001 to 2007 he researched and taught at SOAS in the Departments of Africa and History. He is the author of several articles in the *Journal of East African Studies*, *Social Identities*, and the *Journal of African Cultural Studies*, and of professionally commissioned analytical reports on the North-East Africa region. He joined the Africa Research Group in the UK Foreign and Commonwealth Office in September 2007, covering the Horn of Africa and Kenya.

Lee Cassanelli is Director of the African Studies Center and Associate Professor in the Department of History at the University of Pennsylvania. He is author of *The Shaping of Somali Society* (University of Pennsylvania Press, 1982), *Victims and Vulnerable Groups in Southern Somalia* (Research and Documentation Center, Immigration and Refugee Board, Ottawa, Canada, 1995), and numerous articles on Somali history and society. His co-edited book with anthropologist Catherine Besteman, *The Struggle for Land in Southern Somalia: The War Behind the War*, is now in its third printing (Westview Press, 1996, 2000, and Transaction, 2003). He is currently writing on the effects of the ongoing wars in the Horn of Africa on memory and the production of history in that region.

Christopher Clapham is an associate of the Centre of African Studies, Cambridge University, and editor of *The Journal of Modern African Studies*. He was previously at Lancaster University. His main area of interest is the international relations of Africa, and his books include *Africa and the International System: The Politics of State Survival* (1996) and *African Guerrillas* (edited 1998). He has a specialist interest in Ethiopia and the Horn of Africa.

Francesca Declich teaches anthropology in the Department of History at the University of Urbino, Italy. She has carried out fieldwork in Somalia since before the civil war and continued working with Somali Bantu refugees in Tanzania, Kenya and the US. She now directs an ethnological mission in Malawi and northern Mozambique co-funded by the Italian Ministry of Foreign Affairs, focusing on the Indian Ocean cultural corridor and slavery. Her articles are published in a number of specialized international journals.

Dereje Feyissa completed his PhD at the Max Planck Institute for Social Anthropology/Martin Luther University in Halle/Saale, Germany in 2003. He was a 21st century Centre of Excellence Fellow in the Department of Anthropology, Osaka University, Japan between 2003 and 2005, and has been a Research Fellow at the Max Planck Institute for Social Anthropology in Halle/Saale 2005-2007. Currently he works for the World Bank in Addis Ababa. He has lectured on Ethiopian history at the Alemaya University in Ethiopia and on Social Anthropology at the Martin Luther University and the University of Bayreuth in Germany. He is the author of a forthcoming book entitled *Playing Different Games: Paradoxes of Anywaa and Nuer Identification Strategies in Gambella, Ethiopia* (Berghahn Books) and of numerous articles on social inequality, identity and conflict, ethnic groups and the state, and customary institutions of conflict resolution.

Fekadu Adugna holds an MA in Social Anthropology from Addis Ababa University. He completed his PhD at the Max-Planck Institute for Social Anthropology in Halle/Saale, Germany in 2009 and currently works in Addis Ababa. His research is on the processes of identity construction around the Oromo-Somali borderlands in Southern Ethiopia where he conducted 14 months of field research. He has lectured on Ethiopian history at Debub University and Unity University College and on Social Anthropology at Addis Ababa University, Ethiopia.

Markus Virgil Hoehne holds an MA from Munich University and is PhD candidate at the Max Planck Institute for Social Anthropology in Halle/Saale, Germany. His research is on identity and conflict in northern Somalia (Somaliland and Puntland) where he conducted 22 months of field research between 2002 and 2009. He has lectured at the Martin Luther University in Halle/Saale. His publications include a co-edited volume (with Virginia Luling), *Peace and Milk, Drought and War: Somali culture, society and politics* (Hurst, 2010), a monograph on strategies of peaceful conflict settlement in Somalia (2002, in German), several peer-reviewed journal articles and book chapters as well as consultancy reports on Somalia and Horn-related topics.

Wolbert G.C. Smidt studied Philosophy/History of Humanities, Ethnology and International Law in Geneva, Berlin and Hamburg and holds a PhD in anthropology from Hamburg University (2005). Since 1999 he has been researcher and lecturer at the Asia-Africa-Institute, Hamburg University, and assistant editor of the *Encyclopaedia Aethiopica* at the Research Unit of Ethiopian Studies (Äthiopistik). In 2007 he was professeur invité at the École des Hautes Études en Sciences Sociales, Paris and in 2008 guest assistant professor at Mekelle University/ Tigray. His publications include *Afrika im Schatten der Aufklärung* (2000, 2008), *Ethiopia and Germany* (catalogue, 2005), *Discussing Conflict in Ethiopia* (edited with Kinfe Abraham, 2007), and dozens of articles.

Peter Wafula Wekesa is a lecturer in the department of History, Archaeology and Political Studies at Kenyatta University, Nairobi. He holds a PhD in History from Kenyatta University (2007) and has published several articles on the history of border community relations in East Africa and popular culture, in *African Development*, *Journal of Third World Studies*, *Eastern Africa Social Science Research Review*, *Chemichemi* and *Jahazi*.

Yasin Mohammed Yasin holds an MA in Development Studies at Addis Ababa University (2004), and has worked with the international human rights organization Target as Program Coordinator and as Executive Director of the Lucy Pastoral Development Initiative, a local NGO operating in the Afar region of Ethiopia. Since 2007, he has been a doctoral candidate at the University of Hamburg, Department of Political Science. His publications include journal articles and book chapters on the political history of the Afar and conflict dynamics in the Afar territories.

List of Acronyms

ACANA	Anywaa Community Association in North America
AFIS	Italian Trusteeship Administration
AJC	Anywaa Justice Council
BBC	British Broadcasting Corporation
BMA	British Military Administration
EAC	East African Community
ELF	Eritrean Liberation Front
EPLF	Eritrean People's Liberation Front
EPRDF	Eritrean People's Revolutionary Democratic Front
EU	European Union
FDRE	Federal Democratic Republic of Ethiopia
FRUD	Front pour le Restauration de l'Unité et la Democratie
GPDUP	Gambella People's Democratic Unity Party
GPLM	Gambella People's Liberation Movement
GPNRS	Gambella People's National Regional State
GRO	Gambella Relief Organization
GTZ	Gesellschaft für Technische Zusammenarbeit
HAVOYOCO	Horn of Africa Volunteer Youth Organization
MP	Member of Parliament
NARCK	National Rainbow Coalition Kenya
NFD	Northern Frontier District of Kenya
NGO	Non-Governmental Organization
NPUA	Northern Peoples' United Association
NRS	National Regional State
OAU	Organization of African Unity
OLF	Oromo Liberation Front
OPDO	Oromo People's Democratic Organization
SALF	Somali Abo Liberation Front
SAMO	Somali African Muki Organization
SNM	Somali National Movement
SPLA	Sudan People's Liberation Army
SSDF	Somali Salvation Democratic Front
TFG	Transitional Federal Government
TGE	Transitional Government of Ethiopia
TNG	Transitional National Government
TPLF	Tigrean People's Liberation Front
UN	United Nations
USC	United Somali Congress
UNHCR	United Nations High Commissioner for Refugees

One

State Borders & Borderlands
as Resources
An Analytical Framework

DEREJE FEYISSA & MARKUS VIRGIL HOEHNE

Introduction

In this introductory chapter we offer an analytical framework for researching the resourcefulness of state borders as institutions and borderlands as territories, which is substantiated by the case studies in this volume. The case studies are drawn from the Horn of Africa and eastern Africa, and involve the borders of Djibouti, Eritrea, Ethiopia, Sudan, Somalia, Somaliland, Puntland, Kenya, Uganda and Tanzania. The object of the research is how people who live along and are divided by state borders have adjusted to the borderland situation, and what strategies they use in order to extract different types of resources from borders and borderlands. By resources we refer to immaterial resources such as social relations (across the border), the placement within the territorial, political, or social landscape, or any kind of claim that can be made with regard to state borders and/or borderlands in order to attain social, economic, or political benefits. We also distinguish between borders and borderlands on the following grounds. By borders we mean the institution of inter-state division according to international law; borderlands, on the other hand, are territorially defined as the physical space along the border – on both sides of it (Baud and Van Schendel 1997: 216). Borders and borderlands mutually define one another; the existence of the border constitutes the borderland. We specifically engage with borders as institutions that can be made use of, and borderlands as fields of opportunity for the people inhabiting them.

Borders in Africa have generally been conceived as barriers, whereas they also provide what Asiwaju and Nugent (1996) call 'conduits and opportunities'. As elsewhere in the continent, the academic discourse on state borders in the Horn of Africa is largely focused on the constraints side. Frequently, the Horn is associated with natural and man-made

1

catastrophes, which often have a cross-border dimension, and with violent border conflicts. Many local people as well as external observers perceive the arbitrary colonial borders as one of the causes for these conflicts. In his in-depth study on the early post-colonial border wars of Somalia with Ethiopia and Kenya, Matthies (1977: 6) observed that Africa is the continent of border wars 'par excellence', due to its artificial borders that served colonial interests and disregarded local ethnic and economic conditions. Christopher Clapham (1996a: 237–241) identified three forms of competing conceptions of boundary and territory in the Horn: the territorial (state) nationalism of highland Ethiopia,[1] the expansive pastoral system of the Somali and the Afar, and the ethno-nationalist system of the Oromo. As Clapham noted, these clashing concepts of boundary have contributed to the appalling conflicts in the region (ibid.: 237).[2] Schlee (2003) stressed that the map of the Horn was constantly redrawn over the past decades according to (identity) political considerations, which resulted in the escalation of (partly violent) conflicts on the international, national and sub-national levels. The focus on border conflicts is supplemented by the perception of borderlands as marginal spaces inhabited by under-privileged people who suffer from lack of infrastructure and political participation, from repression, and from inter-state conflict (Markakis 2006). Similarly, Mahmoud (2008: 2) observed that '[b]order politics and the dilemma of divided communities have been a source of strained society-state relations'. Based on observations from northern and north-eastern Kenya, which is largely inhabited by pastoral nomads who are perceived as antagonistic by the state, he concluded that this negative relation between political centre and borderland communities manifested itself in human rights violations, political tensions and economic losses (through not realizing the potential of the pastoral-nomadic economy for the Kenyan state).

A second body of (not necessarily Africa-related) literature perceives borders either as limiting economic and other global exchanges, or, on the contrary, argues that borders are frequently irrelevant when looking at transnational and global processes of exchange and identity formation (Appadurai 2003; Ferguson 2006). Studies of transnationalism and globalization emphasized the de-territorialization (and consequently, the detachment from any fixed borders) of culture, politics and economy (Kearney 1995).

While we recognize these multiple constraints, our interest is not to confirm existing explanations for border-related conflicts, or to offer alternative explanations. We also do not advocate a liberal economy or a transnational agenda. Instead, we examine the (sometimes conflicting) (re)bordering and border-crossing processes within which the agency of the borderlanders is situated. Following Tsing, we emphasize the multiple possibilities engendered by marginal spaces and being marginal. Tsing (1993: 21) argues that 'the image of the border [as a margin] turns attention to the creative projects of self-definition of those at the margins.

By shifting the perspective to that of actors who imagine multiple possibilities, the image raises issues of agency without neglecting the constraints of power and knowledge.' Where Tsing refers to the constraints of power and knowledge, we refer to the constraining powers of the national centres or states.

In the following, we engage with state borders as constraints literature. Subsequently, we briefly touch on important insights of the anthropology of borders and borderlands. From there we develop our analytical framework for studying the opportunities that state borders and borderlands provide, and elaborate on the conditions of resourcing them.

State borders as constraints

ARBITRARY BORDERS

About 42 per cent of the total length of land boundaries in Africa is drawn by 'parallels, meridians and equidistant lines without any consideration of social realities' (Kolossov 2005: 628–9).[3] In his book *The Boundary Politics of Independent Africa*, Touval (1972) asserted that there is something particularly problematic about the manner in which the colonial borders in Africa were drawn. He was referring to the usual perception that borders were demarcated in disregard of the wishes of the local population. Touval, however, did not accept the perspective of the Africans as pure victims. He emphasized that, in a number of cases, African rulers actively engaged with European colonizers. Local chiefs, kings, or sultans profited from these external contacts, through which they were able to stabilize their local authority and gain access to firearms, prestige, education, and so forth. In this way, Touval highlighted African involvement in the colonial project. However, it was mostly the involvement of the ruling elite. A prolific writer on state borders as barriers is the historian A.I. Asiwaju. In his introduction to the volume *Partitioned Africans*, he argued that

> the boundaries have been drawn across well-established lines of communication including, in every case, a dormant or active sense of community based on traditions concerning common ancestry, usually very strong kinship ties, shared socio-political institutions and economic resources, common customs and practices, and sometimes acceptance of a common political control. (Asiwaju 1985: 2)

Asiwaju continued that, although imposed, the borders separating African states were not absolute. Cross-border integration took place every day. Moreover, many clandestine activities across borders, such as smuggling, on occasions posed serious threats to state security and a more or less permanent challenge to the economy (ibid.: v). This micro-sociological approach led him to the position that 'from the viewpoint of border society life in many parts of Africa, the partition can hardly be said to have taken place' (ibid.: 4).

3

Borders were therefore understood as essentially legal limits, which distinguish the jurisdiction of different political regimes and their respective administrations. In the same vein, Schlee (1998: 232) argued with regard to district boundaries in Kenya that 'those boundaries were drawn along the distinctions made by those who drew them'. He identified the dividing lines as 'colonial constructs' that did not recognize African social, political, and economic systems beyond the immediate interests of the colonizers. In addition, he pointed to cognitive differences that play a role in understanding the meaning of a boundary in its local context. 'The result is that people inhabiting the same country have quite different views of the legitimacy and usefulness or even the existence of boundaries' (ibid.: 229). Consequently, border regions in Africa are zones of socio-political ambivalence, 'where the loyalty of the local peoples to either of the states sharing the particular cultural areas has not been, and never could have been, very strong' (Asiwaju 1985: 12). In this perspective, state borders appear to be irrelevant at the micro level, and/or a problem at the political and inter-state level.

CONFLICT-PRONE BORDERS
IN THE HORN OF AFRICA

From a contemporary (2010) perspective, it is bitterly ironical that Asiwaju twenty-five years ago advised the 'politicians' in post-colonial Africa to follow the Somali lead. He referred to the Somali (back then) as the 'only partitioned groups in Africa among whom reactions have taken the form of an active nationalist movement' (1985: 14).[4] Somali nationalism is indeed intimately related to the problem of the arbitrary colonial borders in the Horn (Drysdale 1964; Geshekter 1985). In colonial times, as is well known, the Somali peninsula was divided between France, Italy, Great Britain, and Ethiopia. After the independence of the Somali Republic in 1960, Somalis lived in Somalia, Ethiopia, and colonies that later on became Kenya (1963) and Djibouti (1977). This was seen as a serious problem by Somali nationalists who claimed self-determination for the parts of the Somali nation that remained outside the Somali state (Lewis 1983: 13). Abdirashid Ali Shermaarke, the first Prime Minister of the Somali Republic, outlined his government's position, and the position of many Somalis, when he wrote in the preface to a book on *The Somali Peninsula*,

> Our misfortune is that our neighbouring countries, with whom, like the rest of Africa, we seek to promote constructive and harmonious relations, are not our neighbours. Our neighbours are our Somali kinsmen whose citizenship has been falsified by indiscriminate boundary 'arrangements'. They have to move across artificial frontiers to their pasture lands. They occupy the same terrain and pursue the same pastoral economy as ourselves. We speak the same language. We share the same creed, the same culture, and the same traditions. How *can* we regard our brothers as foreigners? (Information Service of the Somali Government 1962: vi; italics in the original)

4

Already in the 1960s the so-called 'Greater Somalia' policy of the government in Mogadishu, which aimed at uniting all Somalis in one state, led to major conflicts with Kenya and Ethiopia (Matthies 1977). The weakness of Ethiopia after the fall of Emperor Haile Selassie in 1974 prompted Somalia's attack on its neighbour in pursuit of its irredentist dream. This resulted in one of the bloodiest inter-state wars in Africa, popularly known as the Ogaden war (1977–78). The devastating defeat of the Somali national army weakened the regime of Siyad Barre. Mounting militant opposition during the 1980s climaxed in the fall of the government and state collapse, which was followed by internal territorial reorganization. Somaliland seceded in 1991 unilaterally from the rest of Somalia. Puntland was declared an autonomous region in 1998. Most recently, Islamists in the south started fighting for power and Somali unity. This constellation of events as well as external interferences make the Somali-inhabited Horn a 'prime theatre' for ongoing violent conflicts related to, among other issues, state borders.

Another prominent series of border conflicts in the region started with the Eritrean liberation movement. Carved out of northern Ethiopia as an Italian colony in 1890, Eritrea came under British control for a decade (1942–52). Under a UN-mandated referendum Eritrea was federated with Ethiopia in 1952. However, Emperor Haile Selassie annexed Eritrea a decade later, which generated the armed resistance of the Eritrean Liberation Front (ELF). The change of regime in Ethiopia in 1974 and the military rule of the Derg coincided with the rise of a more militant liberation movement called the Eritrean People's Liberation Front (EPLF) that finally liberated Eritrea in May 1991.

The Eritrean wars of liberation have ensconced the establishment of ethno-liberation movements against the centralist state in Ethiopia. The strongest among these was the Tigrean People's Liberation Front (TPLF), which was supported by its ethnic comrades in Eritrea across the border. It also formed an alliance with other ethno-liberation movements and established the Ethiopian People's Revolutionary Democratic Front (EPRDF) in the late 1980s, which seized power in Ethiopia at the same time as the EPLF took over Eritrea. The EPRDF restructured the Ethiopian state into an ethnic federation. The new political order has its own detractors. Centrists oppose it for 'endangering' the very survival of the country, since the constitution theoretically grants the federal states the right to leave the federation. Others complain about the continued centralizing tendencies and the new form of ethnocracy, namely, Tigrean hegemony.

The good relations between the EPRDF and the EPLF benefitted the independence of Eritrea in 1993. Soon, however, conflicting projects of state-building, failure to come up with a mutually acceptable economic arrangement, and a quarrel over the border brought Ethiopia and Eritrea to the devastating 1998–2000 war. Despite the peace agreement the conflict continued, albeit in the form of a proxy war in collapsed Somalia, where the Asmara government supported various Islamist groups whereas

Addis Ababa aided and used different warlords and the Transitional Federal Government (TFG) under President Abdullahi Yusuf (2004–8).

Post-colonial Sudan also plunged into civil wars with regional and border dimensions. At independence from the British in 1957 political elites from northern Sudan sought to monopolize power, mostly through the exclusion of others, particularly Southerners. These politics that reflected regional disparity and differential incorporation into the Sudanese state system were framed in religious terms by the predominantly Muslim Northerners who gave their political aspirations a divine mandate. On that basis they set out to Islamize the whole country, which bred discontent, particularly in the largely Christian south. Post-colonial Sudan has seen two civil wars (1961–72 and 1983–2005) both of which involved external actors and trans-border relations. In answer to Sudan's support for the Eritrean liberation movements, successive Ethiopian governments actively supported southern Sudanese liberation fronts, such as the Sudan People's Liberation Army (SPLA) that was established in 1983. The Sudanese civil wars came to an end after a negotiated peace agreement between the SPLA and the government of the Sudan in 2005. Uncertainties still abound, however; the political future of southern Sudan is to be decided by a referendum in 2011.

Kenya appears to be relatively calm. Except for a brief confrontation with Somalia in 1963 and clashes with Uganda over the area around Mount Elgon in 1976 and as recently as 2006, no hostilities occurred between Kenya and its neighbours. Domestically, the long-standing tensions between the state and part of the Somali population that escalated into the so-called *Shifta* war in the 1960s constituted a prominent and until today smouldering conflict related to the border. Comparatively, however, Kenya is internally and externally more at peace than its neighbours. The 2008 post-election violence was the exception rather than the rule. Nonetheless, the country is deeply involved in the regional conflicts as host to hundreds of thousands of refugees from neighbouring countries. In addition, Nairobi is an important centre for international negotiations that influence dynamics of conflict and peace in the region.

Similarly, Djibouti, apart from recent skirmishes along the border with Eritrea, was not involved in any inter-state war. It had been a French colony until 1977. Its independence dealt a blow to pan-Somalism, since the Republic of Somalia had long sought to drag the Somali part of the Djiboutian population into its 'camp'. Post-colonial Djibouti stayed a close ally of its former colonial 'motherland', hosting French and, after the 9/11 attacks, also US-American and allied troops. Djibouti's economic and political importance regionally and internationally derives from its strategic location on the straits between the Red Sea and the Gulf of Aden. The country is involved in regional conflicts as its harbour is an important lifeline for land-locked Ethiopia. It is also involved in Somali civil war politics, but, mostly 'behind the arras', apart from the peace initiative in Arta in 2000 and the January 2009 Somalia-related conference (Djibouti city).

Despite these empirical facts of border-related conflicts and the arbitrariness of many borders, particularly in the Horn, the argument that the artificiality of the African colonial borders would explain their problematic nature in post-colonial times is not, to our mind, well-founded. Touval (1972) and Herbst (2000) have reminded us that borders in general and state borders in particular are artificial in the sense that they are the product of human imagination put into practice. Moreover, they have often been drawn in the context of wars and conflicts. In Europe, many of the current state borders go back to changes related to either World War I or World War II (Fischer 1949; Kolossov 2005: 607).

IRRELEVANT BORDERS

According to a transnational viewpoint or one informed by globalization theory, borders are inconsequential and even undesirable, given the dynamic nature of cross-border movements and social currents that transgress and make borders irrelevant (Appadurai 1991; Appadurai 2003; Ferguson 2006). The transnational view of borders posits 'a new borderless world, in which the barrier impact of borders became insignificant … Faced with the onslaught of cyber and satellite technology, as well as the free unimpeded flow of global capital, borders would – so the globalization purists argued – gradually open until they disappeared altogether' (Newman 2006: 172). This perspective partly corresponds to what Kolossov (2005: 612) called the 'global paradigm', according to which 'state boundaries are being gradually transformed into virtual lines and are being replaced by economic, cultural and other boundaries'. The scale of interconnectedness engendered by globalization is expressed in various terms. On a positive note, McGrew (1997: 6-7), for instance, evidenced that in the mid-1990s over one trillion US dollars flowed across the world's foreign-exchange markets every day; the number of international tourists reached over 500 million per year; and multinational corporations accounted for between 25 and 33 per cent of world economic output. The downside is that interconnectedness also relates to global warming, massive deforestation, global networks of crime and terror, and so forth. In view of these borderless dynamics, the 'Westphalian order' (built around the territorial integrity of states and the exclusion of external actors from domestic affairs), and related to that, borders, are said to have lost much of their relevance.[5] Amidst high-speed and large-scale mobility, 'the territorial referents of civic loyalty are increasingly divided for many persons along different spatial horizons … that may create disjunct registers of affiliation' (Appadurai 2003: 341). While commenting on the African states' shrinking sovereignty, Appadurai further proclaimed: 'African states care less about policing borders but focus their energies on policing and sanctifying important cities, monuments, and resources at the urban centres of the regime' (ibid.).

The transnationalists' vision of a borderless world fails to capture the reality on the ground in two ways. First, though they are right to note the growing interconnectedness across national borders, globalization is not only about flows but also consists of 'systematic processes of closure and containment' (Shamir 2005: 197). The more borderless the world has become in terms of increased mobility and cultural interpenetration, the more salient borders have become, given the continued relevance of mechanisms of inclusion into a privileged collective self and exclusion of 'others'. Secondly, closure has attained a new lease of life in the post 9/11 world and what Newman called the advent of the securitization discourse: 'in the wake of 9/11 ... governments have begun to reassess their border-opening policies. The securitization discourse has, once again, become prominent as governments move towards re-closing their borders and making them more difficult to cross in the face of perceived security threat' (Newman 2006: 182). While we accept this as a relevant point against the irrelevance of the borders, it has to be noted that the securitization discourse stresses the agency of state institutions along borders. The (re)bordering and border-crossing processes within which the agency of the borderlanders is situated remain opaque.

On a more general level, we reject the borders-as-constraints literature as largely normative. It argues against the 'bad' (arbitrary, conflict-prone, and hindering) or for the 'good' (secured and surveyed) border. In contrast, we propose a non-judgemental perspective. We are interested in people's agency and creativity with regard to state borders and borderlands, turning what appears to be a liability into an asset. This focus has been pioneered by Eric Fischer, a human geographer, and a number of anthropologists working along borders and in borderlands.

Resourcing state borders and borderlands

The earliest non-normative work on modern state borders that we found is Eric Fischer's *On Boundaries* (1949). Based on his study of southern Tyrol, Fischer developed a human geographic perspective on the imprint of boundaries on social life. He posed the pertinent question why the international border should matter, to which he answered that:

> The longer a boundary functions, especially an international boundary, the harder it becomes to alter it. The transportation net gets adjusted to the boundary, market towns take their specific importance from it, habits of the local population are shaped by it, ideas are moulded under the impact of different educational systems. Once established, boundaries tend to persist through their impact upon the human landscape. (Fischer 1949: 197–98)

Fischer's description of the state border between Austria and Italy aptly captures the political developments in Europe in the twentieth century, where, particularly after the World Wars, governments embarked on intensive projects of nationalizing their borders. The borderlanders in the Horn of Africa, however, seem to have gone through different trajectories.

Border regions were often neglected by their respective political centres. As a result, the people residing in these areas are economically and culturally marginalized (Markakis 2006). Yet, as the case studies in this volume and other texts show, marginalization is only one side of the 'border coin'. The other is a huge potential for local agency as we outline below. In contrast to Fischer's study, in which the centre developed an interest in the border, in our cases it is the borderlanders who are becoming active, sometimes up to the level of 'going national'. Thus, like Baud and Van Schendel (1997: 212), we argue for a view from the 'periphery', which sometimes is not peripheral at all. Nonetheless, we keep Fischer's position in mind, particularly when it comes to the issue of borders gaining social and economic validity over time.

Wilson and Donnan (1998: 2), in their seminal introduction to anthropological studies on border identities, stressed the importance of the state for 'new politics of representation, redefinition and resistance'. Following this approach, Rösler and Wendl (1999: 8) argued that 'located at the fringes of nation-states, borderlands usually lack precise boundaries and are more exposed to foreign, trans-border influences and cross-border movements than are the heartlands'. In our perspective, it is exactly this lack of precise boundaries that could create opportunities for the 'borderlanders'. The latter may be physically detached from the centres, but they are partly in control of what happens at the borders, which is in turn vital for the centres. State borders are similar to social borders in the sense that both mark off collective identities. Where they differ is in the degree of rigidity. In state borders national identities are fortified by citizenship, economic regimes, and international legal agreements (concerning the sanctification of state borders), whereas in social borders collective identities exhibit more fluidity. Nevertheless, at a more theoretical level, anthropologists, historians, geographers and political scientists concur in the idea that state borders, despite their 'natural appearance' on maps and in the international system supporting them, are socially constructed (Jackson 1990: 7; Baud and Van Schendel 1997: 211-212; Kolossov 2005: 606).

The constructedness or arbitrary nature of state borders does not mean that they are inconsequential. Related to the just-mentioned state regimes and legal arrangements that admittedly may differ in their rigidity, borders set in motion new economic and socio-political processes that are as much enabling as they are constraining. Furthermore, state borders have intended as well as unintended consequences. They demarcate and separate but also encourage people to explore new connections as well as cross-border opportunities and incentives provided by residing in borderlands. These are sometimes in line with and sometimes opposed to state policies and interests. Raeymaekers (2009: 55) added that 'recent analysis in African borderlands points at the high level of overlap and complicity that often exists between different systems of survival and regulation [including state regulation]'.

Our perspective is further inspired by the works of Fredrick Barth and Paul Nugent. In his study 'Boundaries and Connections', Barth (2000: 17) argued that:

> Throughout history political boundaries have been rich in affordances, offering opportunities for army careers, customs-duty collecting agencies, defence construction contracts and all manners of work and enterprise. They have provided a facility of retreat and escape for bandits and freedom fighters eluding the control of states on both sides; and they are a constant field of opportunities for mediators, traders and middlepersons of all kinds.

According to Barth, the affordances – or, to put it simply, the opportunities – of boundaries derive from their setting the scene for social activities as well as their establishing connections by separating political and economic spaces. In order to profit from borders people have to work and spin connections. Thereby, the boundary becomes shaped by social and material processes 'not by cognitive fiat as the drawing of the boundary was' (Barth 2000: 18). The opportunities that borders provide are not ready-made. Their realization requires effort and varies depending on the particular border site that the people occupy.

Paul Nugent (2002) explored the Ghana-Togo border as what we call a resource. According to his perspective the border as barrier provides opportunities. This is particularly true regarding the formation of national as well as 'informal' economies in which the opportunities are embedded. Nugent criticized the sole focus on the constraints side of the state border as the conventional wisdom about African boundaries (Nugent 2002: 5–8). Once in place, he maintained, the state border creates strong local interests whose proponents seek to preserve the *status quo*. Nugent noted that for the most part, at least in western Africa, national identification proved far more valuable than cross-border ethnic identifications. Rather than disengaging from the state, as many would have predicted, border communities such as those along the Ghana-Togo border have actively sought to shape and utilize the state and its borders. Similarly, Hüsken (2010) observed along the border between Egypt and Libya that the integrity of the different nation-states is not questioned by the cross-border actors, who belong to the same tribal group but consciously adhere to and use their different national identities. With regard to this 'state-shaping' from below, Nugent demonstrated the relevance and limits of Scott's (1990) model of the hidden transcript of power relations. Many scholars working on the constraints side of the border use this model implicitly or explicitly as an analytical frame in which contraband trade, for instance, is viewed as an act of resistance. Instead, Nugent proposed to comprehend the dynamic interplay among various actors in the construction, maintenance and consolidation of borders. Smuggling, in his perspective, is not an act of resistance to state borders, nor is it just the continuation of older trade relations 'by other means'. He argued (2002: 12) that:

10

The very creation of the boundary was bound to have an impact on the local economic geography, opening up avenues of profitable commerce where they had not previously existed. Apart from opening up new trade routes, the smuggling complex also summons forth a new breed of entrepreneurs whose very livelihoods depended upon the perpetuation of the international boundary.

Nugent's focus on the changes that borders introduce, and from which certain opportunities for borderlanders possibly arise, resonates well with Fischer's observation (above) about the impact of boundaries on the human geography. A concept that is very close to Nugent's argument is that of 'arbitrage economies'. Anderson and O'Dowd (1999: 597) defined arbitrage economies as 'economic activities for which the border is the *raison d'être* ... The co-existence of different regulatory regimes on either side of the border generates a form of opportunity structure which invites smuggling, unofficial exchange rates and illegal immigration' (italics in the original). According to their perspective, border dependent activities 'may be seen in terms of "arbitrage" or the exploitation of differentials in prices, interest rates, exchange rates and share prices over time and space' (ibid.).

In their introduction to *Centring the Margins in Southeast Asia*, Horstmann and Wadley (2006) approached borders as opportunity structures. They emphasized how people are not merely constrained by borders but how border-crossing also opens up new options for local agency. They noted (2006: 2) that 'borderlands are unique forms of peripheries as zones between often competing or unequal states. This inter-national character increases the peripherality and ambiguity of the borderlands as inhabitants seek benefits from both sides of the border, and as the states try to control their activities.' The point about state control was also highlighted by Pelkmans, who did research along the Georgia-Turkey border. He argued that '[a]lthough the strategic power of citizens may be higher at the margins, and border dwellers may display more conspicuously ambiguous loyalties, these characteristics may be the precise reason for intensified state regulation, as the history of Soviet borders amply demonstrates' (Pelkmans 2006: 13).

Drawing on these works outlining the complexities of, and the opportunities provided by, state borders and the human actions across them and within the borderlands, we continue to challenge the conventional focus on state borders as constraints. Without denying that borders, particularly in the Horn of Africa, also put limitations on people's lives, and that borderlands are peripheral or marginal zones, we reiterate that we are interested not in what the borders have done to the people, but in what the people have done to the borders, and in what they have made out of living in the borderlands as fields of opportunities. In conjunction with the perspectives of Barth, Nugent, and others outlined above, we argue that borders and borderlands provide different types of resources for local

11

actors. This is the most important assumption, on which the chapters presented in this book are based.

It has already been mentioned that the idea of the border as an opportunity structure, e.g. with regard to smuggling, emanates from the effectiveness of the border in separating national economies, or, more generally, different state systems. In situations of extreme insecurity and violent conflict, which characterize many state borders and borderlands in contemporary Africa and other parts of the global South, 'a border can mean the difference between poverty and material well-being, and occasionally between life and death' (Baud and Van Schendel 1997: 220). Weak and strong states alike are protected by the international legal regime, which defines the state border as sacrosanct (Clapham 1996b, Herbst 1989, 2000). In many regions of the globe, however, statehood has not been translated into spatial hegemony in the borderlands (Horstmann and Wadley 2006: 3). Most states in the Horn of Africa lack the administrative resources, the monopoly of legitimate violence, and, in some cases, the political will to police their borders. This allows for the permeability of the borders, as does the fact that frequently members of the same ethnic group inhabit both sides of a border, but are nevertheless positioned in different political, legal, and economic spaces with their respective opportunity structures. While ordinary people usually have no difficulties with border-crossing, state-agents do. This becomes clear when imagining, for example, an Eritrean soldier or politician crossing to Ethiopia, or vice versa.

The borders we are dealing with are permeable for many people; but permeability, for instance of the thin 'bush-border' between Somaliland and Puntland discussed by Hoehne (this volume), does not mean inconsequentiality. As in the case of Nugent's smugglers, our case studies engage with the permeability of borders at the local level and the rigidity at the inter-state level. The inter-state rigidity of the borders creates different and fluctuating opportunity structures, and the permeability makes access to these opportunity structures possible. In this sense, the state borders we discuss are simultaneously permeable and consequential.[6] The relational mode could be reversed, however. There are cases where permeability is tolerated by the state, whereas a local population might prefer a more rigid form of state border. This is certainly the case regarding the Anywaa's call for the rigidification of the Ethio-Sudanese border (Dereje in this volume).

Analytical framework and application in case studies

We feel that there is a research gap – particularly in the Africanist literature – in the understanding of how people adapt to state borders and make use of them.[7] We recognize the borderlanders as actors in their own right, whereas the view of the borders as constraints perceives them as victims and highlights the agency of the states. Our focus is on the micro level; it stresses the opportunities and the agency of the borderlanders; it acknowledges the permeable but consequential nature of borders; and finally, it is empirically oriented. We are investigating how state borders are made relevant in the everyday lives of the borderlanders. This is close to what Raeymaekers (2009: 57) understood as 'silent encroachment' of the frontier, which 'involves the silent, and at occasions loud, advancement of ordinary people on the propertied and powerful in order to survive hardships and better their lives'.[8] Raeymaekers observed that most of his informants style themselves in resistance to the centre/state while making a living from trans-border trade in the Condo-Uganda borderlands. Our focus on resourcing state borders and borderlands goes even further and actually incorporates the occasional 'co-optation' of the centre (e.g. the state) by the actors at the margin, or the dependence of the state on the borderlanders for security and national identity.

On the basis of the case studies from the Horn we identify four different types of resources that collective as well as individual actors can extract from state borders and borderlands. These are, first, *economic resources* (cross-border trade and smuggling); second, *political resources* (access to alternative centres of political power, trans-border political mobilization, sanctuary for rebels who strive to alter national structures of power, and strategic cooption of borderlanders by competing states); third, *identity resources* (the state border as a security device in an inter-ethnic competition, legitimization of the claim for statehood); and fourth, *status and rights resources* (citizenship and refugee status, including access to social services such as education).

EXTRACTING ECONOMIC RESOURCES FROM STATE BORDERS AND BORDERLANDS

Extracting economic resources from borders and borderlands is a cross-cutting theme of the chapters in this book and beyond. State borders are often markers of different national economies and the price differentials derived from this (Nugent 2002, Little 2006). Echoing Anderson and O'Dowd's (1999) notion of arbitrage economies, Little (2006: 177), who has conducted extensive research on livestock marketing in East Africa, noted that 'the very existence of an international border creates economic opportunities that go well beyond cattle transactions, and distinguish cross-border trade from other types of livestock commerce.' Two of these opportunities are currency arbitrage, which at times can enable borderlanders to earn more profits from money exchange than from the sale of cattle itself, as was the case for the Somali traders in the 1980s, and re-import business, especially in manufactured goods and second-hand clothes (Little 2006: 178). Economic possibilities vary across different border sites depending on the nature of currency exchanges in the area, the volatility of the situation along the border, and local market conditions in the area. In this respect, Little highlighted cross-border settlement patterns as economic capital and outlined that various social and cultural ties shape cross-border trade. He continued that 'these non-economic factors are present in other types of trade but take on added significance in cross-border trade due to its risks, complexity, geographic expanse, and informal nature' (ibid.). Hüsken's (2010) case of the Aulad Ali straddling both sides of the border between Egypt and Libya is a case in point. Their cross-border networks and their 'appropriation' of the border, partly in cooperation with 'friendly' state agents, allow for uncontrolled labour migration of Aulad Ali Bedouins from Egypt to Libya.

In this volume, Wafula introduces us to the world of *magendo*, which is the Kiswahili word for smuggling. His case study is on the cross-border economy of the Babukusu and the Bagisu peoples along the Kenyan-Ugandan border. Prominent trading centres in East Africa such as Lwakha-kha, Suam and Chepkube owe their very existence to *magendo*. Similarly, Cassanelli's contribution shows in a historical perspective how, over the last century, Somalis managed to dominate the cross-border trade in ivory, *miraa* (a plant and mild stimulant), animal trophies, and livestock through the networks they have spun in the four countries in which they live, namely Somalia, Ethiopia, Djibouti and Kenya. The case study by Hoehne shows how settlement along the *de facto* state border between Somaliland and Puntland provides borderlanders with economic gains. By carefully balancing political loyalties, the borderlanders manage to accommodate simultaneously political and military infrastructure from both states. This provides locals with basic salaries paid by one of the respective sides.

A different form of economic opportunity associated with state borders and borderlands is the resources delivered to the refugee camps by the aid agencies. Cassanelli shows how the Somali who live in the northern periphery along the Kenyan-Somali border have paradoxically benefited from neglect by the national government in Nairobi. The UNHCR and countless NGOs poured money and manpower into refugee camps and rehabilitation projects in the region. The globalization of the borderland economy in northern Kenya is reflected in the appearance of new shops, the construction of small airstrips, and the introduction of a regular bus service between the Northern Frontier District (now renamed as North Eastern Province) and Nairobi. Access to the refugee industry has thus had the effect of centring a marginal area in north-western Kenya, at least in relative terms, and compared with the early post-colonial situation.

EXTRACTING POLITICAL RESOURCES FROM STATE BORDERS AND BORDERLANDS

State borders and borderlands also provide resources, discursive as well as actual ones, which help to build political power. According to the case study by Barnes (this volume), the Somali clan of the Gadabuursi extracted political power/autonomy from the colonial border between the Ethiopian empire and the British Protectorate of Somaliland in the context of inter-state competition over the taxation of the borderlanders. The Gadabuursi would have been less successful, had they been wholly and exclusively under either British or Ethiopian rule. Historical records on this border demonstrate that Somalis, far from rejecting borders, actively used them and their position in the borderlands to their advantage against rival Somali groups. This reveals an interesting tension with regard to the Somali claim of resistance against the partition, as outlined at the beginning of this introduction with reference to Asiwaju, Lewis, and the first Somali Prime Minister after independence. It is, however, very much in line with Touval's argument about African participation in the partition.

The competition for political power between the Anywaa and the Nuer in the Gambella region of western Ethiopia discussed by Dereje (this volume) also illustrates how borders and borderlands can be used as political resources. The main political debate in the Gambella region is about who is and who is not a 'real' citizen. According to the 1902 boundary agreement between colonial Sudan and imperial Ethiopia, the majority of the Anywaa became subjects of the Ethiopian state, although a tiny minority were placed within the British colonial administration of the Sudan. The opposite is true of the Nuer. In the context of a changing regional demographic structure and ethnic federalism in Ethiopia after 1991, the border-centred debate on citizenship has in some sense become a new mode of inclusion or exclusion from resources and political power.

Along Ethiopia's eastern border with Djibouti, similar dynamics seem to be at work (Markakis 2003). Yasin (this volume) examines this issue with reference to the changing power relations between the Issa Somali and the Afar along the Ethio-Djibouti border. The Issa live in Ethiopia, Somalia and Djibouti, whereas the Afar reside in Ethiopia, Eritrea and Djibouti. Despite their settlements in three states, the Afar are politically marginal in all of them, whereas the Issa occupy the national centre in the state of Djibouti and are represented in Somalia/Somaliland. Much to the Afar's detriment, the Issa are also more attractive to the Ethiopian state because of their settlements around the strategic route from Addis Ababa to the port of Djibouti, which, in addition to Berbera in Somaliland, has been Ethiopia's main outlet to the sea after the relationship with Eritrea deteriorated in 1998. The net result of this differential access to some of the states in the region is the deep incursion of the Issa into traditional Afar territories.

Fekadu (this volume) examines electoral politics in Ethiopian and Kenyan Moyale, a cross-border settlement along the Ethio-Kenyan border. On each side, political power is contested between various ethnic groups that partly also inhabit both of the two states. The ethnic diversity of Moyale defies any exclusive ownership claim, although some groups constitute a clear majority, whereas others are minorities. A coalition among the minorities, however, could undermine majority rule. In this unstable power structure, cross-border social networks are used for political mobilization in order to enlarge one's constituency, particularly during elections.

The Ethio-Kenyan borderlands also serve as a sanctuary for rebels. Contemporary Oromo political actors are fiercely contesting what they regard as Abyssinian political hegemony over the Ethiopian state, first represented by the Amhara and since 1991 by the Tigreans (Merera 2006). After a brief participation in the Tigrean-led transitional government, Oromo political parties, particularly the Oromo Liberation Front (OLF), left the government and resumed the rebellion. The OLF was able to sustain the resistance against the ruling party, the EPRDF, thanks to the settlement of the Boran-Oromo across the Ethio-Kenyan border. From the Boran-inhabited parts of northern Kenya, the OLF has mounted a series of military attacks on Ethiopian government establishments. More significantly, the continuation of the cross-border armed resistance has nurtured Oromo nationalism, which competes with and seriously undermines Ethiopian nationalism.[9]

EXTRACTING IDENTITY RESOURCES FROM STATE BORDERS AND BORDERLANDS

Relating to and living along state borders also provides identity resources. In this volume Dereje shows that the debate between the Anywaa and the Nuer in the Gambella region is not only about the construction of political power. It is also about building an ethnic security device and preserving one's cultural identity. The Anywaa are not only concerned about the demographic and territorial expansion of the Nuer, but also feel threatened by the Nuer's successful assimilationist system, which has resulted in cultural 'take-over'. The contrasting identity formations of both groups contain within themselves a potential for conflict (Dereje 2003). In this context the Anywaa are eager to construct the international border as an ethnic border, and have sought to mobilize the Ethiopian state in the struggle for cultural identity with varying degrees of success.

State borders may also be used to consolidate collective identities. Hoehne (this volume) outlines how the government of Somaliland strives to validate its claim for international recognition on the basis of its separate colonial history and a long and bloody guerrilla struggle against the oppression of the regime of Siyad Barre.[10] In this and many other cases, statehood clearly serves not only political or economic ends.[11] It is also related to questions of collective identity (Kolossov 2005: 614-15). Young (1994: 33) stressed that the state is an 'ensemble of affective orientations, images, and expectations imprinted in the minds of the subjects'. For Somaliland supporters recognition is not merely a political or legal problem; it is existential: they are Somalilanders. The former colonial border is an integral part of their identity (Hoehne 2009).

The situation of the Tigrinnya speakers along the Ethiopian-Eritrean border has always been what Smidt (this volume) calls pluralist. The creation of this border in 1890, however, has its own share of reducing complexity by setting off the process of bifurcation between the so-called Tegaru people (the Ethiopian Tigrinnya speakers) and the Tigrinnya

16

people (the Eritrean Tigrinnya speakers). As Abbink (2001: 456) noted, 'while political realities since the Italian colonial venture have indeed produced this [division] the ideological effort to consciously buttress the division is still going on, sometimes in bizarre and historically dubious forms.' Smidt's meticulous socio-linguistic and ethno-historical analysis shows that on the Ethiopian side of the border, the Tigrinnya speakers refer to themselves as 'Tegaru', whereas on the Eritrean side the new ethnonym 'Tigrinnya' was adopted. The Tegaru and the Tigrinnya perceive the Ethio-Eritrean border differently. The former regard the border as artificial and seek reunification within existing or new political structures, whereas the latter affirm the validity of the international boundary to the extent that it also coincides with a pre-colonial political boundary. This new process of identity formation is intimately related to the rift between the TPLF and the EPLF and contributed to the violent border conflict between Ethiopia and Eritrea (1998-2000).

EXTRACTING STATUS AND RIGHTS RESOURCES FROM STATE BORDERS AND BORDERLANDS

Borders and borderlands are intrinsically related to the 'refugee industry'. Social services, including education in the refugee camps and getting into UNHCR resettlement programmes, are extremely viable resources for the often marginalized borderlanders. The alternative citizenship of the Nuer who move between Ethiopia and Sudan discussed by Dereje is a case in point. Inhabiting Gambella's outlying districts, the Ethiopian Nuer were peripheral people in a marginalized region. The second southern Sudanese civil war brought hundreds of thousands of refugees to the Gambella region (Hutchinson 1996; Johnson 2003). In this context, the Ethiopian Nuer joined refugee camps in Gambella region that were built for the southern Sudanese Nuer. The quality of the education in the camps was a lot better than in the villages, if there was any at all. The Anywaa did not manage to pass as refugees as they were largely perceived by the aid agencies as Ethiopian citizens. The Nuer effectively used the education provided in the refugee camps in order to strengthen their political standing in the region. Nearly all of the current Nuer government officials and civil servants in the Gambella regional state are 'ex-refugees'.

Similarly, Declich (this volume) outlines how the Zigula succeeded in negotiating their ethnic stigma within the wider Somali society through, ironically, the empowering effect of the refugee experience. The Zigula, as explained by Declich, originally came from Tanzania to Somalia as slaves in the nineteeth century. In their new homeland in southern Somalia they were referred to as *jareer* and recently as 'Bantu' (Menkhaus 2010). As descendants of former slaves they were looked down upon by the so-called 'pure' Somali. Despite social marginalization, the Zigula preserved aspects of their distinct culture such as the Zigula language (a Bantu language) and their matri-kin ritual naming system. After the fall of the Somali government in 1991, they fared better than their former Somali oppressors in the refugee camps in Kenya. They could draw on their language skills as Bantu speakers, which helped to establish some cultural familiarity and even solidarity with the Kenyan aid workers and officials conversing usually in Kiswahili (also a Bantu language). Moreover, the Zigula language became what Declich calls an 'emergency passport' to enter Tanzania. The Zigula could make use of the UNHCR refugee resettlement programme, which is another opportunity structure connected with refugee camps and the refugee industry.

Some thoughts on conditions of resourcing state borders and borderlands

In this section we reflect on the conditions of resourcing state borders and borderlands. We have already emphasized that resources offered by state borders and borderlands are a potential, not a ready-made 'good' waiting for delivery. In fact, people have to strive to realize the opportunities borders and borderlands offer. Who extracts what kind of resource is not, however, determined by sheer effort. There seem to be other intervening variables at work.

The first item to explore is the *demographic size and the cross-border settlement pattern*. From this it appears that the more state borders a group straddles, the greater are its prospects of extracting resources from state borders and borderlands. This link is supported by the ethnographic examples we have provided. In this regard, the Somali and the Anywaa cases represent two extreme ends along a wider spectrum. The Somali seem to be the main beneficiaries extracting various types of resources from three state borders and one *de facto* state border. The Anywaa, on the other hand, were not able to make as much use of their cross-border settlements in Ethiopia and Sudan as their neighbours did, partly because their settlement sizes in the two countries are not proportional, and because they were viewed by the aid agencies as being 'too Ethiopian' to pass as Sudanese.

A second variable to look at is the *distance of the people from the political centre* in the states where they live. Here again the Somali seem to be better positioned than their neighbours. The Somali do not just reside in four established and one emerging state. More critically, with Somalia/Somaliland and, partly, Djibouti, they also dominate politically some of these states. This gives them a competitive edge in making use of state borders and borderlands. Had the demographic size and the cross-border settlement pattern been the sole factor in resourcing state borders and borderlands, the Afar would have been on a par with the Somali because they, too, live in several national states. Except for the regional state of Afar in Ethiopia, however, the Afar occupy a highly marginal position in political affairs at the national level. This is so even in Djibouti where they are a political minority despite their demographic preponderance. The

Afar do not 'own' a state that they can mobilize in local struggles as much as the Somali do.

A third variable is the *significance a specific border possesses for the state actors*. In the volatile inter-state relations in the Horn of Africa, it is self-evident that some borders are more equal than others in the sense that they attain more strategic significance. The Nuer were able to make use of the Ethio-Sudanese border in the 1980s not just because of their effort or significant representation in both states, but also because the dynamics between Ethiopia and Sudan was itself part of broader political processes. The civil war in Sudan is as much locally rooted as it has been entangled with international politics. The Horn of Africa was one of the hottest scenes of the Cold War. Ethiopia and Sudan were clients of the East and the West respectively. The escalation of the civil war and the subsequently thriving refugee industry in the Gambella region and southern Sudan were intimately related to these geopolitics. The passivity of the current Ethiopian government towards the Issa Somali's cross-border political mobilization is also intelligible if it is viewed in the context of the new strategic significance with which Ethiopia's eastern border is imbued. Upon Eritrea's independence in 1993, Ethiopia became a landlocked country. Although it retained access to the Eritrean ports up until 1998, the port of Djibouti has assumed a greater share of handling Ethiopia's international trade. Ethiopia's dependence on the Djibouti port has increased dramatically since the outbreak of the border conflict between Ethiopia and Eritrea in 1998. The strategic route between Addis Ababa and Djibouti is largely inhabited by the Issa Somali. Minding its vital interests, it is no wonder that the Ethiopian government is currently insensitive to the plight of the Afar.

The *depth of the cleavage caused by the border* is another variable to look at. Usually, ordinary people cross the border with relative ease because socio-cultural ties on both sides are still strong. However, in the case of the Ethio-Eritrean border, for instance, the social cleavage seems to be deeper. Sixty years of colonial experience in Eritrea, together with decades of post-colonial civil war, have severely ruptured existing socio-economic ties between the Tigrinnya speakers who live on both side of this border. Despite intermittent strategic alliances, political organizations that claim to represent both peoples have found it difficult to sustain the partnership because of divergent and competing political visions. Echoing Clapham's (1996a) notion of competing conceptions of boundaries, the Ethio-Eritrean border has induced a new differentiation within the highlanders' boundary imaginary. The Eritreans (Tigrinnya) replicate the territorial state nationalism, while the Tigreans/Tegaru invoke an ethno-political boundary system ('Greater Tigray', which straddles the border).

The *degree of inter-state economic differentiation* determines particularly the nature and scale of economic resources extractable from borders and borderlands. The greater the difference between national economies, the more flourishing the cross-border trade is, and the more pervasive the arbitrage economy becomes. It is for this reason that most of the vibrant cross-border trade in the Horn of Africa concentrates along Kenya's borders. Kenya's national economy is not only more developed but is also distinctively organized. Whereas Kenya has followed a neo-liberal economic policy, its neighbours such as Ethiopia and Uganda for long years had a command economy in place. The Kenyan national economy has also responded to the political developments among its neighbours, particularly the military dictatorship of Uganda in the 1980s and the warlordism and continued 'anarchy' of Somalia since 1991. These political differences led to further economic differentiation across the borders concerned.

Furthermore, *entrepreneurial skills* are involved in resourcing state borders and borderlands. People differ in the degree of entrepreneurial skill that they muster. Entrepreneurship entails the existence of a more or less entrepreneurial culture. This point was made by Schlee (1998: 255) who emphasized the ingenuity of herders and traders in the northern Kenyan borderlands. Pastoralists in multi-ethnic settings marked by stiff competition over scarce resources might be particularly prone to the creative use of even minimal chances. Something similar has been observed by Raeymaekers (2009: 63) in the Congo-Uganda borderlands, where smugglers 'developed a talent in avoiding contact with official authorities while at the same time maintaining their physical protection'. In the borderlands between Somaliland and Puntland, members of the local elite – well-trained officers and politicians – manage (sometimes) to pursue a second or even third career on the other side of the border.

Cultural schemes, or what Schlee (1998) calls 'cognitive differences', also condition the resourcing of state borders and borderlands. The strong notion of territoriality among the Anywaa influences the way in which they relate to the Ethio-Sudanese border. In their cultural scheme of interpretation, the national state is represented as an Anywaa village writ large. This caused their disappointment with the national government in Addis Ababa when the latter seemed to be less concerned about the Nuer influx from Sudan than the Anywaa hoped.

Finally, of course, *changes over time* have a bearing on the role of state borders in political, social and economic contexts, and on the opportunities provided by state borders and borderlands.[12] The Ethio-Sudanese border was of differing significance during the Cold War, on the one hand, and during the time of Ethiopian ethnic federalism after 1991, on the other. This provided different opportunities to different border constituencies. In the case of the Somaliland-Puntland border, this *de facto* state border did not even exist before the founding of the Republic of Somaliland in 1991 and Puntland in 1998. The borderlanders in this region can therefore exploit opportunities that, in fact, were only created by the re-creation of (ex-)colonial divisions (on the side of Somaliland) that dealt the final blow to Somali irredentism. Similarly, the importance of the Issa borderlanders for the Ethiopian government increased after the secession of Eritrea and the recent Ethio-Eritrean war that led to the dependence of Ethiopia on goods imported via the port of Djibouti.

Conclusion

The dominant focus on state borders in Africa in general and the Horn of Africa in particular was on borders as constraints. Many writers perceived the artificial colonial borders in the continent as barriers responsible for social, political and economic crises. Borderlands were understood as peripheral spaces inhabited by marginalized people, excluded from state social and other services and suffering from inter-state conflict. We do not deny that particularly the history of the Horn of Africa in the twentieth and early twenty-first centuries provides ample examples of conflicts, marginalization, and suffering along state borders. However – and here we want to make a strong point – careful analysis of cross-border dynamics in the Horn of Africa involving the people being divided by state borders shows that borders and borderlands are more than barriers and marginal spaces. They are also far from irrelevant. While in particular informal economic integration is taking place across state borders in the Horn of Africa, this does not mean that people and states would or could do away with borders. Despite the widening and deepening of the interconnected-ness engendered by globalization, international borders are still main-tained in international law. They are 'sensitive zones' in the relations between states, and with regard to the organization of power within states. They have also assumed an added significance with the rise of the securitization discourse (outlined above).

In this introduction we drew on academic sources, from human geography to history, political science, and social anthropology, as well as on the case studies presented in this volume in order to outline the sometimes counter-intuitive complexities brought about by dividing ethnically related people through state borders. This does not mean that 125 years after the infamous Berlin (Congo) conference (1884), which – contrary to popular opinion – had only a very limited impact on the process of partitioning Africa (Katzenellenbogen 1996), we wish to rehabilitate colonial divisions. Nevertheless, we advocate a more 'sober' and empirically grounded perspective. Since state borders structure social, economic and political spaces, they provide opportunities as well as obstacles for the communities divided by them. Global, national, and local dynamics and regimes of power converge at the borders and charge them with a potentiality that can be grasped in the borderlands. Individuals and groups can extract economic, political, identity, status, and rights resources from state borders, and from the fact that they reside in borderlands. Yet, resourcing state borders and borderlands is not a straightforward process. The opportunities of state borders and borderlands have to be actively seized. Different variables are involved in the process of extracting resources, such as the demographic size and the cross-border settlement pattern, the political distance of the borderlanders from the political centre, the significance a specific border possesses for the state actors, the depth of the cleavage caused by the border, the degree of inter-state economic differentiation, the entrepreneurial skills of the borderlanders, their cultural schemes or cognitive differences, and changes over time. The highlighting of these variables that condition the resourcing of state borders and borderlands should suffice to defend us against the anticipated criticism that we would 'turn a blind eye' to the constraints of the borders.

We tried to be pragmatic for heuristic purposes. We took borders as facts and accepted that they divide as much as they connect. Both division and connection through borders require programmatic action. Borders as dividing lines need powerful state actors to implement their regimes also at the margins. Turning state borders and borderlands into resources for the divided people requires a combination of skills and also involves political, cultural, economic and other variables. Analyzing these internal and external factors and determinants for resourcing state borders and border-lands helps us to understand how people can make the best of being divided by state borders in the Horn of Africa, and elsewhere.

Notes

1 This territorial state nationalism, of course, has had its expansive phase, but it became consolidated through colonial and post-colonial arrangements in the late nineteenth and mid-twentieth century. In opposition to Ethiopian national and pan-African mystification of Ethiopian/Abyssinian history, Geshekter (1985: 6) argued convincingly that before Menelik II (1889-1913) Ethiopia/Abyssinia was not a compact political unit, but 'an association of semi-autonomous principalities' that paid tribute to and, to various degrees, depended on a political center.

2 The political organizations, which claim to represent these divergent conceptions of the border, thus play different 'language games' to the extent that they mean different things when they refer to the border.

3 This is certainly a feature that distinguishes borders in Africa from borders elsewhere in the world. Baud and Van Schendel (1997: 235-240) suggested convincingly that the circumstances of 'border formation' had an impact on the way borders and borderlands have been studied in different parts of the world in the twentieth century.

4 *Ex post*, one could argue that precisely this aggressive nationalism led Somalia into collapse and repartition along former colonial borders (Hoehne, forthcoming).

5 In fact, it is less the Westphalian order than the order of modern nation-states established in the nineteenth century that may or may not lose in relevance (Baud and Van Schendel 1997: 217). Nonetheless, the latter certainly has its origins in the understanding of statehood in the wake of the peace treaties of Westphalia in 1648, which regulated conduct between the important European states of the day.

6 On a similar note, Pelkmans (2006: 13) stressed that 'we need to move beyond the discussion of whether borders are best described in terms of fluidity and rigidity, and examine how these aspects are ultimately interconnected.'

7 Border studies in Europe, including Eastern Europe and the sphere of the former Soviet Union, and certainly along the famous US-Mexican border that is dealt with in a whole

body of literature of its own, seem more advanced; see, for instance, the useful overview articles by Kolossov (2005) and Alvarez (1995), or the instructive case study by Pelkmans (2006). Baud and Van Schendel (1997) have outlined a formidable approach to the (not only) historical understanding of borders and borderlands that certainly is very close to our perspective on the complexities and opportunities along borders and in borderlands. Nonetheless, nowhere did we find the explicit focus on resourcing borders and borderlands that we put forward here.

8 We certainly would prefer the term 'borderlands' to 'frontier'. The latter, in our view, has different political connotations (of 'empty' spaces at the margins of state expansion) compared to borderlands that are located around legally well established borders. The legal existence of borders partly shapes the opportunities provided in borderlands, as outlined above.

9 On a more generic level it can be observed that nearly all ongoing rebellions in Ethiopia occur in the border areas. It seems as if popular discontent needs a cross-border constituency to put up a rebellion and militarily negotiate its interest *vis-à-vis* the government.

10 Contemporary Somaliland nationalists turn Somali nationalism upside down – from being against the colonial border (in the 1960s) to being in favour of it (since 1991).

11 The status of statehood matters in Africa, where the state still functions as the main provider and mediator of critical resources. It is for this reason that the state itself is an object of struggle in Africa (Markakis 1998). This was recently highlighted by Hagmann and Mulugeta (2008) who analyzed pastoral conflicts in the semi-arid peripheries of Ethiopia and showed that these were shaped by ongoing processes of state-building in the context of administrative decentralization.

12 This point has been made before by Baud and Van Schendel (1997: 223–5). These authors were interested in the changing meaning and significance of borders over time, which they tried to capture by referring to the life cycle of borders. We differ from this (as the authors themselves admit) 'evolutionary' perspective by highlighting that borders may be subjected to dramatic and sudden changes, depending on larger (geo)political dynamics.

References

Abbink, J. 2001. 'Creating Borders: Exploring the impact of the Ethio-Eritrean war on the local population'. *Africa* (Rome) 56(4): 447–58.

Alvarez, R. 1995. 'The Mexican-US Border: The Making of an Anthropology of Borderlands'. *Annual Review of Anthropology* 24: 447–70.

Anderson, J. and L. O'Dowd. 1999. 'Borders, Border Region and Territoriality: Contradictory Meanings, Changing Significance'. *Regional Studies* 33(7): 593–604.

Appadurai. A. 1991. 'Global ethnoscapes: Notes and queries for a transnational anthropology', in R. Fox (ed.), *Recapturing Anthropology*. Santa Fe, NM: School of American Research Press, pp.191–210.

—— 2003. 'Sovereignty without Territoriality: Notes for a Postnational Geography', in S. Low and D. Zuniga (eds), *The Anthropology of Space and Place: Locating Culture*. Malden, MA: Blackwell, pp. 337–49.

Asiwaju, A.I. 1985. 'The conceptual framework', in A.I Asiwaju (ed.), *Partitioned Africans: Ethnic relations across Africa's international boundaries*. London: C. Hurst, pp. 1–18.

—— and P. Nugent. 1996. 'Introduction: The Paradox of African Boundaries', in A.I. Asiwaju and P. Nugent (eds), *African Boundaries: Barriers, conduits and opportunities*. London: Pinter, pp. 1–17.

Barth, F. 2000. 'Boundaries and Connections', in A. Cohen (ed.), *Signifying Identities: Anthropological perspectives on boundaries and contested values*. London: Routledge, pp. 17–36.

Baud, M. and Van Schendel, W. 1997. 'Toward a comparative history of borderlands'.

Journal of World History 8(2): 211–42.

Clapham, C. 1996a. 'Boundary and Territory in the Horn of Africa', in P. Nugent and A.I. Asiwaju (eds), *African Boundaries: Barriers, conduits and opportunities*. London: Pinter, pp. 237–50.

—— 1996b. *Africa and the International System. The politics of state survival*. Cambridge: Cambridge University Press.

Dereje, F. 2003. *Ethnic Groups and Conflict: The case of Anywaa-Nuer relations in the Gambella region, Ethiopia*. PhD Thesis. Halle/Saale: Martin Luther Universität Halle-Wittenberg.

Drysdale, J. 1964. *The Somali Dispute*. London: Pall Mall Press.

Ferguson, J. 2006. 'Transnational Topographies of Power: beyond 'The State' and 'Civil Society' in the Study of African politics', in B. Maurer and G. Schwab (eds), *Accelerating Possession: Global futures of property and personhood*. New York: Columbia University Press, pp. 76–98.

Fischer, E. 1949. 'On Boundaries'. *World Politics* 1(2): 196–222.

Geshekter, C.L. 1985. 'Anti-colonialism and class formation: The eastern Horn of Africa before 1950'. *International Journal for African Historical Studies* 18(1): 1–32.

Hagmann, T. and A. Mulugeta. 2008. 'Pastoral Conflicts and State-building in the Ethiopian Lowlands'. *Africa Spectrum* 43(1): 19–37.

Herbst, J. 1989. 'The Creation and Maintenance of National Boundaries in Africa'. *International Organisation* 43(4): 673–92.

—— 2000. *States and Power in Africa: Comparative lessons in authority and control*. Princeton, NJ: Princeton University Press.

Hoehne, M.V. 2009. 'Mimesis and Mimicry in Dynamics of State and Identity Formation in Northern Somalia'. *Africa* 79(2): 252–81.

—— forthcoming: 'Somaliland: The gestation of a *de facto* state', in B. Mesfin (ed), *Regional security in the post-Cold-War Horn of Africa*. Addis Ababa: ISS.

Horstmann, A. and R. Wadley 2006. 'Centering the margins in Southeast Asia: Introduction', in A. Horstmann and R. Wadley (eds), *Centering the Margin: Agency and narrative in Southeast Asian borderlands*. Oxford and New York: Berghahn Press, pp. 1–26.

Hüsken, T. 2010. 'The neo-tribal competitive order in the borderland of Egypt and Libya', in U. Engel and P. Nugent (eds), *Respacing Africa*, Amsterdam: Brill, pp. 170–205.

Hutchinson, S. 1996. *Nuer Dilemmas: Coping with money, war and the state*. Berkeley, CA: University of California Press.

Information Service of the Somali Government. 1962. *The Somali Peninsula: A new light on imperial motives*. Mogadishu: Information Service of the Somali Government.

Jackson, R.H. 1990. *Quasi-States. Sovereignty, international relations, and the third world*. Cambridge: Cambridge University Press.

Johnson, D. 2003. *Root Causes of Sudan's Civil Wars*. Oxford: James Currey.

Katzenellbogen, Simon 1996. 'It didn't happen in Berlin: Politics, economics and ignorance in the setting of Africa's colonial boundaries', in A.I. Asiwaju and P. Nugent (eds), *African Boundaries: Barriers, conduits and opportunities*. London: Pinter, pp.21–34.

Kearney, M. 1995. 'The local and the global: The anthropology of globalization and transnationalism'. *Annual Review of Anthropology* 24: 547–65.

Kolossov, V. 2005. 'Border studies: Changing perspectives and theoretical approaches'. *Geopolitics* 10: 606–32.

Lewis, I.M. 1983. 'Introduction', in I.M. Lewis (ed.), *Nationalism and Self-determination in the Horn of Africa*. London: Ithaca Press, pp. 1–22.

Little, P. 2006. 'Working Across Borders: Methodological and policy challenges of cross-border livestock trade in the Horn of Africa', in J. McPeak and P. Little (eds), *Pastoral Livestock Marketing in Eastern Africa: Research and policy challenges*. Rugby: ITDG Publishing, pp. 169–85.

McGrew, A. 1997. *The Transformation of Democracy?: Globalization and Territorial Democracy*. Cambridge: Polity Press.

Mahmoud, H.A. 2008. *Seeking citizenship on the border: Kenya Somalis, the uncertainty of belonging, and public sphere interactions*. Paper presented at the 12th CORDESIA General Assembly, Yaundé, Cameroun, July 11-12 2008.

Markakis, J. 1998. *Resource Conflict in the Horn of Africa*. Thousand Oaks, CA: Sage Publications.

—— 2003. 'Anatomy of a Conflict: Afar and Ise Ethiopia'. *Review of African Political Economy* 96: 445–453.

—— 2006. *Borders and Borderland Communities in the Horn: The failure of integration*. Paper presented at the conference 'Divided They Stand: The affordances of state borders in the Horn of Africa'. Max Planck Institute for Social Anthropology, Halle/Saale, September 7–8, 2006.

Matthies, V. 1977. *Der Grenzkonflikt Somalias mit Äthiopien und Kenya. Analyse eines zwischen-staatlichen Konflikts in der Dritten Welt*. Hamburg: Institut für Afrikakunde.

Menkhaus, K. 2010. 'The question of ethnicity in Somali studies: The case of Somali Bantu identity', in M.V. Hoehne and V. Luling (eds), *Milk and Peace, Drought and War: Somali culture, society and politics*. London: Hurst, pp. 87–104.

Merera, G. 2006. 'Contradictory Interpretations of Ethiopian History: The need for a new consensus', in D. Turton (ed.), *Ethnic Federalism: The Ethiopian experience in comparative perspective*. Oxford: James Currey, pp. 119–30.

Newman, D. 2006. 'Borders and Bordering: Towards an interdisciplinary dialogue'. *European Journal of Social Theory* 9(2): 171–86.

Nugent, P. 2002. *Smugglers, Secessionists and Loyal Citizens on the Ghana-Togo Frontier: The Life of the Borderlands since 1914*. Athens, OH: Ohio University Press; Oxford: James Currey.

Pelkmans, M. 2006. *Defending the Border: Identity, religion, and modernity in the Republic of Georgia*. Ithaca, NY and London: Cornell University Press.

Raeymaekers, T. 2009. 'The silent encroachment of the frontier: A politics of transborder trade in the Semliki Valley (Congo-Uganda)'. *Political Geography* 28: 55–65.

Rösler, M and T. Wendl 1999. 'Introduction', in M. Rösler and T. Wendl (eds), *Frontiers and Borderlands: Anthropological perspectives*. Frankfurt/Main: Peter Lang, pp. 1–27.

Schlee, G. 1998. 'Some Effects on a District Boundary in Kenya', in M. Aguilar (ed.), *The Politics of Age and Gerontocracy in Africa*. Trenton, NJ: Africa World Press, pp. 225–65.

—— 2003. 'Redrawing the Map of the Horn: The politics of difference'. *Africa* 73(3): 343–68.

Scott, J. 1990. *Domination and the Arts of Resistance: Hidden transcripts*. New Haven, CT and London: Yale University Press.

Shamir, Roxen. 2005. 'Without Borders: Notes on Globalization as a Mobility Regime', *Sociological Theory* 23 (2): 197–217.

Touval, S. 1972. *The Boundary Politics of Independent Africa*. Cambridge, MA: Harvard University Press.

Tsing, A.L. 1993. *In the Realm of the Diamond Queen: Marginality in an out-of-way place*. Princeton, NJ: Princeton University Press.

Wilson, T and H. Donnan. 1998. 'Nation, state and identity at international borders', in T. Wilson and H. Donnan (eds), *Borders: Frontiers of identity, nation and state*. Oxford: Berg, pp. 1–30.

Young, C. 1994. *The African Colonial State in Comparative Perspective*. New Haven, CT and London: Yale University Press.

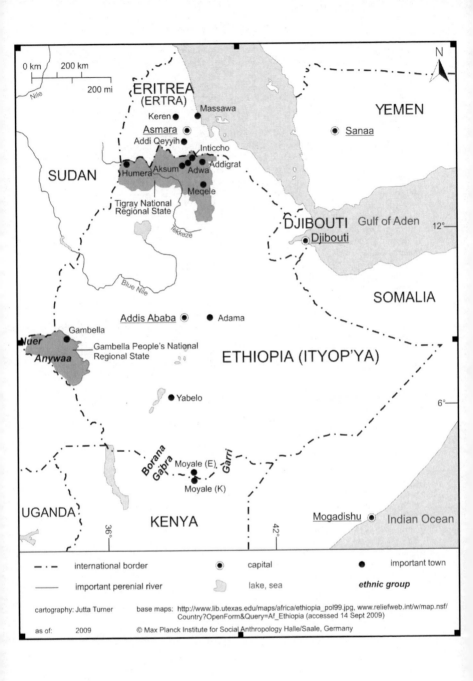

Map 1 *Ethiopian borderlands*

26

Two

~~~~~~

More State than the State?
The Anywaa's Call for the Rigidification
of the Ethio-Sudanese Border

DEREJE FEYISSA

Introduction

State borders have long been viewed as constraints on the people who live in the area, often artificially partitioned by the drawing of the boundary (see introduction to this volume). The Ethio-Sudanese border is no exception to the rule. The 1,600-mile border was demarcated in 1902 as part of the Anglo-Ethiopian treaty (Ullendorf 1967). The study area, the Gambella region, covers the western part of this border extending to the Akobo River in the south, the Pibor River in the west, and the Jikaw River in the north (Collins 1971). This border was drawn on the basis of the economic interests of imperial Ethiopia and colonial Britain and the dictates of the international diplomacy of the day, not the wishes of the people on the ground. The Anywaa and the Nuer, the two largest communities living in Gambella at the time of the delimitation of the international border, were arbitrarily divided between the two states. Where the border was drawn, the majority of the Anywaa were placed within Ethiopia but a section of them was put within the Sudan. The opposite was true for the Nuer; the majority of the Nuer were placed in the Sudan and only a segment of the Jikany Nuer remained within Ethiopia.

In this chapter I focus on how the Ethio-Sudanese border has functioned as an opportunity structure for the Anywaa. The paper briefly sketches the making of the border and the early response of the Anywaa. Against this background it discusses at length how the border is used as a discursive resource in the contemporary ethno-politics of Ethiopia, widely known as ethnic federalism. In the intense political competition between the Anywaa and the Nuer in the newly created regional state of Gambella, the Anywaa construct the Nuer as 'foreigners' through the invocation of the 1902 international border. Fearing the military power and assimilationist drive of their pastoralist neighbours, the agrarian Anywaa evoke the state border to ensure ethnic security and attain a dominant political status in the border region of Gambella. On that basis, the Anywaa view the opportunity cost of separation by the border as being lower than its rewards. Towards that end, they have called for the rigidification of the international border.

There is more to the Anywaa evocation of the border than mere strategic thinking, however. It is embedded in their model of political order that contains a stronger version of territoriality. What the Anywaa have partly done is to project their image of a bounded (ethnic) territory onto the state and its international borders. In effect, the national state is perceived and experienced by the Anywaa through their compartmentalized idea of a political community. Apparently, the Anywaa idea of the border connects with the state's idea of a border. But the (Ethiopian) state operates through multiple concerns about the border, only one of which is asserting political sovereignty. The gap between discursive link and political practice is one of the root causes of the current trouble between the Anywaa and the Ethiopian state. The Anywaa 'rebuke' the Ethiopian state for failing to observe the fundamental premise for modern states, namely, that political sovereignty is identified with bounded territories.

My writing is informed by the poststructuralist notion of 'everyday forms of state formation' in making sense of the Anywaa mode of relating to the Ethio-Sudanese border. Like Nugent, I am interested in 'the ways in which the state is shaped through practices which are on the face of things highly personalized and "un-statish"' (Nugent 2008: 121). The Anywaa evocation of the border is primarily driven by such 'un-statish' reasons, in particular by the project of collective self-preservation in a competitive ethno-space that reacts to the discourse of ethnic extinction, the realization of which has nevertheless the effect of reproducing state ideology (territoriality) at the local level.

The making of the Ethio-Sudanese border and the Anywaa response

The dominant event in the period before the arrival of the Sudanese and the Ethiopian states in what is known today as, respectively, the Upper Nile and the Gambella regions, was the dramatic eastward territorial expansion of the Nuer. The Nuer proceeded at the expense of the Dinka and the Anywaa throughout the second half of the nineteenth century. Before that, 'the Nuer were confined to a small area in southern Sudan in the area west of the Bahr Jebel River. A century later they had pushed eastward to the Ethiopian escarpment expelling all but a few pockets of Anywaa from the Sobat River basin' (Jal 1987: 36). By the early twentieth century groups of Nuer penetrated deep into Anywaa territory as far east as the Laajak hills, near the present-day Anywaa village of Akedo on the Baro River in Gambella (ibid.). Despite their brave resistance, many Anywaa were finally defeated by the Nuer and taken captive (Perner 1997: 144).

Prior to the arrival of the Nuer the Anywaa occupied the land adjacent to the Sobat river and its major tributaries. According to Evans-Pritchard (1940: 8), 'the Anywaa had occupied what is now Jikany Nuer country to the north of Sobat; parts of what is now Jikany and Lou Nuer country to the south of the river; the banks of the Pibor to its junction with the Sobat; and the banks of the Sobat to within a few miles of Abwong.' The Anywaa were pushed into the upland region in the southwest that they currently occupy, while the Nuer ultimately assimilated those who remained. With a four-fold territorial gain, Kelly (1985: 5) described the nineteenth century Nuer expansion as one of the most prominent examples of 'tribal imperialism' in the ethnographic record. The main reason for the dramatic expansion of the Nuer to the east (towards the Anywaa) was access to and control over riverine lands where they could secure dry season water points and pasture (Dereje 2005). The Nuer managed to successfully expand their territories thanks to the amassing effect of the segmentary lineage system and through an elaborate assimilationist system (Evans-Pritchard 1940; Sahlins 1961).

Various travellers and historians reported that by the end of the nineteenth century the Anywaa were said to be on the verge of extinction after waves of displacement by the Nuer. As Collins (1971: 203) noted, 'the Nuer left the Anywaa shattered. Many had died opposing the Nuer advance. Others had perished from the famine which followed, and all suffered the loss of cattle.' The Anywaa were saved by a technological state intervention. Anywaa nobles and headmen acquired firearms from imperial Ethiopia and subsequently managed to consolidate and expand the power of the Anywaa. The 1902 Ethio-Sudanese border was also a border between two different models of political order in the region. The British colonial establishment in the Sudan sought to create a monopoly of violence and homogeneous subjects. The Ethiopian empire, on the other hand, recognized hierarchies of subjects and operated through cooption of local structures of authority with a certain degree of tolerance towards local arms trafficking (Johnson 1986: 221).

Tolerance towards local armament also had an economic rationality. With limited capacity to govern its subjects, the Ethiopian empire had to rely on local leaders to extract wealth from the lucrative international ivory trade (Bahru 1976). Imperial Ethiopia had traded guns for Anywaa's ivory, for more guns had also meant greater capacity to hunt elephants (Collins 1971: 203). The political economy of imperial Ethiopia in the region was very much resented by the British who were more concerned with governing the frontier than extracting wealth from Gambella's natural economy. The other political concern of the British was to protect the waters of the Nile (ibid.: 95). Since both the Anywaa and the Nuer were straddling the border and doing business with imperial Ethiopia, the British were anxious to assert their authority over the frontier. Aspiring to create a homogenous subject (all the Nuer), the British relentlessly negotiated in vain to rectify the border. Imperial Ethiopia, on the other hand, was as much interested in doing business with the agrarian Anywaa as it was in the cattle wealth of the Nuer. Britain's high political stakes and the joint economic interest of the two political regimes in the region, however, helped to limit the escalation of violence between them. As part of the 1902 Anglo-Ethiopian treaty the British leased a trading station in Gambella town to tap into the riches of the western Ethiopian highlands, particularly the coffee and rubber trade for which the region was famous (Bahru 1976).

The creation of the Ethio-Sudanese border impacted differentially on the Anywaa and the Nuer. Taking advantage of their settlement pattern and proximity to the Ethiopian highlands, the Anywaa had earlier access to firearms than the Nuer, who were subjected to a stricter form of political control under the British. Through a series of high-profile military campaigns the British established their authority over the Nuer despite their resistance. Thus, the Nuer had come under pressure from two sides. Between 1910 and 1930 the Anywaa not only recovered from earlier defeats at the hands of the Nuer but emerged as the main local player in the regional power game. At the height of their military power they were said to have possessed as many as 25,000 rifles (Bahru 1976: 112) and constructed political power from this differential access to firearms. This was evident not only from the series of counter offensives they undertook in order to contain Nuer territorial expansion and raid their cattle; they also confronted first the British and then the Ethiopian state. Although these offensives were not sustained, the Anywaa had at least reduced the momentum of the Nuer territorial expansion and attained political autonomy *vis-à-vis* the two states. It was only in the 1930s that the British and the Ethiopian governments established a semblance of government authority in the Anywaa areas. To sum up, in the first three decades of the twentieth century the Anywaa had managed to extract political power from the Ethio-Sudanese border. They established themselves as a 'buffer' between Ethiopia and British Sudan and developed the capacity to contain their neighbours, at least temporarily.

The Ethio-Sudanese border as a political resource in contemporary Gambella

Nuer territorial expansion has continued, albeit in a more 'peaceful' way. Anywaa military resistance had the effect of re-orienting Nuer strategies of access to resources from violent to peaceful means, paralleling the symbiotic exchanges between herders and farmers elsewhere in the world. These exchanges, however, involve a certain asymmetry that favours the Nuer. Flexibility in ethnic recruitment, economic clout (cattle wealth) and numerical preponderance have enabled the Nuer to expand continually into Anywaa territories. This expansion has largely occurred through micro-demographic processes: the instrumentalization of inter-ethnic marriages and friendship networks. Typically, a Nuer man marries an

Anywaa woman. This is initially beneficial to both partners. For the Nuer it is cheaper to marry an Anywaa whose bride wealth payment is lower. For the agrarian Anywaa, marriage with Nuer ensures the flow of cattle wealth. The Nuer anticipate additional gains from such exchanges: marriage ties are used to legitimize settlement in Anywaa territories. Moreover, in virtually all cases, children of the inter-ethnic marriages identify with the Nuer because the Anywaa identity concept is strongly informed by an ideology of ethnic purity that makes it difficult for 'mixed' children to claim Anywaa ethnic identity safely, whereas the Nuer are conspicuously assimilationist. Although the Anywaa form of descent reckoning has a patrilineal bias, attention is given to the patriline of the mother of a person as well. Unlike the emergence of a hybrid identity that often follows inter-group marriages, inter-ethnic marriages between the Anywaa and the Nuer have thus resulted in the expansion of the Nuer. The Nuer families which are tied to the Anywaa through marriage relationships gradually serve as a nucleus for more immigrants. In due course the Nuer immigrants outnumber the Anywaa, who are then left with the option of either joining the Nuer kinship and political structures, or abandoning their villages in order to maintain their cultural identity. The memory of the extensive territorial losses of the nineteenth century, coupled with the continuous encroachment of the Nuer into their lands, has generated the contemporary Anywaa discourse of ethnic extinction – a local discourse which has been magnified by trans-local political processes.

The civil war in southern Sudan and the refugee phenomena that followed it have significantly altered the demographic structure of the Gambella region. By the mid-1980s the number of southern Sudanese refugees in Gambella rose sharply to 300,000, by far outnumbering the local population (Kurimoto 1997). As late as the first national census in 1984, the Anywaa were a demographic majority in the Gambella region. The refugee influx has changed the demographic structure. Most of the refugees were Sudanese Nuer who in due course became localized as Ethiopian citizens through clan networks across the international border. All of the refugee camps were established in Anywaa areas. The fact that many of the refugees were Nuer put further pressure on Anywaa ethnic sensibilities. The Anywaa appealed to the government of Ethiopia, popularly known as the Derg (1974–91), to contain the refugee influx. Their appeal was in vain because the local refugee phenomenon was intricately intertwined with the geo-politics of the time and the associated pattern of political alliances. In the 1980s the governments of Ethiopia and the Sudan were actively involved in mutual subversion, supporting each other's rebels politically and militarily (Johnson 2003). The Derg supported the Sudan People's Liberation Army (SPLA) and the government of Sudan reciprocated by supporting Eritrean liberation movements. This situation was in turn a reflection of yet wider political processes. The Derg was allied to the eastern bloc, whereas the government of Sudan stood on the side of the western bloc during the Cold War (Medhane 2007: 4-5).

31

As part of this pattern of alliances the Derg strategically co-opted the Ethiopian Nuer to enhance the linkage with the SPLA in which the Sudanese Nuer were significantly represented (Dereje 2009). By the end of the 1980s, the Nuer occupied senior administrative posts in the Gambella region. This was perceived by the Anywaa as a political affront that nurtured their sense of abandonment. The Anywaa repeatedly appealed to the Derg to secure the border, but they failed to get a hearing because of the pragmatic alliance between the Derg and the SPLA/Sudanese refugees mediated through the Nuer leadership in the Gambella adminis-tration. The political entrenchment of the Nuer, as well as their demo-graphic growth, accentuated the Anywaa sense of relative deprivation, and their discontent resulted in the formation of a liberation movement known as the Gambella People's Liberation Movement (GPLM). Reflecting a similar pattern of alliances, the GPLM was supported by the government of the Sudan in Khartoum. The GPLM also forged an alliance with the main opposition group known as the Ethiopian People's Revolutionary Democratic Front (EPRDF). This was because the GPLM framed the Nuer territorial encroachment in national terms, as an issue between Ethiopian citizens and foreign nationals. The Nuer-mediated alliance between the Derg and the SPLA made the EPRDF receptive to the Anywaa definition of the conflict situation. With the EPRDF claiming to be the champion of ethnic rights in Ethiopia, the Anywaa's subjection to political repression and cultural uprooting by the Derg also lent plausibility to the Anywaa's self-representation as an endangered ethnic group. The fact that the EPRDF itself was supported by the government of the Sudan and the SPLA by the Derg made the alliance between the EPRDF and the GPLM part of a wider political scheme.

In 1991 the EPRDF overthrew the Derg regime and restructured the Ethiopian state from a rigid form of political centralization to decentraliza-tion in the form of ethnic federalism. Ethiopia's ethnic federalism is a unique experience worldwide (Chabal and Daloz 1999). The 1994 Constitution recognizes ethnic rights which include the right to self-determination up to and including secession. The new political order, however, has not fully delivered on its promises. Only nine ethno-regional states were created out of the more than seventy ethnic groups in Ethiopia. The remaining ethnic groups were placed under the so-called multi-ethnic regional states, with various degrees of political entitlement.

In fact, even in the nine ethno-regional states the political structure does not fully reflect the settlement pattern on the ground. This has necessitated the insertion of a wide variety of sub-autonomous adminis-trative units for the new regional minorities. The Gambella People's National Regional State (GPNRS) is a case in point. The GPNRS 'belongs' to five 'indigenous' ethnic groups: the Anywaa, the Nuer, the Majangir, the Opo and the Komo, who together make up 76 per cent of the state's population. The remaining 24 per cent are migrants who came to Gambella from different regions of the country at various times and for different reasons. They are generically referred to as the 'Highlanders'. The bulk of the Highlanders, however, came to Gambella in the mid-1980s as part of the government's policy of resettling famine-affected people from the northern and southern highlands into regions of lower population density such as Gambella (Dereje 2008). It is for this reason that the High-landers are identified by the Anywaa and the Nuer with the Ethiopian state. In the new political dispensation, however, the Highlanders occupy the status of 'outsiders' because by definition they belong to other regional states than Gambella on the basis of their respective ethnic identity.

Although all indigenous ethnic groups have constitutionally equal political rights in the multi-ethnic regional states, in reality one or the other ethnic group dominated the political process over the past two decades through various ideologies of entitlement. Throughout the 1990s the Anywaa were the dominant force in the GPNRS. The GPLM-EPRDF alliance was a turning point in inter-ethnic power relations in post-1991 Gambella. With EPRDF backing, the Anywaa seized political power in the GPNRS. One of the discursive strategies used by the Anywaa power elites to justify their dominant political status was the definition of the situation in terms of natives versus outsiders. Represented as outsiders, the Nuer were not just a competing ethnic 'other' but 'foreigners' who troubled 'citizens'. The Anywaa found evidence for their definition of the Nuer as foreigners by making reference to the 1902 international border which placed the majority of the Nuer in the Sudan. According to this formulation, all Nuer migrations into the Gambella region after 1902 became, retrospectively, 'illegal'. The Anywaa also referred to the recent Nuer practice of alterna-tive citizenship between Sudanese and Ethiopian national identities as further evidence of the 'foreignness' of the Nuer. When commenting on Nuer pragmatism, the Anywaa often employ an Amharic expression, *behulet bila yemibelu* (those who eat with two knives), in reference to the alternative citizenship which was widely practised by the Nuer.

In the 1980s many Ethiopian Nuer switched to Sudanese national identity and joined the refugee camps that had been established in the Gambella region, with the consent of the Derg. Dozens of NGOs, under the auspices of the UNHCR, operated in the camps providing social services particularly health and educational facilities. The educational support package included scholarships (food, shelter and allowance) all the way up to college and university levels. As a result, a lot of Ethiopian Nuer flocked into the camps to gain access to better educational facilities. The deteriorating security condition in the border district of Jikaw in the second half of the 1980s was an additional push factor for the Ethiopian Nuer to switch their national identity to Sudanese, since the refugee camps appeared safer than the villages. Throughout the second half of the 1980s all the schools but one were closed down in the Nuer-inhabited areas in Ethiopia because of the military clashes between the SPLA and the Sudanese government inside Ethiopian territory. This complex system of political alliances had the effect of blurring the international border.

Reacting to this fluidity, the UNHCR relaxed its screening procedures and refugees were admitted *prima facie*. This worked much better for Nuer refugees of Ethiopian origin who instrumentalized the image of Nuer as 'Sudanese' than for the Ethiopian Anywaa who were conspicuous with their 'Ethiopian' national identity. Attached to the refugee camp was also an opportunity structure called the refugee resettlement programme. Making use of this opportunity structure within the aid agencies, a significant number of Nuer have been resettled in North America and Australia. The Nuer diaspora there is estimated at 10,000, a significant number of whom are from the Gambella region.

The 1990s brought a new opportunity structure for the Nuer. As already mentioned above, in 1991 Ethiopia was restructured along federal lines. In this context, Gambella regional state became a prime example of the integration of historic minorities (Dereje 2006). Designated by the federal government as one of the 'indigenous' peoples of the GPNRS, the Nuer have sought to use the chances offered by Ethiopia's ethnic federalism. With the new political space being dominated by the Anywaa throughout the 1990s, however, the Nuer had to engage in local politics of inclusion.

With the GPLM's seizure of political power in the GPNRS, the Nuer were marginalized in the power-sharing and distribution of state-mediated resources. Playing the national card brought the Anywaa not only ethnic security but also a dominant political status in the newly constituted border state of Gambella. This political dominance was evident in the disproportionate political representation in the regional council and preferential treatment in the government job market. In the first three rounds of local and regional elections (1992, 1995 and 2000), the Anywaa disproportionately dominated the regional council and occupied key managerial posts in the GPNRS:

Table 2.1 Ethnic profile of the MPs in the Gambella regional Council

Group	1992	1995	2000
Anywaa	11	24	28
Nuer	5	10	19
Majangir	3	5	4
Opo	-	1	1
Komo	1	1	1
Highlanders	1	-	1
Total	21	41	54

Source: Compiled from field notes

Reacting to the Anywaa's exclusionary practices, the Nuer resorted to various counter-strategies in their politics of inclusion. In 1992 they established a political party, the Gambella People's Democratic Unity Party (GPDUP), to challenge the political dominance of the Anywaa. Operating within multiple constraints, the GPDUP remained a minor political force throughout the transitional period (1991–4). The 1994 census, however, provided it with a new political 'fact' which it was able to use to renegotiate the asymmetrical power relations between the two parties, and therefore between the Anywaa and the Nuer. According to the census, the Nuer constituted 40 per cent and the Anywaa 27 per cent of Gambella's population. Overnight the Nuer were transformed from a largely 'foreign' people to an 'ethnic majority'. This new political context now aggravated the Nuer sense of relative deprivation.

Ever since the census result was made public, Nuer politics has gravitated towards a demographic strategy of ethnic entitlement. The Anywaa have fiercely contested the census result, arguing that the Nuer population was inflated by migrants from southern Sudan and from the refugee camps. The controversy surrounding the census has raised the level of mutual antagonism between the Anywaa and the Nuer and radicalized their respective political strategies. The more demographic the Nuer case becomes, the more the Anywaa cling to their historical justification for their dominant status and the greater the interest they have developed in the international border. The entitlement issue has permeated various domains: from power-sharing to access to natural resources and social services. In this political debate, the Anywaa used the 'citizenship card' to mobilize the Ethiopian state in a local struggle. As the following narrative by a principal Anywaa political actor of the 1990s suggests, the Anywaa extended the discourse of an 'impending danger' eventually to the Ethiopian state itself, if the Nuer 'peril' was not averted:

> Today the Nuer are taking over our lands. Tomorrow they will go to the highlands. They are already in Dambidolo, even Addis Ababa. What do they do there? During the SPLA time [in the 1980s], the Nuer commanders used to say Gambella was part of southern Sudan because there are no black Ethiopians. The Nuer are not just expanding into Anywaa territories but have a hidden agenda of annexing Gambella to southern Sudan. If the Nuer do not stop pushing us we will also finally go to Bure, even to Gore [the two nearest highland towns]. Where else could we go then? What makes Ethiopia a country if it does not secure its border? (Opamo Uchok, former Head of Gambella Bureau of Education, Gambella town, interviewed in Ruiru, Kenya, February 22, 2002)

In the discussion I had with Opamo in Ruiru where many of the Anywaa refugees in Kenya live, we were joined by his friend, Abula Obang, who was also a one-time influential Anywaa political actor in the GPNRS. While elaborating on Opamo's 'statish' outlook, Abula further justified the Anywaa's call for the rigidification of the border in 'global' terms by making a reference to the western cultural imagery of the border that distinguishes and differentiates clearly marked territories and groups:

> It is migration that is affecting politics in Europe. The Germans and the French are angry because a lot of people are going there and disturbing their systems. They are concerned because if more and more people go

there, to whom will the land then belong? They fear that they will be a minority in their own country. That is exactly what we are saying. We are not saying that the Nuer should not be allowed to use the land and the water or even to live together with the Anywaa, but they should respect that the land belongs to the Anywaa. Germany and France are concerned about immigration because they know that democracy favors majorities and more foreigners would mean more power to them. Once they are in, you cannot say 'no' because they start claiming. Even after the EU was established the state borders are still valid in Europe. (Abula Obong, Head, Social sector, Gambella regional council, Gambela town, January 20, 2001)

The cultural construction of the state border

The Anywaa's call for the rigidification of the international border is not only a strategy in the politics of entitlement, but is also embedded in their cultural world. Territoriality features prominently in the social organization of the Anywaa. Territoriality is acted out above all in the two mutually constituted concepts of *jobur* (first-comers of a village) and *welo* (latecomers who are considered as guests of the *jobur*). Guests of a temporary or permanent nature are highly respected by the Anywaa but they are not really integrated fully into the *jobur*. The *welo* may contribute to the economic or military strength of the village, but they can also leave at any time. Within the *jobur* there are earth priests called *wat-ngomi*. In addition to ensuring fertility (human and agricultural) and maintaining the dignity of the earth, the *wat-ngomi* also ensure the separation between the human and animal (wild) territories. At times when a wild animal encroaches on a human territory the *wat-ngomi* performs a ritual that 'reminds' the encroaching animal to leave the 'human' territory (Perner 1994). Evans-Pritchard (1940: 37) described Anywaa territoriality in the following manner: 'the Anywaa are strongly attached to the sites where their ancestors lived and often tenaciously occupied them in face of extermination.' In a later work he further noted (1947: 93): 'however long strangers and their descendants live in a village and however much they intermarry with the dominant lineage or *jobur* they can never become members of it but remain *welo*, strangers.'

For the Anywaa, being a guest/stranger is a permanent status, a concept that is also used in inter-group (inter-village) relations within Anywaa society. For the Nuer, being a guest is a temporary status, a phase in the localization process, a concept that is also applied intra-ethnically. Among the Nuer the notion of a first-comer (*dil*) is a framework of inclusion for newcomers (other Nuer and non-Nuer alike), within which localization occurs through adopting the lineage name of the *dil*. For the Anywaa, the Nuer immigrants to their villages, related through affinal ties, are defined as *welo*, no matter how long they stay. The Anywaa mode of identification is closely tied to a specific territory, where they till their lands, go hunting and have their fishing grounds. When forced to settle in a new place, they have to become one with the land by dissolving clumps of earth in the water they drink. As noted by Perner (1997: 180–81), the Anywaa village has clear-cut territorial boundaries (*kew*), known to both its own inhabitants and those of other villages. He continued that 'each village in fact does have its territory with boundaries, well known by every-body' and 'the borders of a village's territories were outlined by runners who went to circumscribe the limits of a site, fixing certain points (such as trees, mouths of rivers, etc.) as boundary posts. The Anywaa believe that clear demarcation of a territory is extremely important as it helps to avoid conflicts between people of different territories.' The concept of *kew* also features in Anywaa cosmology. The Anywaa belief system recognizes three 'spheres of existence', which Perner (1994) calls the human sphere, the sphere of the earth, and the sphere of spirituality. Each being is entitled to exist within its own specific sphere. God (*Jwok*), a resident in the sky, is in charge of the sphere of spirituality. According to the Anywaa cosmological scheme, *Jwok's* border-crossing (intrusion into the human sphere), evident in the prevalence of misfortunes in a village, is the root cause of the human predicament.

Against the backdrop of such a radical formulation of territoriality, Nuer territorial and cultural encroachments have created a sense of bewilderment on the side of the Anywaa. This is evident in the scheme of interpretation the Anywaa often employ to make Nuer territorial expansion intelligible:

> God gave each people a language, a land and a system. If the Nuer would stay in the land, which we give them, it would be good. Anywaa have a system called *kew* [boundary]. There is *kew* between Jwok and humans; *kew* between countries; *kew* between neighbours; *kew* between brothers and even between father and son. The British made a *kew* between the Anywaa and the Nuer [the creation of homogeneous ethnic administrative units] to create a system so that there would be no problem between us. But the Nuer just move and take other people's land. The Nuer have no system. They move like the Felata [the Fulbe in the Sudan]. People like the Nuer and the Felata have no system. (Extracted from interview with Reverend Pastor James, Presbyterian Church of Sudan, Khartoum, March 2002)

A similar scheme of interpretation was used by another informant from a different social background, while reflecting on the Nuer territorial and cultural encroachments:

> The problem with the Nuer is too much democracy. Anybody can go to a Nuer village and live with them and become Nuer. That is what happened to the Jingmir Anywaa. Jingmir were originally Anywaa but now they have become Nuer. Some even have *goro* [sic, *gaar*, the Nuer male initiation mark]. We are fighting with the Nuer in Akobo but the Jingmir are not siding with us. In fact, some of them support the Nuer. If I go to Bentiue the Nuer will give me a wife so that I gradually become Nuer. With us it is

different. Anywaa reproach those who leave their village and join others. Only people who have problems leave their villages and live with other people. This is because the Nuer have no system and that is why they do not respect system where it exists. We got system from our kings. We respect our kings; wives respect their husbands. Other people say Anywaa are selfish and don't want to live with others. That is not true. We respect the system because we do not want to create problems. Kings bring systems, and you find kings in the bible as well. (Omot Agwa, Director, Gambella Peace and Development Programme)

The repeated reference to a 'system' in the aforementioned narratives is related to the Anywaa's model of a political order which is distinct from that of their neighbours. The relatively centralized political organization of the Anywaa, described extensively by Evans-Pritchard (1940) and Lienhardt (1957), sharply contrasts with their pastoralist neighbours such as the Nuer, whose non-centralized model of political order (the segmentary lineage system) is often referred to as 'ordered anarchy'. In traditional Anywaa society there were two kinds of political communities: the *ji-nyieya* ('people of the kings') and *ji-kwari* ('people of the chiefs'), which Evans-Pritchard called, respectively, nobles and headmen. Despite some differences in their political status, both the *ji-nyieya* and the *ji-kwari* were attached to specific territories, and they hardly embarked on territorial aggrandizement. The object of the struggle between the nobles and the headmen was not territory but royal emblems. The Anywaa take pride in their model of political order as an 'index' of civilization and often contrast it with their 'state-less' pastoralist neighbours, a status claim which is increasingly inserted into the contemporary identity politics, as is evident in the references to a system in the quotations above.

The Anywaa perception of the international border is partly conditioned by their own model of political community based on bounded territories. The state border is perceived and experienced as *kew*. Although the Anywaa were politically dominant in the GPNRS throughout the 1990s, they did not manage to fix the international border as much as they would like to have done. Management of international borders is a federal mandate. Lack of interest or determination by the federal government to police the border so that Nuer border-crossing could be checked is interpreted by the Anywaa as evidence of their status as 'second-class citizens' in Ethiopia, as the following statement by an Anywaa suggests:

Some borders are well protected and the government provides security to the border people. Hasn't the entire nation gone to war with Eritrea because of Badime? The government swiftly declared war on Eritrea because the people who live in the border town of Badime are Tigreans, the same people who also rule the country. The Gambella border is 360 degrees open. Sudanese Nuer could cross the border any time and take over Ethiopian land. (Interview with Abula, Nairobi, August 2002)

Collins, the principal historian of the Nilotic societies, shares Anywaa's grievances against the Ethiopian state. He identifies 'the failure of Ethiopia to control the frontier, administer the Baro Salient, and provide good governance' as one of the root causes of the Anywaa's troubles with their neighbours (Collins 1971: 156). He further embeds the government's apathy about protecting the Anywaa, which the latter refer to as evidence of their 'second-class citizenship', in the 'racist' framework of Ethiopia's national identity which is constructed in the language of skin colour, namely, that the blacker one is the less Ethiopian one becomes: 'underlying much of Ethiopian policy or lack thereof is the historic disdain by the Highlanders ... for the Africans on the Sudan plain below the escarpment ... Racism is compounded on the plains below the highlands by their isolation, swampy and forested terrain, and a porous frontier' (ibid.).

The Anywaa's changing perceptions of the border

The Ethiopian government is ambivalent towards the Anywaa's call for the rigidification of the border. More generally, Ethiopia has often seen itself as surrounded by potential enemies, and has worried about the extent to which its minorities would be loyal in the event of war with its neighbours – a classic example of what Kymlicka (2006) calls the 'securitization' of state-minority relations. In the context of highly volatile relations with the Sudan, the Nuer were occasionally regarded by the Ethiopian government as a security threat. In 1997, for instance, the two countries were on the brink of war, with Ethiopia accusing the Sudanese government of exporting Islamic fundamentalism to Ethiopia (Medhane 2007). A Nuer rebel leader, Riek Machar, was allied with the government of Sudan. As a result, the EPRDF, allied with the Anywaa, undertook a tight screening procedure to distinguish between Nuer citizens and refugees in the Gambella region. Towards that end, the Newland, the Nuer settlement area in Gambella town, was raided by the federal army and the regional police. The EPRDF's military action, however, was not driven by principle (enacting sovereignty), but rather was conducted on the basis of political expedience.

Moreover, in the volatile relations with the Sudan, the larger presence of the Nuer in the Sudan could also be regarded as a resource by the Ethiopian government in the geo-political game. Thus, instead of tightly policing the border, as suggested by the Anywaa, the EPRDF seems to have taken an ambiguous position towards the Nuer. The clue to this could be found in the following narrative by a government cadre. As part of enhancing political legitimacy, the EPRDF opened a political indoctrination school at Tatek, some 70km west of the capital city Addis Ababa, particularly for elites from the peripheral regional states such as Gambella which are not directly governed by the EPRDF. In the 1998 political training of the Anywaa and Nuer cadres the issue of citizenship was addressed in the following manner:

One of the issues which we discussed in this training was 'What would happen to Gambella should southern Sudan become independent?' The Nuer cadres said, 'We will remain as Ethiopian citizens' but the Anywaa said, 'No, the Nuer will be the first to go to the Sudan because even now they identify as Sudanese.' After a long debate, the EPRDF told us the answer: 'it is not right to say the Anywaa are Ethiopian and the Nuer are Sudanese. Both of you come from the Sudan [in reference to Nilotic migrations] and nothing will change the fact that Gambella is an Ethiopian territory. Both the Anywaa and the Nuer have the right to live in Gambella'. The EPRDF cadre then posed this question to us: '...but what is this Nuer Christian prayer which says "May God liberate our land"? Are you not living in an already liberated land? Why should you pray for southern Sudan?' We told them that we pray like that because the Nuer church came from the Sudan and we simply adopted their prayer. (Peter Kayier, GPDUP cadre, interview, Nairobi, August 2002)

A similar ambivalence is observable among the Highlanders, who are identified categorically with the Ethiopian state by the Anywaa and the Nuer. Represented as such, the Highlanders emerge as 'significant others' in evaluating the 'depth' of the Anywaa's and Nuer's commitment to Ethiopian national identity, although they have been politically marginalized in post-1991 Gambella. The following narrative by a Highlander from Gambella town illustrates how the Highlanders often position themselves in the citizenship debate between the Anywaa and the Nuer:

The Anywaa are familiar to us. We have a history of living together. You can trust them as Ethiopians. The problem with the Anywaa is rather their ownership claim over the Gambella region. They want Gambella for themselves. The Nuer, on the other hand, are foreigners [Sudanese]. The good thing about the Nuer is they are hard working and they don't discriminate between people. Economically they are also useful. We don't get anything from the Anywaa. At least we see Nuer cattle in the butchery. But you cannot trust the Nuer. Their heart is with the Sudan. You do not find them in Ethiopian history books. How can you trust somebody whom you do not know? (Extracted from an informal discussion with a highlander civil servant, Gambella town, July 2000)

The Anywaa, for their part, present themselves to the Ethiopian government and the Highlanders as genuine Ethiopian citizens who represent the national interest better than the Nuer. In return for this they expect government protection from the cross-border Nuer territorial expansion and, in their perspective, the ultimate 'extinction' of Anywaa society. In effect, the Anywaa have appealed to the Ethiopian government to live up to their expectations of fixing and policing the international border. Drawing on their own notion of a border as bounded territory, coupled with a relative abundance of land in the Anywaa-inhabited areas, the rigidification of the international border gives the Anywaa more security than its permeability. Although there is a low-level cross-border movement, the migration of the Sudanese Anywaa to the Gambella region is virtually non-existent, save for a small trickle to the refugee camps. The Anywaa in the Gambella region feel that they are positioned to benefit from the international border in as much as it could help them at least to contain further Nuer territorial expansion, if not as a discursive strategy in the politics of exclusion in ethno-politics. In the competitive ethno space the border is signified as a guarantee of the survival of the Anywaa, not a cross-border resource for ethnic mobilization. This is so because pan-Anywaa political mobilization could provoke a similar pan-Nuer mobiliza-tion in which the Anywaa are destined to lose, given the stark numerical imbalance and the differential accumulation of military power between the two.

As a result, the Ethiopian Anywaa overstated their Ethiopian national identity, whereas they were conspicuously silent about their Sudanese connection until they fell out with the EPRDF after 2002. In March 2001, for instance, the reigning king, *Nyiya* Adongo from Utalo village in South Sudan, paid a visit to the Gambella region and attempted unsuccessfully to make contact with the Ethiopian Anywaa officials in order to set up a cross-border ethnic political network. As a last resort, *Nyiya* Adongo held a secret meeting with a group of disgruntled educated Anywaa to enhance pan-Anywaa sentiment. This incident revealed the existence of alternative discourses in the Anywaa project of containing their neighbours. The Sudanese Anywaa and those in the diaspora propound a pan-ethnic strategy, whereas the Anywaa power elites in the Gambella region pursued a national strategy throughout the 1990s.

The Anywaa's disappointment grew sharply in the early 2000s when they failed to get the support they expected from the EPRDF during a deadly power struggle with the Nuer between June 2002 and January 2003 that cost the lives of many people from both sides, particularly in Gambella and Itang towns. With this conflict, the government introduced a new power-sharing arrangement ostensibly to balance the Anywaa historical and the Nuer demographic arguments for political entitlement. This greatly alienated the Anywaa who once again felt abandoned by the Ethiopian state. As a result, there has been a discursive convergence among the various Anywaa political actors who earlier followed divergent strategies of containment.

Disgruntled groups of Anywaa expressed their anger by attacking government establishments and ambushing civilian Highlanders. On 13 December 2003, a car carrying eight employees of the government was ambushed some 30 kilometers outside of Gambella town. The occupants of the car, all of them Highlanders, were killed in the attack and their bodies were mutilated. The individuals who carried out the attack were reportedly never caught, but 'it was widely assumed both by the Highlanders and the government that the ambush was the work of an armed Anywaa group' (Human Rights Watch 2005: 12). Whoever killed the eight Highlander government officials, the manner in which they were killed was brutal. The severely mutilated bodies were paraded in a vehicle to the regional council offices for public display before they were taken to the hospital mortuary. Assuming that the murders were committed by the Anywaa, and agitated by the gruesome display of the mutilated bodies, a mob of Highlanders went on the rampage, indiscriminately killing Anywaa males with rocks and machetes. Some members of the federal army deployed in the region, who were exclusively Highlanders, also partici-pated in the killing using automatic weapons. Estimates of the casualties vary. Anywaa sources and international human rights organizations put the Anywaa death toll as high as 424 (Human Rights Watch 2005; Anuak Justice Council 2006), whereas the government acknowledged only 67.

The border has assumed a new meaning in the Anywaa imagination of ethnic security since December 2003. Thousands of Anywaa have crossed the border and taken shelter with the Sudanese Anywaa in Pochalla County. This new political experience has led to a re-strategizing of ethnic security, from a national to an ethnic and pan-Anywaa consciousness spearheaded by their diaspora.

The formation of the Anywaa diaspora is itself a result of the pragmatic use of the international border. By the 1990s some Anywaa had already drifted away from a national strategy (ethnic security framed in national terms) to alternative citizenship, following in the footsteps of the Nuer. In the mid-1990s a small group of Ethiopian Anywaa went to southern Sudanese refugee camps in Kenya where they managed to pass as Sudanese Anywaa, in order to make use of the UNHCR's refugee resettle-ment programme to North America. It was more difficult for Anywaa to pass as Sudanese refugees in Ethiopia where they were perceived by the aid agencies as 'Ethiopians'. On that basis, the aid agencies accepted the Ethiopian Nuer as refugees *prima facie*, while the Anywaa had to undergo tight screening procedures. Alternatively, the Anywaa went to refugee camps in Kenya where they could pass as southern Sudanese with relative ease. Buying into the discourse on skin colour in Ethiopia the Anywaa were perceived by the Kenyan refugee camp authorities as 'too black' to be Ethiopian. Thus, what is a source of discrimination in Ethiopia enabled the Anywaa not only to negotiate their marginality through resettlement in North America but also to connect their troubled ethnic compatriots in Gambella with a global audience. While claiming southern Sudanese national identity in reference to the cross-border settlement, the Anywaa have extracted a different type of resource from the international border by crossing it. As part of their engagement in homeland affairs, Anywaa diaspora political organizations and support groups have proliferated, such as the Anywaa Community Association in North America (ACANA) and the Gambella Relief Organization (GRO) based in Minnesota, and the Anywaa Justice Council (AJC) based in Canada. There is a higher degree of reflexivity in the 'fear of extinction' by the Anywaa diaspora. Unlike their homeland compatriots who have for a long time used a national strategy for ethnic security, the Anywaa diaspora have reframed Anywaa claims for resources, political power and identity maintenance in the new global claim structure of an indigenous minority persecuted by a genocidal state (Ethiopia) and 'bad' neighbours (Dereje 2006).

Concluding remarks

Cognizant of the larger cross-border settlement pattern of their competing neighbour, the Nuer in southern Sudan, the Anywaa in the Gambella region of Ethiopia constantly refer to the international border as a frame of reference to define the parameters of inclusion/exclusion in the competition for political power and claims for resources, and as a mechanism of identity maintenance. The state border as a reference point has enabled them to frame an ethnic concern (fear of extinction) in national terms, in which the Nuer are not only encroaching into Anywaa lands but their expansion is becoming an issue between 'natives' and 'outsiders'. They are presented as 'foreigners' who trouble 'citizens'. Framed in this way, the Anywaa anticipate mobilizing the Ethiopian state in a local struggle. It is for this reason that they invoke the state discourse (sovereignty) more than the state. The Anywaa's call for the rigidification of the border, typically a state discourse, resonates with the notion of an everyday form of state formation. Nugent (2008: 121) confirmed that 'the margins of the state … are spaces of creativity where the actions of ordinary people help to configure the state'.

While actively reproducing the state ideology through enactment of the border, what drives the Anywaa discursive practice is not commitment to a national identity but rather a national framework within which ethnic interests are protected and renegotiated. Viewed from this perspective, the opportunity cost of separation by the state border is viewed by the Anywaa political actors in the Gambella region of the 1990s as lower than the rewards of the cross-border mobilization. There is more to the Anywaa discourse of the border than mere strategic thinking. The perception of the state border also has cultural roots: the overarching theme of territoriality as an organizational principle in the Anywaa imagination of the social world. The new sets of political experience and the changing perceptions of the Anywaa towards the Ethio-Sudanese border since 2003, on the other hand, illustrate how a state border can be variously signified by the borderlanders.

References

Bahru, Z. 1976. *Relations between Ethiopia and the Sudan on the Western Ethiopian Frontier 1898-1935*. Ph.D. dissertation. University of London.
Chabal, P. and J.-P. Daloz 2001. *Africa Works: Disorder as Political Instrument*. Oxford: James Currey.

Collins, R.1971. *Land beyond the Rivers: The Southern Sudan, 1898–1918*. New Haven, CT: Yale University Press.

Dereje, F. 2003. *Ethnic Groups and Conflict: The case of Anywaa-Nuer relations in the Gambella region*. Ph.D dissertation submitted to Martin Luther University.

—— 2005. 'Land and the Politics of Identity: The Case of Anywaa-Nuer Relations in the Gambella Region', in S. Evers, M. Spierenburg and H. Wels (eds), *Competing Jurisdictions: Settling Land Claims in Africa*. Leiden: Brill Academic Publishers, pp. 203–22.

—— 2006. *The Affordances of Framing Local Struggles in Global Terms: The Identity Politics of the Anywaa Diaspora in North America*. Paper presented at the Graduate School Colloquium, Martin Luther University, Halle, June 12 2006.

—— 2008. 'Layers of Conflict in the Gambella Region: An Interactive Approach', in E. Bruchaus and S. Sommer (eds), *Hot Spot Horn of Africa Revisited: Approaches to Make Sense of Conflict*. Münster: LIT, pp. 146–58.

—— 2009. 'Conflict and Identity Politics: The Case of Anywaa-Nuer Relations in the Gambella Region', in E. Watson and G. Schlee (eds), *Changing Identification and Alliances in Northeast Africa*. Vol II. New York: Berghahn Books, pp. 181–203.

Evans-Pritchard, E.E. 1940. *The Political System of the Anuak of the Anglo-Egyptian Sudan*. New York: AMS Press.

—— 1947. 'Further Observations on the Political System of the Anuak'. *Sudan Notes and Records*. 28: 62–97.

Human Rights Watch. 2005. *Targeting the Anuak: Human Rights Violations and Crimes against Humanity in Ethiopia's Gambella Region*. 17(3A). New York: Human Rights Watch.

Jal, G. 1987. *The History of the Jikany Nuer before 1920*. Ph.D. dissertation. History Department, School of Oriental and African Studies, University of London.

Johnson, D. 1986. 'On the Nilotic Frontier: Imperial Ethiopia in the Southern Sudan, 1898-1936', in D. Donham and W. James (eds), *The Southern Marches of Imperial Ethiopia*. London: James Currey, pp. 219–54.

—— 2003. *Root Causes of Sudan's Civil Wars*. Oxford: James Currey.

Kelly, R. 1985. *The Nuer Conquest: The Structure and Development of an Expansionist System*. Ann Arbor, MI: University of Michigan Press.

Kurimoto, E. 1997. 'Politicization of Ethnicity in Gambella', in K. Fukui, E. Kurimoto and M.Shigeta (eds), *Ethiopia in Broader Perspective: Papers of the 13th International Conference of Ethiopian Studies*. Kyoto: Shokado, pp. 798–815.

Kymlicka, W. 2006. 'Emerging western models of multination federalism: Are they relevant for Africa?', in D. Turton (ed.), *Ethnic Federalism*. Oxford: James Currey, pp. 32–64.

Lienhardt, G. 1957. 'Anuak Village Headmen I'. *Africa* 27(4): 341–55.

Medhane, T. 2007. 'Gambella: The Impact of Local Conflict on Regional Security'. Addis Ababa: Centre for Policy Research and Dialogue. http://www.eprdhorn.org

Nugent, P. 2008. 'Border Anomalies: The Role of Local Actors in Shaping Spaces along the Senegal-Gambia and Ghana-Togo Borders', in A. Bellagamba and G. Klute (eds), *Beside the State: Emerging Powers in Contemporary Africa*. Köln: Köppe Verlag, pp. 121–38.

Perner, C. 1994. *The Anyuak – Living On Earth in the Sky. Vol. I. The Sphere of Spirituality*. Basel: Helbing & Lichtenhahn.

—— 1997. *The Anyuak – Living On Earth in the Sky. Vol. II. The Human Territory*. Basel. Helbing & Lichtenhahn.

Sahlins, M. 1961. 'The Segmentary Lineage: An Organisation of Predatory Expansion'. *American Anthropologist* (New Series) 63(2:1): 322–45.

Ullendorf, E. 1967. 'The Anglo-Ethiopian Treaty of 1902'. *Bulletin of the School of Oriental and African Studies* 30(3): 641–54.

Three

Making Use of Kin beyond the International Border

Inter-Ethnic Relations along the Ethio-Kenyan Border

FEKADU ADUGNA

Introduction

International borders, particularly those in Africa, have been perceived as constraints to the livelihoods of the people divided by them (see Chapter 1 by Dereje and Hoehne in this volume).[1] Gufu Oba (2000) has succinctly explained how the Borana Oromo who were divided by the colonial border between the two empires, Ethiopia and Great Britain, suffered enormously at various times. He elucidated in particular the agony of the Obbu Borana who reside along the Kenyan-Ethiopian border, mainly because of the closure of access to water sources on the Ethiopian side which is highland and rich in water resources. The problem of the Obbu Borana climaxed during the Italian occupation.

Without deeming this perspective unimportant, this chapter explains the advantages of the same borders, but in post-colonial times. I shall try to explain how individuals and groups instrumentalize the border at present as a resource in order to win the competition and conflict among themselves, on the one hand, and between themselves and the states to which they 'belong', on the other. I start by briefly introducing the three communities which serve as a case study to substantiate the argument.

The Borana are predominantly cattle pastoralists. They inhabit the southern rangelands straddling the Ethio-Kenyan border. In Ethiopia they live in the Borana and part of the Guji Zones of the Oromia National Regional State. In Kenya their home areas are the districts of Moyale, Isiolo and Marsabit. Ethnically, the Borana are one of the groups that make up the Oromo nation. In fact, they provide the core symbols of Oromo nationalism, such as a functioning *gada* system, which lies at the heart of the Oromo discourse of their egalitarian and republican form of administration (Legesse 1973, 2000; Bassi 2005).

The Garri, on the other hand, inhabit Ethiopia, Kenya and Somalia. They live in the Moyale and Hudet districts of the Somali National Regional State in southern Ethiopia, in the Mandera district of northern Kenya, and around El-Waq in the southern part of Somalia. The Garri are a bilingual group that speaks Somali as well as Oromo. Also their cultural traits are mixed, including Somali and Oromo features. These multiple identity markers put the Garri in the advantageous position of being able to switch between being Somali and Oromo at different times and in different situations (Schlee 1994; Fekadu 2009). Recently, in the context of the formalized and state-led ethno-national federal arrangement in Ethiopia, the Garri overwhelmingly opted for being part of the Somali community rather than joining the Oromo.[2]

Among the Gabra, the third group featuring in this chapter, ethnic identity proved to be very fluid and instrumental. Based on their location, there are two groups of Gabra who consider each other as kin: the Gabra Miigo and Gabra Malbe inhabiting southern Ethiopia and northern Kenya, respectively. While the Gabra Miigo live mixed with the Borana in the Oromia National Regional State of southern Ethiopia, the Gabra Malbe have an exclusive constituency in the Marsabit district in northern Kenya. With a long history of nomadic life and cultural adaptation, the Gabra are endowed with thick cultural markers that can 'make' them both Oromo and Somali similarly to the Garri. But in contrast to the latter, they are not bilingual. They speak *Afaan* Oromo. They have a socio-cultural organization of the *gada* kind, close to that of the Borana, but with some fundamental differences in their organizations and calendars. On the other hand, they have a Somali housing style, camel-centred rituals, and follow a calendar similar to that of the proto-Somali people (Schlee 1989; Tablino 1999; Kassam 2006). The Gabra elite are effectively employing these cultural means at their disposal in order to take advantage of the possibility of 'dual identification' as both Oromo and Somali.

My empirical data come from Moyale (in Ethiopia and Kenya). The name Moyale has been used for two districts, the Ethiopian and the Kenyan Moyale. On the Ethiopian side, Moyale is divided into the Oromo Moyale and the Somali Moyale districts. Both districts use the same town, the Ethiopian Moyale town, as administrative centre. As a result, this town and its surroundings are severely contested between the Oromia and Somali National Regional States of Ethiopia. Borana, Garri and Gabra reside right across this setting. My main concern is to examine how these seemingly divided actors use the presence of their kin on the other side of the border in conflict situations and/or during election campaigns for building extended networks of support, hosting and supporting rebels, and also easing/mediating disputes.

Local conflict, state policies, and the opportunities of borders

CONFLICTS OVER REGIONAL STATE BORDERS IN ETHIOPIA

The defeat of the military regime that ruled Ethiopia for seventeen years (1974–91) and the subsequent coming to power of the Tigrean Peoples Liberation Front (TPLF)-led coalition, the Ethiopian People's Revolutionary Democratic Front (EPRDF), radically changed the political structure in Ethiopia. The transitional government charter adopted in 1991 and the 1994 Constitution of the Federal Democratic Republic of Ethiopia (FDRE, 1995) revolved the terms of the political game both at the national and local levels, turning ethnicity from a taboo topic into a concept facilitating co-existence in a divided nation (see Vaughan, 2003; Turton, 2006).[3] The Constitution divided the country into nine putatively autonomous ethnic-based regional states and two multi-ethnic city-states. Ethiopia was 're-mapped' by this new political structure after more than a century of unitary state organization (James et al. 2002; Schlee 2003).

Such state policies and provisions of the Constitution, and the ensuing political dynamism, have several effects, two of which are very important in the sort of identity politics I am discussing here. First, ethnicity became a defining principle of the state organization in Ethiopia; as such it is inter-twined with resources. As a result, ethnic identity politics have become more important than ever before. Second, by equating ethnic groups and administrative units – an overlap of ethnic and administrative borders – the system made territorial borders between ethnic groups more important than ever before. This has played a significant role in solidifying ethno-territoriality (Aalen 2006; Hagmann 2007).

The Oromia and Somali National Regional States, which officially belong to the Oromo and Somali peoples respectively, are among the ethno-national states. These two regional states have been engaged in protracted conflicts and claims and counter-claims over territory along their borders.[4] The Ethiopian government argues that the strategies to settle conflicts around the ethno-national borders, such as the Oromia–Somali border conflict, are included in the constitutional framework. The central tool regarding these 'in-built mechanisms of conflict resolutions' is undertaking a referendum to decide the fate of the contested resources (territories) by a majority vote (50% +1 formula). After years of negotiation brokered by the national state institutions such as the House of the Federation and the Ministry of Federal Affairs, the two regional states reached an agreement to undertake a referendum in the 430 *kebele* (territorial units of the lowest level of administration) along their border.[5]

Most pastoralists rejected the decision to undertake the referendum. Their major argument was that the referendum would not take into consideration their socio-economic situation. The livelihood of the local communities depends on nomadic and/or transhumant pastoralism, which requires seasonal mobility and the extensive use of the environment beyond administrative territorial borders, while the referendum is a political solution to impose solid borders. In fact, the constitutional arrangements clearly disregarded the pastoralists' methods of resource management by limiting their opportunistic use of the rangelands. The Borana further argued that, besides the necessities of the pastoral economy, the resolution of any conflict based on rivalry over territorial claims should be related to historic and traditional ownership rights rather than to a referendum (Fekadu 2004, 2009). Notwithstanding the local objections, the state (both the federal and the two regional states) continued with its project of undertaking the referendum.[6]

The National Electoral Board was given the responsibility of coordinating and supervising the whole process. The state-owned national media broadcasted the need for and the procedures of the referendum. Accordingly, after a decade of territorial contestations and partly violent conflicts most of the border between the Oromia and the Somali National Regional States was delimited in a referendum in November 2004. The inhabitants of the borderlands including the pastoralists were forced to cast ballots to decide their fate, also with regard to resource use and ethnic identification. The process was 'successfully' undertaken in 422 *kebele*, according to official sources.[7] The Oromia National Regional State won 323 and the Somali National Regional State 99 of the contested *kebele*. However, the referendum failed to materialize in four *kebele* in Moyale town and the surrounding area. The ballots of another two *kebele* were rejected for technical reasons.

Ethiopian officials argued that the referendum served administrative purposes, but for the local actors it was a question of either losing or gaining resources mainly related to territory endowed with water wells, grazing land, ritual places and towns. Furthermore, the process had enormous implications for the ethnic identity of the groups inhabiting the borderlands between the two regional states. The referendum not only failed to resolve the existing conflicts but also intensified them in some areas, quite contrary to the claim of the state to have solved the issue. For instance, the Garri and Borana fought two deadly conflicts over their borders during the long dry season of 2008 and another in February 2009. According to a BBC journalist who reported from Moyale town in Ethiopia, in the last conflict alone more than 300 people died and some 70,000 were displaced.[8] Paradoxically, through state interference and the ensuing violence, this internal administrative border has become more solid following the referendum than the Ethio-Kenyan international border, which is the focus of the rest of this chapter. For instance, in most of the areas where the district border was delimited by the referendum the previous social relations based on holding a common market, attending school together, and bond friendship relationships across the district border came to an end. Ensuing violent clashes deepened political and ethnic divisions.

LOCAL POLITICS AND ALLIANCES ACROSS
THE ETHIO-KENYAN BORDER

In the conflicts mentioned above, the Ethiopian Moyale district has been seriously contested between the Borana and Garri at the local level and between the Oromia and Somali National Regional States at the national level. The two levels are not separated, but closely connected. The Borana are considered to be representatives of the Oromia National Regional State, while the Garri are perceived as belonging to the Somali National Regional State. The Gabra have a presence in both the Oromia and Somali National Regional State. This presence depends on political and economic opportunities on either side. Since 1995 Moyale town hosts two district administrations, one related to the Oromia and the other related to the Somali National Regional State. Each administration comprises a mayor, a police force, a customs office, a prison, and so forth. In Moyale 'everything is double', as locals mockingly told me. They have: double flags, double uniforms, double taxation, double police force, double live-stock market and double prison building. The town has also been wit-nessing occasional clashes between the police forces of the two regional states with injuries and casualties.[9] The continued conflict situation led the Borana and the Garri to mobilize their trans-national ethnic networks. They called upon their kin across the border in Kenya for support particularly during the referendum. In October 2006, I interviewed an official in the National Electoral Board of Ethiopia in Addis Ababa, who was in charge of the referendum that was supposed to be undertaken in Moyale, but failed to materialize. He put the blame for the failure of the referendum in Moyale town and its surroundings on Moyale's location on the international border and the transnational presence of the Garri.

> We have undertaken a referendum in 422 *kebele* from Miesso in the east to Arero in Borana [to the west]. We failed to do the same in Moyale. In Moyale we have registered the voters. At the end of the registration, we found that the number of the registered voters by far exceeded the actual population of the town. We heard that thousands of Garri from Kenya have been registered to vote. Few of them were captured and imprisoned.[10]

Leaving out other variables, such as the overall results of the referen-dum, this quotation precisely elucidates how the Garri used the opportunity of the border by mobilizing their kin in Kenya to win the competition over territory in Ethiopia. The Ethiopian official and other Ethiopian policy-makers, including those who negotiated the referendum, perceived the border as solid. However, for the pastoral communities whose settlements transcended the international border, the border was superficial. This is because members of ethnic groups, clans and extended families live on both sides of the border and cross it on a daily basis without being particularly aware of it (especially in times of peace). They cross the border in search of pasture and water, to visit markets and schools, to go to hospitals and to see family members, without any official documents (i.e. ID cards). They exploit ethnic/clan communal resources such as clan-owned wells. Mobilizing ethnic or clan resources during competition and conflict is just part of this. One of my Garri informants, who was involved in local politics, differentiated ethnic (clan) matters from citizenship. According to him, 'any conflict between Garri and their neighbours involves all the Garri regardless of where they live, in Ethiopia, Kenya or Somalia. They participate by providing financial and human resources, and by giving information. It is an ethnic (clan) matter rather than [a matter of] nationality.'[11] In March 2006, about 200 Ethiopian Garri were sent to support their kin in El-Waq, southern Somalia, in the conflict with the Marrehaan Somali.[12] Similarly, a recent publication reveals a rumour that the Kenyan Garri used the Garri militia from the area occupied by the Rahanweyn Resistance Army (RRA) in southern Somalia during the local conflict with the Ajuran Somali in northern Kenya (Schlee 2007: 429).

The Garri's mobilization of transborder alliances in order to strengthen their positions in local conflicts goes back to the Italian period. The Italian army that occupied southern Ethiopia in 1936 came from Italian Somaliland (currently southern Somalia), where the Garri have their kin. Immediately following the Italian occupation, the Garri on the Ethiopian side established good contacts with the Italians. This was facilitated by Garri from southern Somalia who were part of the *banda*, the 'native' troops of the Italians. Many *banda* were Garri from southern Somalia to whom the Ethiopian Garri are related. According to archival documents, the Italians 'armed the Gurre [Garri] under Hassan Gababa [the then clan head of the Garri] and incited them to attack the Ethiopians and the Boran who had remained loyal to the Ethiopians. The Gurre [Garri] at once fell upon the Gabra and raided many hundred head of stock and camels from them ...' (quoted in Oba 2000: 93). Thus, already in the past the Ethiopian Garri effectively used the presence of their kin in Somalia to establish a political relationship with the 'new power' (the invading Italian force) and make use of it in the local competition with their neighbours, the Borana and Gabra. In the next section I shall present similar trans-border networks highlighting the advantage of the border for liberation fronts in the post-colonial era.

BORDERS AS RESOURCES FOR
LIBERATION FRONTS

The Ethiopian government's relations with the local communities are skewed in the interests of the state, not the other way round. No Ethiopian regime has 'liked' equally the different communities at the periphery. So far, at least one of the groups has been labelled as a 'security threat'. In the

1960s and 1970s the Garri, and to some extent the Gabra and other Somali clans inhabiting the region, were in this category, while the Borana's relations with both the Imperial and the Derg regimes had been good.

Before the state collapse in Somalia in 1991, the Garri and other Somali groups sought support from the Republic of Somalia through assumed kinship relations and ideology. The Republic of Somalia was hosting, training and fully sponsoring the Somali Abo Liberation Front (SALF), a rebel group overwhelmingly supported by the Garri and the Gabra in their conflict with Ethiopia and their local rival, the Borana (Gebru 1996; Markakis 1987). In fact, Mogadishu declared that 'the government of [the] free Somali state has a special duty towards its countrymen across the borders, who have a common cultural heritage and origin' (Information Service of the Somali Government 1962: ix). In fact, the SALF was established to fulfil the irredentist interests of the Republic of Somalia, and the Ethiopian Garri used it to obtain access to military and financial support from Somalia, which they needed in their local conflict with the Borana. The Borana, on the other hand, sought support from the Ethiopian regime. Their interest coincided with the interest of the governments in Addis Ababa that sought to check the Somali who were considered a security threat due to Somali nationalism and irredentism. As a result, Haile Selassie as well as Mengistu provided the Borana with arms. This state support even transcended the international border to reach the Kenyan Borana who were under similar pressure from their Somali neighbours. In 1962 the representatives of the Northern Peoples' United Association (NPUA), a party established by the Borana and other Oromo groups in northern Kenya, met Emperor Haile Selassie and were given logistical support to set up offices and other facilities for their party (Oba 2000: 104–5).

In the 1990s the pattern of alliances between the Ethiopian government and the local groups changed. The Borana's relations with the centre in Ethiopia were reversed. The Borana were accused of supporting the Oromo Liberation Front (OLF), and therefore categorically labelled as an enemy of the state. Following the total collapse of the Republic of Somalia, the Garri and the Gabra became associated with the Ethiopian state.[13] Many Borana either joined the OLF or left for northern Kenya to escape harassment by the EPRDF regime. They were hosted by their kin in northern Kenya, the Kenyan Borana. On 6 June 2006 I interviewed Hassano Arero, a Gabra, then top official in the militia and security office in the Borana zone. The interview was conducted in Moyale. He told me about the activities of the OLF and the response of his government around that border:

> Look at that mountain, just this mountain. It is on the Kenyan side of the border. That is the military base of the OLF. Because most of the OLF fighters are Borana, the Kenyan Borana host them. We have repeatedly tried to uproot them but unsuccessfully. Currently we are undertaking a

joint operation with Kenya, but so far the result is nil. Do you know what they do? They just melt into the society and one cannot identify them; because they are the same [people].[14]

The presence of the OLF army on the mountain at which the official was pointing may not even be true, but that is not the point here. Rather, the quotation clearly explains how the OLF uses the opportunity created as a result of the separation by the international border. The OLF spearheaded the construction of Oromo nationalism and, as a liberation front, fought different Ethiopian regimes. It has a long history of operating in eastern and western Oromia, as compared with the south, where it became active only recently. With its cross-border constituency, the southern front currently seems to be more important than the other fronts in sustaining the Oromo rebellion against the Ethiopian state.

The border is porous, however, not only for the OLF but also for the Ethiopian army that occasionally penetrates deep into Kenya in pursuit of the OLF fighters and their local 'hosts', the Kenyan Borana. This practice does not undermine the advantage of the border; rather it is part of the state's project of holding back the affordances of the border from the other actors.

The political attraction of the border has been even more clearly revealed as the current Ethiopian government, represented by the Oromo People's Democratic Organization (OPDO), the Oromo arm of the EPRDF, recently engaged in the competition to make use of the political space across the border.[15] For about fifteen years (1992-2007) the OLF enjoyed exclusively the political space across the Ethio-Kenyan border, while the Ethiopian state has been operating in the area to check its movements. In the last two years (since 2007), it seems that Ethiopian state actors have gone beyond fencing the border to engage in the competition over the Oromo constituency beyond the border. In March 2007 Ethiopian officials from the Borana Zone visited Sololo (a small town in the Moyale district of Kenya, allegedly the OLF's centre) to discuss with their counterparts on the Kenyan side what they called the common wellbeing of the Borana on both sides of the border. On 16 September 2007 top Ethiopian officials including the President of Oromia National Regional State, ministers and diplomats celebrated the Ethiopian Millennium in Moyale, thus turning the periphery into a centre.[16] Large numbers of Borana from Kenya, mostly MPs, officials and elders, were invited and attended the celebration. Among them 200 individuals led by an MP from Saku constituency (Marsabit district in Kenya), accompanied by officials from the Borana Zone of Ethiopia, visited central Oromia based on the invitation from the Oromia National Regional State administration. The team was warmly received in Adama town (100 km east of Addis Ababa) and was accompanied by top regional officials in their travel to different parts of central Oromia. Obviously, this was an attempt by the Ethiopian state to make use of the Borana across the border and to engage in the competition for the political space across the border.

On the other hand, the Kenyan Borana, Garri and Gabra need the support of their kin on the Ethiopian side during national elections in Kenya.[17] Ethnicization of administrative borders in northern Kenya can be traced back to the 1930s when the British established a 'tribal grazing area' following the Oromo-Somali line. The two ethnic groups were restricted to the west and east of the line respectively (Schlee 2007, 1989). In the 1980s, the ethnicization process was intensified at the smaller district level. For instance, Marsabit district was sub-divided into Saku (Borana), North Horr (Gabra) and Laisamis (Rendile) constituencies. Moyale was separated from Marsabit and became a district in 1995. The Borana dominate the Moyale district, but there are significant numbers of Gabra and Garri.

Over the two decades since 1990, many inhabitants of the Ethiopian Moyale town had acquired Kenyan identity cards, and were therefore eligible to vote in Kenya. To enlarge their constituency, chiefs, councillors and Members of Parliament had to multiply the numbers of their supporters. So they distributed more ID cards to their kin, regardless of the arbitrary international border. During the 2006 by-election the three contenders representing different political parties were all Borana. This did not preclude the participation of the Gabra and Garri. Regardless of their conflict-ridden relations with the Borana, they were still interested in voting in order to support the one Borana candidate whom they considered best for promoting their own interests.

Serious competition was expected between two contenders, one labelled a 'religious' man, the other considered to be a 'nationalist' in the local arena. The first, Mr Adan Wachu, was a former head of the Kenyan Muslim Council. He was regarded as more religious than nationalist. The second was Mr Wario Galgalo, a university student and a brother of one of the previous MPs, the late Dr Guracha Galgalo. He was suspected to be a supporter of the OLF and Oromo nationalism in Kenya. The Muslim Gabra (Miigo) who mostly inhabit Ethiopian Moyale, backed Mr Wachu. In contrast, the Borana on both sides of the border favoured the alleged Oromo nationalist, Mr Galgalo. In particular, among the Ethiopian Borana, Islam is not very strongly rooted. For them ethnicity and the OLF factor are more vital than religion. Adan Wachu's supporters worked hard to persuade the Ethiopian Borana that his religious position did not undermine his representing the Borana and that he was equally a nationalist. On the final day of the election, the Ethiopian army attempted to close the border and detained a few Borana found with Kenyan ID cards at the main border check point. This revealed the usual interest of the centre to restrict and control access of local people to the opportunities arising from the border (Nugent 2002).

On the other hand, however, there were rumours that Ethiopian security officials were encouraging the Gabra voters to cross the same border into Kenya in order to vote. Thus, the Ethiopian government implicitly supported the candidate of the National Rainbow Coalition Kenya (NARCK), Adan Wachu, despite his alleged religious agenda (at a time when Ethiopian troops crushed the Union of Islamic Courts that had come to power in southern Somalia in 2006).

This shows the ambivalent attitude of the Ethiopian state toward its border with Kenya, that, in the Borana case, had to be closed, but in the Gabra case was clandestinely opened in order to influence the results of the elections in Kenya. This, of course, could not prevent many Borana who knew the routes to Kenya better than the Ethiopian soldiers.[18] A rumour that Adan Wachu and his party – NARCK – had promised to give Kinissa, a location east of Kenyan Moyale town that was contested between Gabra and Garri, to Gabra undermined the support for him expected from the Garri.[19] Other variables, particularly sympathy for Wario Galgalo's claim to 'inherit' his deceased brother's seat with all the related family responsibilities involved, were also important factors influencing the election.

THE GABRA AND THE BORDER

Among the three groups mainly discussed in this chapter, the Gabra are minorities on both sides of the border. In the post-1991 pattern of state-community alignment in this peripheral area, the Gabra stood with the EPRDF against the OLF which has been supported by the Borana. The Ethiopian state needs the Gabra on both sides of the border to deal with the OLF factor. This seems to have helped the Gabra elite to organize themselves and co-operate across the border and to build up strength *vis-à-vis* their neighbours, mainly the Borana. The late Dr Godana Bonaya, MP for North Horr and former Foreign Minister of Kenya, and Shano Godana, MP of Yabello District, Ethiopia, and former head of the Borana Zone Militia and Security office, are said to have synchronized these cross-border relations of the Gabra. In June 2006, Shano Godana was accused of supporting the Kenyan Gabra in the conflict with the Ethiopian Borana. Ethiopian officials argued that that he was supporting 'foreign powers' against his own citizens by providing them with information. He was forced to give up his career.[20] This was just a further episode of local political struggle across the border.

The Gabra make use of the presence of their kin on the Kenyan side of the border not only during conflicts with their neighbours but also with regard to the internal struggles and competition. Currently, the Gabra Miigo are in dispute among themselves along the Oromo and Somali ethno-national boundary. It pits those who identify with the Oromo against those who identify with the Somali, and therefore highlights competing version of Gabra ethnic identity. This is one result of the post-1991 political reforms in Ethiopia.

The Gabra are not only a people situated on the border between two major ethnic groups, but they also have a deep-rooted ethno-historical substratum that 'makes' them both Oromo and Somali, rather than either of them. Their 'camel culture', which manifests itself in their everyday life and rituals, their cross-cutting ties with the Garri clans, and their calendar, which is recognizable in the Arabo-Islamic world, compel the Gabra to consider themselves closer to the Somali than the Oromo. Yet, other identity markers such as their language (Afaan Oromo), their age and generation set, through which they have developed strong ritual associations with the Borana, and the territory in which they resided peacefully with the Borana, make them part of the Oromo nation rather than the Somali (Schlee 1989; Tablino 1999; Kassam 2006; Fekadu 2009). In the context of intensified competition and contestation between the Garri and the Borana and/or between Somali and Oromo, the Gabra are pressed to decide on their identity and show allegiance to one or other side. To fit into the framework of the politics of ethnicity currently dominating in Ethiopia, the Gabra elites identified themselves with the ethnic group that offered them jobs: those who got a job in the Somali National Regional State claimed Somali-ness and those who secured a job in Oromia National Regional State claimed Oromo-ness. In this way, even brothers ended up as members of different ethnic groups. Both camps within the Gabra co-opted elders to help them legitimize their identity claims and used aspects of their cultural repertoire selectively to strengthen their claims to either Oromo-ness or Somali-ness (Fekadu 2009).

The Kenyan Gabra, who are well educated, active in business, and citizens of a different state with different opportunity structures, are considered resource-persons for giving advice and reconciling the Gabra Miigo of Ethiopia. During research on the Ethiopian side of the border I interviewed two Gabra elders who had talked to the late Dr Godana Bonaya, the already mentioned Gabra politician on the Kenyan side. My informants represented the different versions of the Gabra identity, namely, Oromo-ness and Somali-ness. In 2004 Arero Abdi Jilo, a popular Gabra elder, visited Dr Godana Bonaya in Nairobi and requested his personal advice to solve the problem the Gabra faced in defining their ethnic identity within the context of identity politics in Ethiopia. Arero Abdi argued for the Oromo-ness of the Gabra.[21] My other key informant, Haji Hassan Qalla, a *de facto* representative of the Gabra in the Somali National Regional State, and obviously in favour of the Somali-ness of the Gabra, visited Dr Godana more than once to secure his support in the project of (re-)defining the Gabra identity.[22] In 2007, a larger number of Kenyan Gabra elders, intellectuals and officials became involved in the project of 'deciding' on the ethnic identity of the Ethiopian Gabra.[23] This was an attempt to unite the group in a social environment characterized by internal and inter-ethnic competition. At the time of writing this text (2009) the outcome of this process was yet unclear.

Conclusion

This chapter has examined the long-standing and complex inter and intra-group alliances and conflicts in the southern Ethiopian borderlands and the opportunities provided to locals by the state-border between Ethiopia and Kenya. Particular emphasis has been given to the way Borana, Garri and Gabra make use of their kin connections across the border in different contexts: for instance, during violent conflicts and in election periods. Kin support each other militarily and/or by providing shelter. Sometimes, delegations of elders from across the border also engage in conflict settlement. The chapter showed how the Garri employed their access to political space in the Republic of Somalia in the 1960s and 1970s in their local conflict in Ethiopia, and at the same time, how the Somali government attempted to make use of its 'countrymen' across the border in Ethiopia based on the ideology of Somali nationalism and irredentism. Recently, the Kenyan Garri mobilized the Garri in southern Somalia to gain their support in a local conflict in Kenya; the Garri in Somalia, on the other hand, were aided by their kin in Ethiopia in a conflict with the Marrehaan in southern Somalia. Similar processes of cross-border mobilization could also be observed with regard to the Borana since the early 1990s. The Ethiopian Borana have been hosted by their kin in Kenya as their relations with the Ethiopian state deteriorated after they were accused of supporting the OLF.

Above all, the border has facilitated the activities of various rebel groups operating across the discussed borders. The SALF, overwhelmingly supported by the Garri and other groups who claim Somali origin, enjoyed the support of the Somali government in Mogadishu (before 1991), which provided weapons, ammunitions and logistic support. Similarly, the OLF benefited from the separation by the international border. The Kenyan Oromo are a tiny minority as compared with the whole Oromo population. However, the fact that the Kenyan Oromo live under a different government/political regime and within different opportunity structures made their contribution to the Oromo cause vital in the war between the OLF and the Ethiopian state. I shall conclude this chapter by reiterating Fredrick Barth's highly accurate assessment, that 'boundaries have been rich in affordances, offering opportunities for army careers, customs-duty collecting agencies … . They have provided a facility of retreat and escape for bandits and freedom fighters eluding the control of states on both sides' (Barth 2000: 28–9).

Notes

1 The data used in this chapter are extracted from the fieldwork I undertook for my PhD research, which was sponsored by the Max-Planck Institute for Social Anthropology. I wish to thank Dereje Feyissa, Markus Hoehne, Mamo Hebo and Dejene Gemechu for their critical and constructive comments on the first draft of this paper.

2 The current switching of the Darawa lineage of the Garri to the Oromo and the negotiations with the Oromia National Regional State officials and discussions with different offices at federal level such as the House of Federation and Ministry of Federal Affairs are ongoing. It is too early to comment on these processes.

3 However, other scholars argue that the new political line reflected in the charter of the Transitional Government of Ethiopia (TGE) and in the FDRE 1994 Constitution was simply an empty promise designed to mask the regime's totalitarian goals (see Sorenson 1998: 225).

4 These conflicts have been defined as conflicts triggered by drought and competition over scarce resources (Hussein 2002; Dejene and Abdurahman 2002), by ecological or environmental degradation (Medhane 2002), and as a conspiracy involving a divide-and-rule strategy employed by the Ethiopian state (Merera 2003).

5 This has drawn its legitimacy from the country's Constitution (Article, 48), which asserts that 'all state border disputes shall be settled by agreement of the concerned states. Where the concerned states fail to reach agreement, the House of the Federation shall decide such disputes on the basis of settlement patterns that include undertaking of a referendum on the disputed territories.'

6 The term 'federal state' indicates the national level here.

7 The financial expense of the referendum was about four million Ethiopian Birr, US$470,000.

8 http://news.bbc.co.uk/2/hi/africa/7929104.stm, accessed on 13 March 2009.

9 Two 'town wars' erupted in the summer 2007; one erupted later, in January 2008, after I had left Moyale. Most of these clashes happened unexpectedly and were triggered by police forces that ran into each other when patrolling the town at night. Only one clash had a 'real reason' such as a quarrel between the two administrations in Moyale over plots of land in the town.

10 Interview with an official in the National Electoral Board of Ethiopia, Addis Ababa, 5 October 2007

11 Interview with Hassan Shina, head of the Somali Moyale district administration, Moyale, 6 November 2007.

12 Interview with Adan Alio, Moyale, 10 August 2006.

13 For the local dynamics of the war and aspects of ethnic identification see Schlee and Shongolo (1995).

14 Interview with Hassano Arero, a Gabra top official in the militia and security office, Borana zone. 6 June 2006, Moyale. His Gabra background made him loyal in the eyes of the state and gave him the confidence to talk openly about the issue, which was otherwise considered very sensitive.

15 The OPDO was founded in 1990 by the TPLF in northern Ethiopia. The TPLF has managed to recruit members of the OPDO from Oromo-speaking war captives then under the control of the TPLF and the Eritrean People's Liberation Front (EPLF).

16 The Ethiopian calendar retains the old Egyptian Coptic calendar, which is 7–8 years behind the Gregorian calendar. The celebration of the 'Ethiopian Millennium' that depends on Orthodox Christianity has been contested by different ethno-national and religious groups.

17 This section is based on my observations during the 2006 by-election to replace the MPs who died in a plane crash in April 2006. In that accident five MPs from northern Kenya

(Moyale, North Horr, Sakku, Laisamis and Isiolo) lost their lives. This election showed how porous the international border is to the people who live there. I did my fieldwork mainly on the Ethiopian side of the border and observed how much the population on the Ethiopian side was engaged in the election campaigns on the Kenyan side.

18 Interestingly enough, election politics on the Ethiopian side of the border never attracted the Kenyans. The local perception in Moyale (Kenya) was that what matters on the Ethiopian side of the border is military strength rather than elections. The referendum which was supposed to determine the fate of Ethiopian Moyale (whether it belongs to Oromo or Somali), discussed above, was the only case for the Kenyans to take Ethiopian ID cards.

19 It is interesting to note that, because of this competition with the Gabra during the by-election, the Garri supported the candidate accused of being a Borana/Oromo. This happened regardless of the social and cultural 'bonds' (common religion, and assumed kinship and history) between both groups that in other contexts are stressed to explain the relatively amicable relations between the Garri and Gabra. This illustrates the instrumental character of alliance formation in this context.

20 Interview with Wario Galgalo, Borana Zone official, Yabelo, 29 October 2006.

21 Interviews with Arero Abdi, Gabra elder, Moyale and Yabelo, in July 2006.

22 Interview with Haji Hassan Qalla, Moyale, 26 October 2006 and August 2007.

23 Interview with Chief Qalla Bante, the chairman of the committee established for this purpose, Moyale, 25 August 2007.

References

Aalen, L. 2006. 'Ethnic federalism and self-determination for nationalities in a semi-authoritarian state: The case of Ethiopia'. *International Journal of Minority and Group Rights* 13(2-3): 243–61.

Barth, F. 2000. 'Boundaries and Connections', in A. Cohen (ed.), *Signifying Identities: Anthropological perspectives on boundaries and contested values*. London: Routledge, pp. 17–36.

Bassi, M. 2005. *Decisions in the Shade: Political and juridical processes among the Oromo-Borana*. Trenton, NJ: Red Sea Press.

Dejene, Aredo and Abdurahman Ame 2002. *The Root Causes of Conflict Among the Southern Pastoral Communities of Ethiopia: A Case Study of Borana and Digodia*. Paper presented to OSSREA.

Federal Democratic Republic of Ethiopia 1995. 'The Constitution of the Federal Democratic Republic of Ethiopia'. *Federal Negarit Gazeta*. First year, No. 1, Addis Ababa: Birhanina Selam Printing Press.

Fekadu, A. 2004. *Inter-Ethnic Relations between the Oromo and Somali: The Case of Borana, Digodia and Marehan*. MA thesis. Department of Sociology and Anthropology, Addis Ababa University.

—— 2009. *Negotiating Identity: Politics of Identification among the Borana, Gabra and Garri around Oromo-Somali Boundary in Southern Ethiopia*. Ph.D. dissertation submitted to Martin Luther University, Halle.

Gebru, T. 1996. *Ethiopia: Power and Protest Peasant Revolts in the Twentieth Century*. Lawrenceville, NJ: Red Sea Press.

Hagmann, Tobias 2007. *Pastoral Conflict and Resource Management in Ethiopia's Somali Region*. Ph.D. Dissertation. Swiss Graduate School of Public Administration, Lausanne.

Hussein, J. 2002. *Competition over Resources and Ethnic Conflict in Federal Ethiopia: The Case of the Recent Guji–Gedeo Conflict*. Research Report submitted to OSSREA.

Information Service of the Somali Government. 1962. *The Somali Peninsula: A new light on imperial motives*. Mogadishu: Information Service of the Somali Government.

James, W., D.L. Donham, E. Kurimoto and A. Triulzi (eds) 2002. *Remapping Ethiopia: Socialism and after*. Oxford: James Currey.

Kassam, A. 2006. 'The People of the Five "Drums": Gabra ethnohistorical origins.' *Ethnohistory* 53(1): 174-193

Legesse, A. 1973. *Gada: Three Approaches to the Study of African Society*. New York: The Free Press.

—— 2000. *Oromo Democracy: An indigenous African political system*. Asmara: Red Sea Press.

Markakis, J. 1987. *National and Class Conflict in the Horn of Africa*. Cambridge: Cambridge University Press.

Medhane, T. 2002. 'Traditional Mechanisms of Conflict Resolution versus State Intervention: The Borana Oromos and Merihan Somalis in Ethiopia', in G. Baechler, K. R. Spillmann and M. Suliman (eds), *Transformation of Resource Conflicts: Approach and instruments*. Bern: Peter Lang, pp. 185–214.

Merera, G. 2003. *Ethiopia Competing Ethnic Nationalisms and the Quest for Democracy, 960–2000*. Addis Ababa: Chamber Printing House.

Nugent, P. 2002. *Smugglers, Secessionists and Loyal Citizens on the Ghana-Togo Frontiers: The Life of the Borderlands since 1914*. Athens, OH: Ohio University Press; Oxford: James Currey.

Oba, G. 2000. ''Where the Bulls Fight, it is the Grass that Suffers': The Impact of Border Administration on the Drought Coping Strategies of the Obbu Boran during the Twentieth Century'. *Journal of Oromo Studies* 7(1+2): 87–107.

Schlee, G. 1989. *Identities on the Move, Clanship and Pastoralists in Northern Kenya*. Gideon S. Nairobi: Were Press.

—— 1994.'Islam and the Gadaa System as Conflict-Shaping Forces in Southern Oromia', in Harold Marcus and G. Hudson (eds), *New Trends in Ethiopian Studies: Papers of the 12th International Conference of Ethiopian Studies*, Vol. II. Lawrenceville, NJ: Red Sea Press, pp. 975–97.

—— 2003. 'Redrawing the Map of the Horn: The Politics of Difference'. *Africa* 73(3): 342–68.

—— 2007. 'Brothers of the Boran Once Again: On the Fading Popularity of Certain Somali Identities in Northern Kenya'. *Journal of Eastern African Studies* 1(3): 417–35.

Schlee, G. and A. Shongolo 1995. 'Local war and its impact on ethnic and religious identification in Southern Ethiopia'. *GeoJournal* 36(1): 7–17.

Sorenson, J. 1998. 'Ethiopian Discourse and Oromo Nationalism', in J. Asefa (ed.), *Oromo Nationalism and the Ethiopian Discourse, the Search for Freedom and Democracy*. Lawrenceville, NJ: Red Sea Press, pp. 223–54.

Tablino, P. 1999. *The Gabra: Camel nomads of northern Kenya*. Nairobi: Paulines Publications.

Turton, D. 2006. 'Introduction', in D. Turton (ed.), *Ethnic Federalism: The Ethiopian Experience in Comparative Perspective*. Oxford: James Currey, pp. 1–31.

Vaughan, S. 2003. *Ethnicity and Power in Ethiopia*. Ph.D. Dissertation. University of Edinburgh.

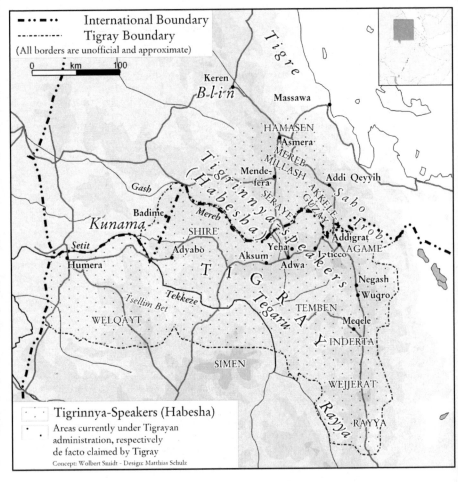

Map 2 *Tigray, ethnic and political*

Four

The Tigrinnya-Speakers across the Borders
Discourses of Unity & Separation
in Ethnohistorical Context

WOLBERT G.C. SMIDT

Imagine there's no countries. /It isn't hard to do /Nothing to kill or die for
(John Lennon)[1]

Introduction

The Tigrinnya-speakers discussed in this chapter are the dominant group
of the state of Eritrea, independent from Ethiopia since 1993 (*de facto* since
1991), and also form the predominant majority in the northern Ethiopian
Regional State of Tigray, just south of the Eritrean border. Thus, today a
state border that became a war border in 1998 separates Tigrinnya-
speakers into two halves. With the help of ethnonyms and ethnohistorical
examples, it is shown in this chapter that the establishment, reinforcement
and weakening of boundaries were and are integral parts of Tigrinnya
history and of today's political reality. Boundaries separating Tigrinnya
subgroups from each other were and are marked by changes of discourse,
following both ancient subgroups' identities and actual political-dynastic
interests. Discourses have often made pre-existing boundaries more visible
– or created some anew – and caused others to disappear from view, while
often persisting at a lower level of discourse and socio-economic practice to
be possibly revived later on.

The chapter shows that boundaries are nothing artificial for Tigrinnya-
speakers, but rather are a typical heritage of this large ethno-regional
group composed of many sub-groups. These sub-groups are marked by a
tendency both towards regionalism and at times towards feelings of unity
encompassing virtually all Tigrinnya-speakers. While the existence of
boundaries is nothing new, the existence of a state boundary has added a
new quality, the consequences of which are not yet fully foreseeable. The
traditional tendencies of separation are replaced by a state-sponsored
division. However, these days one can observe the growing importance of

another aspect of Tigrinnya tradition: In the situation of persisting political hardship in Eritrea, one can hear more and more Eritreans saying in private conversations that 'we – the Tigrinnya-speakers – are all one and only separated by political leaders'. This chapter aims to demonstrate that the mere existence of a boundary separating the Tigrinnya-speakers is not surprising from an ethnohistorical point of view, and even not a problem in itself; the problem – and the new phenomenon – is rather the absolute-ness of the separation by that boundary.[2]

Discourses of separation and of unity are both an integrative part of Tigrinnya tradition and identity. 'We have never been one' (a discourse prevalent in Eritrea) versus 'We are one and the same' (prevalent in Tigray) are both based on historical facts. This seemingly paradox situa-tion makes it very tricky for any observer, especially for those close to one or the other discourse, to find a way through the chaos of contradictions. However, the basic phenomenon is not difficult to understand, as it is widespread and familiar to most ethnic groups. Within many ethnic groups there are lines of separation within the framework of a feeling or discourse of unity or belonging, which are the basis for the formation of a we-group as Elwert (1989) called it (for a discussion in the context of the Horn of Africa see Zitelmann 1994). It depends on the respective situation, as to which of the two discourses prevails in an ethnic group. It is not so rare for groups to split up along these internal lines of separation.

Particularly in south-western and western Ethiopia a number of examples of such splits could be found during the past 15 years, when a number of new ethnic groups suddenly began popping up, all of them claiming to have 'always' been there, but having been overlooked. There are also movements in the reverse direction, separate groups becoming 'one' with another, bigger one (such as the Omotic-speaking Anfillo, today most of them considering themselves Oromo).[3] These movements into unity or separation should not be misunderstood: the changes are often more changes in the discourse than real socio-cultural transformations. The situation of an ethnic group in fact stays largely the same as before, but one speaks differently about it.

On the one hand, in a situation of unity, internal lines of separation normally continue to exist, but become less important. These lines of separation may shift within the group, successively including some groups previously excluded and excluding others previously included, following socio-economic changes. But lines of separation are there, even if they are hidden. On the other hand, in a situation of separation, a feeling and tradition of unity can be easily revived or (re-)created. Another factor can be added: if unity or separation prevails can sometimes simply be a question of perspective – within the ethnic group itself. Some see the group as united (separated by external forces only), while others under-line the separated-ness. The Tigrinnya-speakers[4] are a good example of this. 'Within unity' there is no unity. The 'we' within the we-group is pluralistic.

Names: 'Tigre' or -?

A closer look into the naming of the ethnic group already helps to understand the complexity of the situation. Naming reflects well the degree of 'one-ness' and of separation. Names reflect boundaries. The Tigrinnya-speakers, wherever you ask them, affirm themselves as being one, ethnically. But politically they are today marked by a boundary which separates them into two big halves. Some Tigrinnya-speakers (especially in Ethiopia) say that this boundary is artificial, others (especially in Eritrea) claim that it has been inherited from the past. The function of this boundary within the ethnic group will be discussed further below. We start here with the technical question: Is there one designation for this ethnic group? Outsiders in fact do have one ethnic designation for the Tigrinnya-speakers: *Tigre* (derived from the Amharic term for the province).[5] It is clear, however, that this term should not be used in academic literature as the ethnic designation for the Tigrinnya-speakers, as it is only used by non-Tigrinnya-speakers.[6]

But how do they call themselves? It is significant that the self-designation of Tigrinnya-speakers differs between the larger regions and also according to social / rural-urban context. There is no term unifying the 'Tigre' as one ethnic group separated from others. The only term everyone accepts (and which is also mostly used in daily conversation) is H̲abesha. This ethnonym, however, in principle includes all Christian Highlanders speaking Ethio-Semitic languages. Younger Tigrayans (i.e., inhabitants of the Regional State of Tigray) call themselves *Tigray* (or more properly *Tigraway*; plural form: *Tegaru*), and use this as an ethnic term; implicitly, they understand that this encompasses all Tigrinnya-speakers. However, it is rejected by Eritreans, who understand it as a purely geographical term. If you ask educated Eritreans stemming from the highlands to which ethnic group they belong, they will answer *Tigrinnya*. They use the name of their language as the ethnic self-designation. Generally, one means all the Tigrinnya-speakers by this term, but it is only accepted as an ethnic term in Eritrea.

We see already here that ethnic self-designations used by Tigrinnya-speakers depend on the context (geographical, but also socio-cultural and political). This multitude of terms is an indication of the existence of boundaries within the group, and one may ask if this multitude is an integrative part of the group's culture and history. It is therefore methodologically helpful to look into ethnic terms used among different groups of Tigrinnya-speakers.

SELF-DESIGNATIONS OF TIGRINNYA-SPEAKING GROUPS

Table 4.1 lists different groups of Tigrinnya-speakers with their state of residence, sub-group and self-designation. It is important to note that some groups are not listed in this table: the Cushitic-speaking Irob (a Tigrayan mostly Catholic 'subgroup' of the Muslim Saho in Eritrea, considering themselves independent from them), the Nilosaharan-speaking Kunama (some of whom have shifted to Tigrinnya in Tigray), and the Agaw-Cushitic-speaking Bilen (self-designation Blin), as they still consider themselves as ethnically clearly separated (Smidt 2006b). But it should be noted here that boundaries between these groups are shifting; members of all these groups do also speak Tigrinnya, some of them exclusively.

Table 4.1 *Ethnic and linguistic self-designations in urban and rural context*[7]

Ethnic (sub)group	Ethnic self-designation	Self-designation for the language
Tigrinnya-speakers of Tigray [8]	Tigray[9]	Tigrinnya *(qwanqwa*[10]*) Tigray*
	Tigraway (sg.) Tegaru (pl.) *Habesha*	*(qwanqwa) Habesha*
Rayya	*Rayya* Tigray (etc., as above) <u>H</u>abesha	*(qwanqwa) Rayya* Tigrinnya
Wejjerat	*Wejjerat* Tigray (etc., as above) *<u>H</u>abesha*	*Wejjerinna (Wejjerinnya)* Tigrinnya
'Tsellim Bet' of Mezega	Tsellim Bet Tigray (etc., as above) *Ch'aré* (<u>H</u>abesha[11])	*(qwanqwa) Tigray* Tigrinnya
Tigrinnya-speakers of Eritrea (except Jeberti)	Tigrinnya *<u>H</u>abesha*	Tigrinnya *(qwanqwa) <u>H</u>abesha*
Jeberti of Eritrea	(Tigrinnya) *Jeberti* (*<u>H</u>abesha*)	Tigrinnya *(qwanqwa) <u>H</u>abesha*

Only a few groups exclude themselves from the most general and dominant self-designations. However, the Tigrinnya-speakers consist of numerous subgroups, who, in daily conversation, would often rather tend to use their local self-designation than the more general one: the <u>H</u>amasénay in <u>H</u>amasén, the Tsen'adegle in Akkele-Guzay,[12] the Tembénay in Tembén, the Agame in Agame, and so forth. Table 4.1 shows, however, that there is no term which is used by all Tigrinnya-speakers, but a great majority call their language Tigrinnya, and almost all call themselves <u>H</u>abesha (on this ethnonym more below).

The exceptions are interesting. A group existing in both Eritrea and Tigray are the Jeberti, as Muslim Tigrinnya-speakers are generally called. They mainly live in towns or cities, and along ancient trade routes in Tigray, mostly as merchants, sometimes as peasants, such as in Inticc'o. Their most important settlements lie along the trade route between Aksum and the east (via Adwa, Dibdibo, Inticc'o up to Addigrat), and on the eastern trade route from the Red Sea southwards (via Akkele-Guzay in eastern-central Eritrea, Addigrat, Negash, Weqro, Agula', Kwiha, Meqele, etc.). The centralist political tendencies of recent decades have strengthened the formulation of a separate Jeberti identity – as a counter-reaction. They reject the terms 'Tigrinnya' and 'Habesha', which are associated with Christianity (but elders still call their language *qwanqwa* Habesha, in contradiction to these evidently more recent tendencies).[13] In contrast to these, however, some Tigrayan Jeberti refuse to call themselves Jeberti, declaring themselves to be 'the same' as the others, Tegaru and Habesha.

Another separate and largely unknown group are the Tsellim Bet in the hot western lowlands of Tigray, near the Tekkezze river.[14] Due to their dark complexion/'blackness' and supposedly ancient 'African' origin (recent research shows their connection to the Gumuz[15]), they are not Habesha. Usually they also do not call themselves Habesha, and Tigrayan highlanders also do not include them in this self-denomination. But Tigrayans call them Tegaru, as they speak Tigrinnya, live in Tigray and practise Christianity (in a version characterized by syncretism). In modern discourse they are, therefore, included; but they tend to define themselves as a separate entity.

The Rayya are also a group of 'foreign' (Oromo) origin. The idea of a patrilinear heritage of ethnicity has an interesting effect in their case. Young Rayya[16] will insist that they are Tegaru (Tigrinnya-speakers of Tigray), Habesha *and* Rayya-Oromo. In this case the Oromo in a way became an ethnic 'subgroup' of the ethnic group of Tegaru. The inclusive identity of Tegaru is today accepted by them, but they have also inherited the identity of being Oromo. In addition, their Tigrinnya is strongly influenced by Oromo vocabulary, therefore even educated youngsters will use the term Rayya for their dialect, in differentiation from the term Tigrinnya used for the language of other Tegaru (even if Rayya is clearly a dialect of Tigrinnya).

Migration is one factor in the creation of ethnic subgroups and clans. Generally, however, these groups are not excluded, but fully included. But, too much pressure of inclusion could also lead to rejection from the side of the subgroup concerned, as the case of the Eritrean Jeberti illustrates. A new internal boundary is in the making. In all other cases, unity is in the making.

MAIN SELF-DESIGNATIONS OF THE TIGRINNYA-SPEAKERS
Table 4.2 provides an overview of the terms used by 'typical' Tigrinnya-speakers (i.e. excluding groups with a separate status) when they speak of the whole group of Tigrinnya-speakers.

Table 4.2 *The most general self-designations in Tigray and Eritrea*

Self-designation	in Tigray	in Eritrea
Habesha (used in the primary sense of Tigrinnya-speakers)	x	x
Tigray	x	
Tegaru	x	
Tigrinnya		x
(Tigrinnyi)[17]	x	

Eritreans cannot call themselves Tigray, as this term is connected with a province beyond their state borders. But even historically the term Tigray does not seem to have been dominant in Eritrea.[18] This is not surprising as there was already another ethnic term: Habesha. One can summarize that almost all Tigrinnya-speakers call themselves Habesha, with the exception of some 'separatist' Jeberti-groups and 'foreign' groups such as the 'black' Tsellim Bet.

In the local context Habesha do not understand this self-designation as synonymous with Ethiopian;[19] it is widespread also in Eritrea. Highland Eritreans generally accept the translation 'Abyssinian', which is not primarily a political but a cultural term. An analysis of Eritrean texts (e.g., discussions of the Eritrean diaspora in the internet) shows that the term Habesha is largely preferred rather than Tigrinnya. It provides a strong, warm feeling of belongingness, thus revealing itself as being a truly ethnic term; the term brother (*hawey* – my brother) is often quickly used, when someone outs himself as Habesha in an internet chat. It is an extremely inclusive term, providing all the emotional promise of belongingness and closeness typical of an ethnonym.

But some further explanation on the well-known, but in its complexity often underestimated, term Habesha is necessary. First, it can generally be observed that this term (with the variations Habesha or Abesha in Amharic) is used to self-designate the Tigrinnya and Amhara Highlanders living in the realm of the pre-nineteenth-century Christian kingdom of the highlands, Ityop'ya.[20] It is from this ethnic term that the European terms Habessinia (seventeenth century), later Abyssinia (from [H]Abesha = Arab. al-Habasha = Abessinians/Abyssinians) was coined. That is the wider sense of the term.

Second, in the local context the term shows its exclusivity, when it is used as an ethnonym. When Tigrayan elders speak of Habesha and *qwanqwa* Habesha, there is always the connotation of a 'highlander' belonging to the same ethnic group and speaking the same language (sometimes implicitly including the common religion, Christianity). But what exactly is meant? In fact, in daily conversation one often means the Tigrinnya-speakers exclusively, which can be understood from sentences in which one speaks of 'us Habesha', clearly the we-group, in opposition to 'the Amharu' (the Amhara), the others. Only when asked further, it might be admitted that the Amhara should be included, but only in the sense that they are also the heirs and descendants of the Aksumite Empire; but they are not the 'original' Habesha. In this context it is not surprising that the term *lingua abissina* had been suggested by a conservative Eritrean linguist, who did not want to use the new-fashioned 'Tigrinnya' and preferred the old-fashioned term *'qwanqwa* Habesha' for Tigrinnya (Agostinos 1994).

The diversity in the existing language designations is significant. Today, as we see in Table 4.1 above, the term Tigrinnya is widely accepted for the language. But it is an Amharic word, which had only been introduced slowly through the use of Amharic in cities, administrative centres and schools. The Amharic ending -*innya* does not exist in Tigrinnya. When one speaks of a language in Tigrinnya, including their own, it is enough to add *qwanqwa* (language) to the name of the ethnic group or province, or even leave *qwanqwa* out, if the context is clear enough. So Habesha speak Habesha. Tigray speak Tigray. And Tigrinnya speak Tigrinnya – or *qwanqwa* Tigrinnya.[21]

A closer look at the meaning of the word Tigrinnya helps. In fact, Tigrinnya in Amharic means 'Tigré-ish' (Tigray-language). It is interesting in this context that local tradition in Tigray, still followed today by Tigrayan elders, never uses the term 'Tigray' for the whole province, but exclusively for its centre, i.e. Adwa with the ancient cities of Aksum and Yeha; the term is therefore associated with the oldest centre of the state (excluding the Tigrayan provinces of Tembén, Inderta, Agame, Welqayt etc. etc.; in this sense Agame is outside Tigray). When people spoke of the 'language of Tigray' this meant the language of the centre – i.e. of Aksum and of the *tigré mekonnin*. This is quite logical: the centre, to which one is connected through tribute (or some other rather loose political connection) and strong religious ties, gives the name.[22] This makes it also understandable why especially those groups which had kept a high degree of political autonomy, as is known from the Wejjerat, did *not* call their language 'language of Tigray', as they were politically not part of Tigray proper. Their language could only be called 'language of Wejjerat' (Wejjerinna). The same phenomenon can be observed with the formerly completely independent Rayya, who speak the 'language of Rayya'. Even if Wejjerat and Rayya both speak dialects of Tigrinnya, they do not call their language Tigrinnya, as this signifies a connection with the province of that name. The use of the term marks a boundary.

DIVERGING IDENTITIES WITHIN AN ETHNIC CONFEDERACY

It should not be regarded as surprising that Tigrinnya-speakers are marked by such a multitude of diverging identities (which are not always very visible to outsiders).[23] They are quite a large group, living in an extended area, which was at times an important princedom and sometimes split into several often autonomous provinces or princedoms. In ancient times it was a state (the Aksumite kingdom) and as such necessarily included diverse socio-political groups and groups of different origins. This pluralistic situation of the Tigrinnya-speakers can in some ways be compared with the Amhara or the Oromo, who are also conglomerates of groups unified under a common linguistic and to some degree political label rather than simply an ethnic group. As it is difficult to speak of a German ethnic group, it is difficult to simply treat the Tigrinnya-speakers and the Amhara etc. as ethnic groups like any others.[24] Each of them forms a sort of ethnic confederacy, a conglomerate of partially separate groups unified under the label of some common identity and common language – a confederacy which can always split again along pre-existing boundaries (but also in the midst of the split remembering an idea of mutual belonging). This is somehow true for many ethnic groups, particularly for huge ones inhabiting large territories. While I do not wish to refute the use of the term ethnic group for such peoples, I propose the use of a more complex term in contexts where it is useful to be precise. Consequently, one may speak of an ethno-political nation, an ethno-regional group, or better still an ethnic confederacy, for example. The last term in particular has the useful connotation that the unity is partially due to a specific political situation (as a break occurring in the unity would also be). So, there is nothing natural in the unity, and nothing artificial in the separation; both are part of the 'game'.

Internal boundaries in modern politics

Woldeab Woldemariam, a journalist and politician and the greatest and most prolific Tigrinnya writer of the 1940s, propogandized in his earlier publications political union between Tigray and Eritrea. He himself was born in Seraye in southern-central Eritrea, but was of Tigrayan origin, thus originating from the other side of the colonial-border (on this period, see Ullendorff 1985). After the Italian occupation of Ethiopia in 1936, Tigray was immediately united with Eritrea. British occupation of *Africa Orientale Italiana* in 1941 led to a subsequent restoration of the pre-war borders, and Tigray and Eritrea were again separated. There were strong groups among Tigrayans and Eritreans, who were advocating re-unification and the formation of a Tigrinnya nation-state; but it was never made clear what it would be called. Eritreans would expect the continuation of the post-1936 situation, i.e. the creation of a greater Eritrea, Tigrayans would tend towards the restoration of the ancient pre-1855 Tigrayan princedom (with its confederated provinces). Woldeab Woldemariam seemingly avoided discussions on the name of the future entity; he spoke of the *Tigray Tigrinnyi* and their need of union.

Later British involvement with Emperor Haile Selassie who had returned from exile and subsequently ended the *de facto* British Protectorate over Ethiopia (from 1941 to 1944) made a union between Tigray and Eritrea impossible (Astier Almedom 2006). In Eritrea, the question now was: union with all of Ethiopia or complete separation? The followers of the idea of a greater Eritrea split. A majority of Tigrinnya-Highlanders, religiously connected with the Ethiopian Orthodox Church, followed the idea of 'union with motherland Ethiopia', while a minority, among them influential reformist intellectuals such as Woldeab, who today is considered the father of Eritrean independence, chose the smaller Eritrea option and independence from Ethiopia. If Tigray and Eritrea could not be independent together, at least Eritrea should get this chance.

A closer look at the term *Tigray Tigrinnyi* is instructive, as the term itself refers to a boundary. When speaking of unity, the promoters of Tigray-Eritrean unification did not simply use the term Tigray; there are also others, such as the Tigrinnyi, and they have to be included. Who are they? In Eritrea the term Tigrinnyi is known exclusively from historiography referring to that period of the 1940s; it did not enter the language. Some believe that it was a pure invention of Woldeab. In Tigray, however, the term is used in non-political conversation. *Tigray Tigrinnyi metsi'om* means: Many people came. It may, for example, be said when many people come to a great feast. The phrase indicates that *not only* all Tigrayans came, but even other Tigrinnya-speakers from beyond Tigray. Again there is the notion of 'the other'. The term shows that the language takes into account that Tigray is too narrow a term to include all Tigrinnya-speakers. As the expression has this fixed meaning in everyday conversation, it can be concluded that it predated Woldeab's political (re-)interpretation. In fact, it corresponds to the historical situation that the Tigrayan centre only very rarely controlled all Tigrinnya-speaking areas.

The historical moment when the Ethiopian-Eritrean border became most virulent, was the Ethiopian-Eritrean war of 1998 to 2000.[25] The war started with clashes at the border near Badime, a village of Tigrinnya-speakers of Tigrayan and Eritrean origin, near the Kunama territories. The boundary changed from a simple state border to a frontline. The Ethio-Eritrean border had already been a subject of heated discussion from the moment of the creation of the Eritrean state in 1993 (*de facto* in 1991).[26] Local identity formation was now connected with the formation of this state border (Tronvoll 1999; 2003). The 'separatist' Eritrean identity had already accepted this boundary as given well before 1991, while in Ethiopia the urban public generally assumed that there was no need for an independent Eritrea and thus no need for a border. This meant that the existence of a quite fundamental feeling of separated-ness on the Eritrean side (thus, also a need for protection from incursions) was widely overlooked or not recognized.

On the Tigrayan side, feelings were mixed: even if the Eritrean border had existed since 1890, it was completely open most of the time. Over generations Tigrayans had migrated to Eritrea mainly for job opportunities, or for trade. In this sense the boundary was connecting people

69

and providing them with opportunities, since Eritrea beyond the border offered important economic resources. In *this* sense, Eritrea was perceived as a separate entity and a separate sphere of opportunity. Clearly, borders are not automatically barriers. However, a feeling that all Tigrinnya-speaking groups belonged to each other was animated especially starting from the 1940s. This led, especially on the Tigrayan side, to ideas that the boundary should be abolished for the sake of uniting of all Tigrinnya-speakers.

Finally, another factor came on the scene: Eritrea defined itself as a modern nation-state, created by colonialism. In this sense Eritrea has no ancient historical claims, and does not need them; the state defines itself through modernity (Dorman 2005; Hirt 2001; Ruth Iyob 1993). The boundary could therefore only be explained through international law, which stipulated that the colonial boundary (defined by treaties and international practice) was the official Eritrean boundary.

On the Tigrayan side, however, things were conceptually very different. Tigray defines itself through its ancient history and the history of its settlements. Boundaries are not known through international treaties, but are created by local practice. This was the case also in Badime. By practice, the Tigrayan majority in this settlement had always kept their links with Tigray, with the effect that it was included into the administration of the Tigrayan sub-province of 'Adyabo. This logically follows ancient patterns of belonging. The settler keeps his contacts with his home region, juridically as well as administratively. Due to the Tigrayan definition of territory and boundaries through heritage and ancient (local) rules, a conflict with the radically different definition of boundaries by the Eritrean state was foreseeable. In fact, already in 1993 there were numerous (local) reports about such problems. Local committees met and discussed the exact location of the boundary, but in many cases did not come to any solution. Until 1997 there were repeated reports on conflicts over farm and grazing land and cattle rustling in border areas, which showed that the diverging concepts of the boundary caused continuous problems.[27]

In 1997 Eritrea introduced the new Eritrean currency, which was followed by the establishment of restrictions on cross-boundary trade from the Ethiopian side. This led to a sudden increase in the practical importance of the border that now did not connect the regions any more, but dramatically separated them. Local problems over the definition of the exact location of the boundary thus increased in their importance. When an Eritrean army unit occupied Badime, this location was incorporated into Eritrea in violation of local concepts of boundary (which, however, contradict international law). Badime has later been defined as belonging to Eritrea by the international court of arbitration set up after the Ethiopian-Eritrean war. It needs to be emphasized, however, that local realities also exist, leading to differing concepts of boundaries, which are very strong, as they are generally accepted locally, where international law is unknown (Smidt 2002; 2006a; 2008).

The place-name Badime has today acquired a highly symbolic meaning in Eritrean and Tigrayan political discourse. Whenever it is used, this toponym expresses a deep grief over the boundary, always in the sense that Badime had been taken 'unrightfully' by the other (taken away from Tigray by the Eritreans in May 1998/taken away from Eritrea by the Tigrayans before 1998). The term crystallizes the fundamental dissent between the diverging concepts of the concrete border. It is thus an example of a border which only exists on one side. Yet, borders do only have a stabilizing effect if they are located unanimously. This is the condition for a border connecting people and providing basic protection to both sides. A border that is only clearly defined for one side will necessarily be challenged by the other side, and will lose its stabilizing effect. It may even become a reason for war. But those who blame the border as the cause of the problem misconceive the situation. It is not the border itself – as long as it is defined unanimously by those separated by it – that is the problem, but the *lack* of a clear-cut border, or, in other words, the existence of two opposed perspectives on the border. The problem is the unfinished establishment of a 'real' border.

When Badime is evoked, this problem is normally not seen. One sees only the bad deed of the other. In Tigray, as in Eritrea, bars and restaurants are often named after Badime. Music bands in Ethiopia and in Eritrea are called Badime. Badime symbolizes the bad other and the claim to be right, on both sides. There are also other allusions to the border in daily life. The Geza Gerlasé is a famous traditional restaurant in Meqele, the capital city of Tigray. It was founded by a Tigrayan who had lived in Eritrea before. His family was already deeply rooted in Eritrea before the outbreak of the war. The war led to the re-adoption of a strong Tigrayan identity. Literally the restaurant's name means House of Gerlasé (the short form of Gebre-Sellasé, the name of the owner). However, it also contains an allusion. Gerlasé is also the name of a small settlement on the boundary between Eritrea and Tigray, which was successfully defended against Eritrean occupation at an early stage of the war. This name therefore re-affirms the Tigrayan identity of the restaurant's owner. His history is the history of mixed identities, exchanged for a new strong identity created by war and symbolized by the border that in fact is a military front up to the present. Both countries, Ethiopia and Eritrea, continue their war of words; hot war has been followed by cold war (Tronvoll and Tekeste Negash 2000; Jacquin-Berdal and Plaut 2005). The contradiction between the Ethiopian point of view (based on local traditions about borders) and the point of view of the international court of arbitration (supported by Eritrea) remains unsolved.

A problem for the non-recognition of the boundary as perceived by the other was, as shown, the fundamentally different characters of Tigrayan and Eritrean political identities. On the Tigrayan side, for example, the concept of a 'Greater Tigray' was developed, which was to include all areas of Tigrinnya-speakers. However, the groups promoting this concept did not gain political control over the Tigrayan People's Liberation Front (TPLF) (Hammond 1999; Berhe Kahsay 2005), even if Eritrean authors tend to explain the problems in this way. In fact, the idea of the unity of all Tigrinnya-speakers shifted with time. Today's TPLF no longer pursues the idea of a 'Greater Tigray', but focuses on unity *within* Tigray. The TPLF and EPLF illustrate well the complexity of inner-Tigrinnya tensions, separations and connections. The two organizations at times worked closely with each other. Eritreans (living in Tigray) were and partly still are active in the TPLF, and vice versa. This was strongly helped by a sense of belonging to the same group of Tigrinnya-speakers. But the history of the struggle recounts that such connections rarely stayed 'brotherly' for a longer period of time; they were often only 'strategic'. Different historical claims and identities and political aims resulting from this regularly led to most dramatic shifts of alliances (for example, alliances between the TPLF and ELF, the mortal enemy of the EPLF) and the re-establishment of separating boundaries. While the idea of a common identity often facilitated collaboration, the internal boundaries often led to a serious lack of possibilities of mutual understanding. One is tempted to say that we are observing here the problem that the idea of unity itself caused such problems, as this idea leads to blindness towards boundaries; differences are not seen until it is too late. In a way, also in this case the non-recognition of differences (i.e., borders), which were not negotiated, contributed to the problem.

In a totally different context, boundaries also play a constructive role in modern Tigrayan politics. Border areas were, in the past, characterized by *shifta*, groups of bandits and outlaws. However, today the government establishes new settlements especially in border areas, thus pacifying them and establishing control. Modern boundaries in Tigray are therefore more and more characterized by chains of modern settlements set up by the government. The new settlement of Dansha near the Sudanese border, where former fighters obtained farming land, is an example of this (Krug 2000). It demonstrates the positive function of a border as a factor of stabilization.

During the Eritrean war of liberation, Eritrea was denied the right of existence by most foreign observers and the Ethiopian central government, which rejected the establishment of a new boundary. However, from the Eritrean point of view, they were simply defending an already existing boundary against 'foreign' dominators or intruders, who were violating it. In a sense, the whole liberation struggle was a struggle to defend this boundary and fight for its final recognition. In 1993 the international community, including Ethiopia, recognized the new state of Eritrea. From the Eritrean point of view the existence of that boundary, for which they had fought for three decades, was finally acknowledged. Even if some observers claimed that the establishment of new boundaries entailed new dangers, one has to admit that at least this recognition stopped a bloody and never-ending war. The new boundary guaranteed a recognition which was so urgently needed that it led to war; it was a new guarantee against suppression (Young 1996; 1997). This protective function of boundaries is often overlooked.

Also within Ethiopia itself, numerous new boundaries were established, following a similar idea. With the recognition of existing separate entities and the cessation of their integration by force into an artificial centralist state, peace finally became possible after years of war. This separation entailed the opportunity of establishing new connections, this time based on mutual recognition. This recognition could only become possible through the definition and establishment of boundaries, including the recognition of pre-existing internal boundaries within Ethiopia. The chances of this historical moment cannot be disproved by the later outbreak of war, which was, as we have shown, not caused by the boundary itself, but by the mutual non-recognition of the boundary as perceived by the other. This in fact contradicted the very concept of a boundary.

Internal boundaries as a historical and ethnological phenomenon

Until now we have only seen that the Tigrinnya-speakers are split into different groups, the dominating ones being those calling themselves Tegaru (in Tigray) and those calling themselves Tigrinnya (in Eritrea), while the boundaries between both terms remain fluid. Are there any deeper reasons for this split, going beyond modern politics?

BOUNDARIES SEPARATING HISTORICAL TIGRINNYA PROVINCES

The discourse of unity is misleading, as is the discourse of total separation. Assumptions based on these discourses lead to gross misunderstandings of what is going on at present. It is, however, important to stress that both discourses, the one of unity and the other of separation, have to be considered and taken seriously. Any we-group is a dialectical construction. Defining the modern boundary as purely artificial underestimates its function, by ideologizing it, and underlining its illegitimacy (this is the discourse followed by Alemseged Abbay 1998). Boundaries had already played a crucial role in Tigrinnya history well before modern conflicts: today's state boundary at the Mereb was already established as a provincial boundary in the eighteenth century and occasionally before (Kolmodin 1915; Smidt 2007b; Alemseged Abbay 1997). At the same time, ancient interconnections between Tigrinnya groups also continued to exist from ancient times until today, even if the colonial Eritrean boundary created a boundary which was more pronounced than those previously. The centre of common Tigrinnya identity was Aksum, the centre of the ancient Empire and still the centre of the Orthodox Church. Pious pilgrims went to Aksum, disregarding any boundaries.[28] Colonial expansion in Eritrea entered into local realities, transforming them. An ancient inner <u>H</u>abesha boundary changed into an international boundary (we know this well from Austrian-German history etc., which no longer considered the Austrian-German boundary illegitimate).

What has already been outlined in detail by Dereje Feyissa and Hoehne in Chapter 1 of this volume should be borne in mind here: that every boundary is artificial, and that every boundary is potentially fluid. The coming and going of boundaries is normal. It is therefore not possible to use a discourse of artificiality to make one specific boundary illegitimate. If we underline their artificiality, all boundaries are illegitimate ultimately. So, characterizing a boundary as artificial does not say much. Artificial or not, they are there, and they have a function.

In the case of Tigrinnya-speakers, interaction with boundaries seems to be ancient. One might come close to understanding, when one says that boundaries are an integral (and historical) part of Tigrinnya identity and identities. The history of this ethnic group shows us that even the Tigrinnya identity itself is based on a vivid and flexible interaction with boundaries, a dynamic inclusion of borders within their political identity. Tigrinnya politics in the past was a politics of networks, across boundaries, linking different nobles and autonomous groups within a half-feudal, half-democratic confederacy (Perini 1905). These borders could be crossed, and also defended, when local interests were endangered. It is not by chance that the TPLF model for the creation of a new Ethiopia was largely based on the recognition (and partially creation) of boundaries, a model already followed to some degree by the Tigrayan *atse* Yohannes IV. Different from his predecessor Tewodros II, who zealously subjugated the Ethiopian princedoms and forced them under his absolutist-reformist strong hand, Yohannes IV recognized half-autonomous leaders in the different provinces and princedoms of Ethiopia. By recognizing their autonomy he was successful in his demand for partial submission. By recognizing pre-existing boundaries, he could use the services of his potential counterparts. The recognized boundaries could be crossed, due to their recognition.

A closer look into Tigrayan dynastic history makes this clearer. One often thinks of Tigray as a princedom with its own dynasty, similar to the other Ethiopian princedoms or kingdoms like Shoa or Gojjam. This is incorrect. One speaks, for example, of a Tigrayan dynasty (meaning Yohannes's descendants); again this is quite wrong, a strange copy of the Shoan, Gojjame, Amhara models. It was rarely that Tigray was unified under one leader. If one tries to get a complete list of Tigrayan leaders from oral tradition, for example, one will get quite different answers in Agame and in Adwa, Tigrayan provinces which are very close to each other. When one leader managed to control most of the Tigrinnya provinces, he was able to do this regularly for two reasons. First, he could base his power on a complex network of genealogical connections with the different key provinces, each of which got its share (many examples of the political role of genealogical connections are given by Perini 1905; see also Tronvoll 1996). Secondly, he also respected – a *conditio sine qua non* – the local land rights of the local leaders and peasants. Consequently, after his downfall the leader of another province would get the chance to grasp his power.

So, no dynasty was ever established over the whole of Tigray (in contrast with the Tigrayan provinces, more locally, where some dynasties managed to stay in power for many generations). One Tigrayan prince was *re'esi* Welde Selassie around 1800, whose descendants did not inherit any power. The next, after an interim, was Subagadish of Agame, but his heirs only succeeded him in their home region, Agame. Another was Kasa Mercha (later Yohannes IV) of Tembén and again with him another province and all the members of his local networks got the chance to inherit. When Eritrean historians claim today that their ancestors in the highlands had already lived independently before colonization, it is based on the same facts. Hamasén had its own petty dynasty, governing autonomously and participating in the networks of Tigray. A member of this dynasty, Ande Haymanot, took control of much of Tigray, thus entering into the always same game of separation and inclusion. It was with him that the Mereb was established as a provincial boundary in the eighteenth century, his power base being behind the Mereb ('Mereb Mellash') (Smidt 2007b).

TIGRINNYA ETHNIC TERMINOLOGY

The networking character of Tigrinnya identities and boundary construction can be seen also, to some degree, in their ethnic terminologies, which are fluid.

Table 4.3 *Tigrinnya ethnic terminology*

Tigray (informant: Agame)	Eritrea (informant: Akkele Guzay)
hizbitat Ityop'ya – the peoples of Ethiopia	*hizbi Ertra* – the people of Eritrea
hizbi Tigray – the people of Tigray	
behere Tigray – the ethnic group of Tigray	*behere Tigrinnya* – the ethnic group T.
hizbi Agame – the population of Agame	*hizbi Akkele Guzay* – population of A.
beheresebat Irob – the small ethnic group I.	*weledo Tsen'adegle* – the subgroup Ts.
'Inday weledo – the lineage (clan) of 'Inday	*inda Hayet* – the lineage of Hayet
inda Nguse – the house of Nguse	

An interesting difference lies in the term *weledo* (sometimes: *tiwiledi*), meaning: 'the ones born of'. This term is used in both Eritrea and Tigray. Eritrea, especially Akkele Guzay, is characterized by strong descent groups, which had reached a high degree of internal autonomy, culminating in the creation of their own regional law books starting from the seventeenth century (Kemink 1991; Favali and Pateman 2003; Smidt 2006c; 2007a). Most of Tigray, closer associated with the Ethiopian king of kings, did not go through such a development. The Tsen'adegle in Akkele-Guzay, for example, managed to keep themselves autonomous, only following their own war leaders, selected by the elders' assemblies. They are *weledo*, a descent group with strong binding ties of 'brotherhood' (*hawinnet*).[29] This helped them to create strong boundaries, which, however, were not fully territorial, but are connected with the descent group. In Tigray, the term *weledo* is also used, but includes much smaller units, which are likewise bound to each other. The *weledo* '*Inday* mentioned in Table 4.3 are a clan, which is found in a few villages in 'Addi Da'iro (Agame), named after an ancestor only four generations distant.

The term *weledo* expresses a strong feeling of belongingness within a network of family obligations. These are important examples: the creation of subgroups is based on the idea of common descent, which creates security through mutual obligations. Boundaries are set up between the different groups and can become quite permanent. But below the *weledo* there are smaller units, smaller lineages which include mother lines, which can cross the boundaries that were set up by the *weledo*; such 'houses' are often called *inda*. A looser term which is widespread is *deqqi* (children of), which can mean the children of a still living elder or even all the inhabitants of the country (*deqqi* Ertra or *deqqi* Tigray), thus creating a strong quasi-parental link between all the people. The network of cooperation can be largely extended.

Finally, anyone 'belonging to us' can be included through the rhetoric of parentage. The Tigrayans in this sense are all brothers; they eat the same things, and they have the same root ('*zer'i*' corresponding to the English idea of 'being of the same blood').[30] This discourse can include all Tigrinnya-speakers, who all participate in the idea of belongingness through ancient descent. Most highland Eritreans claim descent from '*negus* Meroni' who had come from the south (i.e. Tigray) in medieval times to settle in Eritrea, or at least claim common descent from the Agi'azyan (as they are called in local legend, i.e. the historical Agi'azi population in pre-Aksumite times) or Sabawiyan (the South Arabian immigrants in the first millennium BC). Descent is not just a word; through common descent one becomes a brother. But only if an existing boundary does not provide better chances of growth or protection.

MODERN POLITICS AND LOCAL TRADITIONS
OF BOUNDARIES

Modern politics can exploit the two great concerns of Tigrinnya identity: (i) the preservation of boundaries, i.e. the defence of the age-old autonomy of your well-functioning *local* networks of mutual help, or (ii) the feeling of belongingness and *hawinnet* across all boundaries, which is another form of assuring economic success even in the difficult circumstances of drought and war.

The politics of separation and inclusion which can be observed in modern Tigrayan and Eritrean politics fits well into this. President Isayas

Afeworqi was the son of a worker in the Asmara government office of the Ethio-Eritrean Federation, who was of Tembén descent; his family is still well-known in Tembén in Tigray. Minister President Meles Zenawi's mother, who died a few years ago in Adwa, Tigray, was an Eritrean from Seraye. While tens of thousands of Eritreans and Ethiopians of some kind of Eritrean descent (e.g. through the paternal grandfather) were deported for economic and propaganda reasons at the beginning of the Ethio-Eritrean war of 1998, Meles's mother fulfilled all the criteria of someone to be deported, but of course remained. The Information Minister in Meles's government, Bereket Sim'on, is an Eritrean from both his father's and his mother's side – again, if descent is the decisive criterion. These examples have puzzled many observers, especially within Ethiopia itself. Without a good understanding of the function of boundaries, this cannot be well understood. Within unity, boundaries were always set up. In the midst of separation, boundaries were overcome. Boundaries protect different spheres, and change with changing interests. When the close interaction between the EPLF and the TPLF is discussed, one tends to overlook their often fundamentally diverging interests, despite their relatedness in some respects. This constellation made them strategic partners and even 'brothers'; yet, with changing circumstances their relationship easily changes into deadly enmity, which, like the relatedness, follows an age-old Tigrinnya tradition.

Relations can cross almost all boundaries; a Tigrinnya-speaker can find 'cousins' in even the remotest regions. But in the case of rupture, which is an integral part of a long history of local feuds, everyone has a clear set of rules in his mind, as to whom he should belong (and who is no longer a cousin). In the rural context this is defined through genealogical descent from the paternal line (real or imagined). Cases of adoption exist, where the genealogy of an outsider is replaced by a fictive local one to include his family in the local network of rights and obligations. In a more modern urban context, which can especially be observed in colonial-built cities like Asmara or Mendefera, belongingness becomes more political, but still expresses itself with the vocabulary of descent (*deqqi*) and brotherhood (*ḥawinnet*).

Concluding remarks

The Ethio-Eritrean boundary has allegedly separated one huge unified ethnic group, the Tigrinnya-speakers, since 1993. In both local and international discourses the existence of this boundary has often been used to point to the wrong directions that modern Ethiopia has taken. These discourses are based on the widely held idea that the state borders of post-colonial Africa are artificial, and that, in the Ethiopian case, there would be some sort of eternal 'Greater Ethiopia', which makes any new boundary illegitimate. This chapter has shown how mistaken this discussion is.

First, the Tigrinnya-speakers are not one 'ethnic bloc'. The idea of the unity of all Tigrinnya-speakers is an artificial modern creation. Historically, the Tigrinnya-speakers rather identified with more local entities, defined through descent and political leadership (such as the Agame in eastern Tigray or the Akkele-Guzay in central Eritrea, etc.), and this is largely the case still today, especially in the rural context. At the same time, strong interconnections between all Tigrinnya-speakers (in the sense of an ethnic confederacy) have always been presented and repeatedly also became politically important.

Second, the boundary is not simply a colonial creation. The boundary separating the Tigrinnya-speakers is in many parts pre-colonial, a heritage of older boundaries separating half-autonomous units or petty princedoms under the suzerain or sovereign rule of the king of kings of Ityop'ya. The colonial history changed a fluid traditional boundary, however, into an inflexible, more divisive boundary.

Third, boundaries are always subject to change, and they are not illegitimate simply because they are new. Particularly in discourses among highland-Ethiopian intellectuals, the idea prevails that Ethiopia is illegitimately cut into pieces and destroyed by 'new' boundaries (be they the boundaries of the regional states or the post-colonial boundaries). This idea refutes the historical reality that boundaries in Ethiopia are (a) old, (b) frequently changed, acquiring greater or lesser importance according to context or even 'wandering', or (c) being newly created following new political developments, new alliances and new cleavages.

Fourth, recognized boundaries are a chance for stabilization. One of the current political diseases is the rejection of the validity of borders. Borders define the respective spheres of influence and, negatively, exclude arbitrary interference in one another's affairs, but do not necessarily separate populations from each other. Boundaries define where which set of rules is valid, but allow commercial and other relations and can in this sense encourage exchange, where it is felt to be needed, but also protect local interests from interference.

The Tigrinnya-speakers in the Eritrean highlands and Tigray are a classic example of an ethnic group, which has 'always' existed with territorially defined internal boundaries separating the autonomous sub-groups from each other, and has always witnessed a wide set of interconnections across these boundaries (political alliances, educational/religious exchanges of personnel and ideas, commerce, marriage, etc.). The relationship between the great number of independent local identities (in some cases so strong that it is doubtful if they still belong to an ethnic group called Tigrinnya-speakers) and a common Tigrinnya identity has always opened up two possibilities: to follow a common Tigrinnya project and/or local interests and alliances. The diverse self-designations used by different Tigrinnya-speaking groups – cultural and social groups – illustrate this well.

The state boundary has led to new developments on both sides of the boundary (in Tigray people tend to call themselves Tegaru or Tigray, in

Eritrea the term Tigrinnya is used – in both cases including the others in the term, but refusing the validity of the other's term). The modern boundary separates two spheres of re-definition of identity or cultural-political positioning, but this development of two new ethnic terms also reflects a conviction of belongingness. However, both by their very conception exclude each other. In addition to these modern developments, other local terms (like Rayya) still exist, excluding, to some extent, an artificial Tigrinnya unity even within Tigray. This reality of diversity and plurality is to be seen in the context of local traditions of cross-border relations.

To repeat and underline some of the most important ideas of this chapter: borders are constructions, but are well enrooted in Tigrinnya history; identities had been formed along these borders, borders are therefore an integral part of Tigrinnya identity construction. Like all constructions, they were sometimes replaced by new constructions, and identities were re-formed. The new political identities of Tigrayans or Eritreans are in this sense part of a long tradition of identity-formation along changing internal boundaries. A new and currently unsolvable problem is certainly that, through the possibilities of modernity, i.e. modern weaponry and infrastructure, which freezes specific boundaries, boundaries can become more dangerous and destructive than ever before, as they lose their fluidity. The situation becomes even more dangerous when different boundaries are imagined, which logically exclude each other, as is the case with the Tigrayan border of Badime contradicting the Eritrean version of the border. Borders are the result of the mutual recognition of each side's diverging identities and interests. It is in fact mainly the lack of recognition of the other (which includes, by definition, a border) which leads to conflicts and even war, not the border itself.

Notes

1   Quoted by the German-Tigrinnya singer Senait Mehari, who sang Lennon's song after having returned from a journey to Addis Ababa and Khartoum (2005), see her book *Wüstenlied* (2006), p. 309.

2   In the case of Eritrea, the boundary meant the recognition of the wish to live without foreign domination (including domination by a remote imposing state centre), and thus meant a chance for mutual recognition and renewed contact across the boundary before it became a war boundary, and before Eritrean soldiers started to patrol the boundary to hinder Eritreans escaping to Ethiopia or the Sudan.

3   A small ethnic group in western Ethiopia, who once formed the core of the defunct Anfillo kingdom, which had been included in Oromo rule from the mid-19th century. The Omotic language Anfillo, related to Kaficho, is about to die out, being replaced by Oromiffaa as a result of a long interaction with the Oromo, the dominant ethnic group (Smidt 2003: 262-64). This is linked to a process of devalorization of its own origin (the majority of Anfillo-speakers were in fact serfs of the Anfillo rulers) and assimilation into a culturally and economically more attractive larger group, the Oromo.

4 For technical reasons I chose to use this term in this chapter, as it is the most neutral one, not part of any political discourse or historical tradition; it simply encompasses those people(s) speaking Tigrinnya and does not pre-judge their exact status within this group. This is also the term predominantly used in the *Encyclopaedia Aethiopica*. I do not exclude the fact that other terms might be more suitable in other contexts. The Tigrinnya language is an Ethio-Semitic language, closely related to Amharic, Tigré, Gurage and Gi'iz. Different from Amharic, it has preserved several features of ancient Ethio-Semitic languages spoken in the region in antiquity (of which Gi'iz has been preserved as the Church language); the area in which Tigrinnya is spoken very roughly corresponds to the core of the ancient Aksumite kingdom.

5 This term is regarded as inappropriate in modern discourse in Ethiopia today – particularly in Amharic publications of the government – and has been replaced by the plural form 'Tigrawiyan'.

6 In addition, the term 'Tigre' is already the (modern) self-designation of another group: the Tigre are an important and well-known ethnic group in the Eritrean lowlands, speaking Tigre. And, adding to the complexity of the situation, in the local context there is also the term *tigre*, meaning 'vassal group', among the Blin, Beni Amer and several leading groups among the Tigre, such as the Bet Asgede etc. (Munzinger 1864). The term 'Tigre' in the sense of 'Tigrinnya-speaker' should therefore be dropped in ethnological literature.

7 Self-designations dominating in the respective rural context, i.e. the most traditional ones, are printed in *italics*; the table shows the most common self-designations used in Tigray and in Eritrea, and the notable exceptions, such as those used by the Rayya and other more peripheral subgroups.

8 i.e. today's Regional State of Tigray (Biherawi Kililawi Mängisti Tigray); different from the pre-1991 situation, this state encompasses all territories inhabited by Tigrinnya-speakers in Ethiopia today.

9 This term only appears occasionally as an ethnic self-designation. In rural contexts, the terms Tigray, Tigraway and Tegaru are used rather in a geographical context, not as an ethnonym. The only real ethnonym used is mostly Habesha, and occasionally more local ethnonyms designating subgroups.

10 The word *qwanqwa* (= language, in Tigrinnya) can be omitted, if the context makes it clear that the language is meant. Interestingly it is also occasionally used in connection with 'Tigrinnya', somehow a tautology.

11 No longer used in the original *ethnic* sense, but expressing a diffuse feeling of Ethiopian-ness. Further below the difference between the very traditional, local meaning of 'Habesha' and the meaning of 'Habesha/Abesha' in the wider Ethiopian context is discussed.

12 On the ethnic structure of Eritrea see Nadel 1944.

13 For further details see Smidt 2005.

14 No ethnographic research has ever been carried out among them. It seems that they have been virtually overlooked as a distinctive group both by researchers and administrators.

15 A publication on them, based on field research in April 2008, is in preparation (Smidt and Habtom Gebremedhin 2009; Smidt 2005). Local Habesha tradition claims that they are former slaves from Begemdir, other sources suggest a connection with the border sultanate of Gallabat (Metemma), while their own tradition rather suggests that they were the original inhabitants of the whole region and were later subjugated by Ethiopians coming from the Welqayt highlands and Begemdir. The Ethiopian People's Revolutionary Army, operating in their region in the 1970s, tried to free them, but could not fully abolish the client-master relationship of the then 'Bet Barya' (later replaced by the term Tsellim Bet) with the Habesha highlanders.

16 I am speaking here of the Rayya of Oromo origin; there are also Rayya groups of Tigrinnya origin, who claim to be the original settlers.

17 This term is rarely used in Tigray, when speaking of Tigrinnya-speakers outside Tigray (plural form of Tigrinnya as understood as a group)

18 On this in detail see Smidt 2005.

19 In contrast to people in central Ethiopia, who use this term (and its variant Abesha) quite generally for 'Ethiopian'.

20 See, for example, the internet site www.habesha.com. They write: 'The name of this web page was chosen due to our desire to select a neutral and commonly shared term of reference for both Ethiopians and Eritreans. Since the site's inception, however, we have learned that many in Ethiopia do not associate with the term h/abesha, as it excludes groups such as Oromo, Somali, and the many Southern Nationalities and Peoples. We have also learned that there are a number of Eritreans who do not refer to themselves as 'habesha' such as Rashaidas, Kunamas and others. Perhaps, the biggest lesson we have learned is that the term 'h/abesha' is a complex phrase that has specific social, geographical and sometimes political connotations and we will reserve it as a name that is quite vulnerable to constant modifications.'

21 This literally means: language of *Tigray-language*.

22 There is an open discussion on how the term Tigray came to be identified with the province of Aksum. In ancient inscriptions there are Aksum and the Aksumites, but no Tigray; but 'Tigretai' are mentioned in an ancient Greek text, who were seemingly living at the coast (Lusini 2004).

23 'Outsider' in this context does not only mean the Amhara outsider, or the German visitor, but also a member of any Tigrinnya group living geographically or socio-politically separate from the others. A Jeberti, for instance, might have a definition of his own Tigrinnya identity which is quite different from what his neighbour supposes.

24 Am I, being an ethnic Frisian by paternal heritage, really an ethnic German, or just a German by citizenship and language?

25 For an excellent discussion of local identities involved in this conflict see Reid (2003). For references to pre-twentieth century developments of inner-Tigrinnya-boundaries see Trivelli (1998).

26 There are numerous publications on how Eritrea came into existence as a state. I shall not therefore repeat here what is widely known (Hirt 2001; Ruth Iyob 1993). The basics of this recent history are also mentioned by Dereje Feyissa and Hoehne in Chapter 1 of this volume.

27 This local news did not reach international newspapers. Eritrean and Ethiopian society traditionally tends not to publicize conflicts; it is believed that it is better to solve them behind closed doors.

28 This fact had been used by the British officer Stephen Longrigg in the 1940s when he suggested that 'the middle and highland part of Eritrea … with its Tigrinya-speaking inhabitants should be united and receive British aid and support' (quoted in Astier Almedom 2006: 120). Longrigg thus used a factor interconnecting the different groups for his idea of unification, while his concept disregarded the still separating factor of strong local identities.

29 On the importance of this concept for the social structure of Tigrinnya-speakers see Smidt 2008, 2007c.

30 In Tigrinnya, family relations are not defined through blood, even if it is repeatedly said in the Anglophone literature on Ethiopia and Eritrea that 'blood' or 'blood relations' play a central role in the region, which is somehow a terminological eurocentrism. What links families is not 'blood' but the common origin; one is the 'seed' of the forefathers. Sometimes this common origin is defined through the bones: the bones are inherited from the ancestors, because they are only things which last; they grow first, and the flesh grows around them.

References

Agostinos-Tädlá [= religious name: Agostino da Hebo] 1994. *La lingua abissina. qwanqwa habesha* [ed. by Tawaldabrhán Saggáy]. Asmara: Edizioni 'Adveniat Regnum Tuum'

Alemseged Abbay. 1997. 'The Trans-Mareb Past in the Present'. *The Journal of Modern African*

Studies 35(2): 321–34.

—— 1998. *Identity Jilted or Re-imagining Identity? The Divergent Paths of the Eritrean and Tigrayan Nationalist Struggles.* Lawrenceville, NJ and Asmara: Red Sea Press.

Astier M. Almedom 2006. 'Re-reading the Short and Long-Rigged History of Eritrea 1941-1952: Back to the Future?'. *Nordic Journal of African Studies* 15(2): 103–42.

Berhe Kahsay 2005. *Ethiopia. Democratization and Unity. The Role of the Tigray People's Liberation Front.* Münster: Monsenstein und Vannerdat.

Dorman, S.R. 2005. 'Narratives of nationalism in Eritrea: research and revisionism'. *Nations and Nationalism* 11(2): 203–22.

Elwert, G. 1989. 'Nationalismus und Ethnizität. Über die Bildung von Wir-Gruppen'. *Kölner Zeitschrift für Soziologie und Sozialpsychologie* 41: 440–64.

Favali, L. and R. Pateman 2003. *Blood, Land, and Sex, Legal and Political Pluralism in Eritrea.* Bloomington, IN: Indiana University Press.

Hammond, J. 1999. *Fire from the Ashes. A Chronicle of the Revolution in Tigray, Ethiopia, 1975–1991.* Lawrenceville, NJ and Asmara: Red Sea Press.

Hirt, N. 2001: *Eritrea zwischen Krieg und Frieden. Die Entwicklung seit der Unabhängigkeit.* Hamburger Beiträge zur Afrika-Kunde, 62. Hamburg: Inst. für Afrika-Kunde.

Jacquin-Berdal, D. and M. Plaut (eds). 2005. *Unfinished Business, Eritrea and Ethiopia at War.* Lawrenceville, NJ and Asmara: Red Sea Press.

Kemink, F. 1991. *Die Tegreñña-Frauen in Eritrea: eine Untersuchung der Kodizes des Gewohnheitsrechts 1890–1941.* Stuttgart: Steiner.

Kolmodin, J.A. 1915. *Traditions de Tsazzega et Hazzega, II: Traduction Française,* Uppsala: *Archives d'Études Orientales,* Vol. 5.

Krug, S. 2000. *Anthropologie der Kriegs- und Nachkriegszeit in Äthiopien.* Münster, Hamburg and London: LIT.

Lusini, G. 2004. 'Note linguistiche per la storia dell'Etiopia antica', in V. Böll, D. Nosnitsin, T. Rave, W. Smidt and E. Sokolinskaia (eds), *Studia Aethiopica in Honour of Siegbert Uhlig on the Occasion of his 65th Birthday* [Festschrift]. Wiesbaden: Harrassowitz, pp. 67–77.

Munzinger, W. 1864. *Ostafrikanische Studien.* Schaffhausen: Hurter.

Nadel, S.F. 1944. *Races and Tribes of Eritrea.* Asmara: British Military Administration.

Perini, R. 1905. *Di qua dal Marèb (Marèb-Mellàsc').* Florence: Tiografia Cooperativa.

Reid, R. 2003. 'Old Problems in New Conflicts: Some Observations on Eritrea and Its Relations with Tigray, from Liberation Struggle to Interstate War'. *Africa* 73(3): 369–401.

Ruth Iyob 1993. *The Eritrean Struggle for Independence. Domination, Resistance, Nationalism. 1941–1993.* Cambridge: Cambridge University Press.

Smidt, W. 2002. 'Äthiopien: Falsche Grenzen ein internes Kriegsinstrument? Anmerkungen zum Urteil im Grenzstreit Äthiopien/Eritrea'. *Afrika-Bulletin* 28(107): 8–9.

—— 2003 'Anfillo ethnohistory', in S. Uhlig (ed.), *Encyclopaedia Aethiopica,* Vol. 1.Wiesbaden: Harrassowitz, pp. 262–64.

—— 2005. 'Selbstbezeichnungen von Təgrəñña-Sprechern (Ḥabäša, Tägaru, Təgrəñña u.a.)', in B. Burtea, J. Tropper and H. Younansardaroud (eds), *Studia Semitica et Semitohamitica. Festschrift Rainer Voigt.* Münster: Ugarit-Verlag, pp. 385–404.

—— 2006a. 'Friedensräume in Tigray im Konflikt', in A. Hornbacher (ed.), *Ethos, Ethik, Ethnos* [Festschrift für Hermann Amborn]. Bielefeld: Transcript Verlag, pp. 367–89.

—— 2006b. 'Discussing ethnohistory: The Blin between periphery and international politics in the 19th century'. *Chroniques yéménites* 14: 131–44.

—— 2006c. 'Tigrinnya, Soziale Kohäsion, Landrecht und lokale Geschichte der Tigrayer in Äthiopien und der Hochland-Eritreer', in S. Wenig (ed.), W. Smidt, K. Volker-Saad and B. Vogt (co-eds), *In kaiserlichem Auftrag: Die Deutsche Aksum-Expedition 1906 unter Enno Littmann,* Vol. 1. Stuttgart: Verlag Lindensoft, pp. 63–72.

—— 2007a. 'Traditional Law Books', in Siegbert Uhlig (ed.), *Encyclopaedia Aethiopica,* Vol. 3. Wiesbaden: Harrassowitz, pp. 516–18.

—— 2007b. 'Märäb', 'Märäb Mellash', in Siegbert Uhlig (ed.), *Encyclopaedia Aethiopica,* Vol. 3. Wiesbaden: Harrassowitz, pp. 772–75.

—— 2007c. 'A Society of Unity: The Refusal of Conflict in Tigray', in W. Smidt and Kinfe Abraham (eds), *Discussing Conflict in Ethiopia, Proceedings of the Conference on 'Ethiopian and*

German Contributions to Conflict Management and Resolution', Addis Ababa 11–12 November 2005. Münster: LIT, pp. 86-98.

—— 2008. 'Unvereinbare Rechts- und Weltentwürfe: Grenzverläufe zwischen Äthiopien und Eritrea aus zwei Perspektiven – ein versteckter Kriegsgrund', in R. Tetzlaff, Abdulkader Saleh, N. Hirt and W. Smidt (eds), '*Friedensräume' in Tigray und Eritrea unter Druck – Identitätskonstruktion, soziale Kohäsion und politische Stabilität*. Münster: Lit-Verlag, pp. 293-321.

Smidt, W. and Habtom Gebremedhin 2009. 'S̲ällim Bet', in S. Uhlig (ed.), *Encyclopaedia Aethiopica* 4. Wiesbaden: Harrassowitz (forthcoming).

Trivelli, R.M. 1998. 'Divided histories, opportunistic alliances: Background notes on the Ethiopian-Eritrean war'. *Afrika Spectrum* 33 (3/1998): 257-89.

Tronvoll, K. 1996. *Mai Weini, a Highland Village in Eritrea. A Study of the People, Their Livelihoods and Land Tenure During Times of Turbulence*. Lawrenceville, NJ and Asmara: The Red Sea Press.

—— 1999. 'Borders of violence – boundaries of identity: demarcating the Eritrean nation-state'. *Ethnic and Racial Studies* 22(6): 1037–60.

—— 2003. *Identities in Conflict. An ethnography of war and the politics of identity in Ethiopia 1998-2000*. PhD thesis, London: Department of Anthropology, London School of Economics and Political Science, University of London.

Tronvoll, K. and Tekeste Negash 2000. *Brothers at War, Making Sense of the Eritrean-Ethiopian War*. Oxford: James Currey; Athens, OH: Ohio University Press.

Ullendorff, E. 1985. *A Tigrinya (Tegrenna) Chrestomathy, Introduction – Grammatical Tables – Tigrinya Texts – Letters – Phrases – Tigrinya–English Glossary – Select Bibliography*. Wiesbaden: Steiner.

Young, J. 1996. 'The Tigrayan and Eritrean Peoples Liberation Fronts: A History of Tension and Pragmatism'. *The Journal of Modern African Studies* 34(1): 105–20.

—— 1997. *Peasant Revolution in Ethiopia, The Tigray People's Liberation Front 1975–1991*. African Studies Series 90. Cambridge: Cambridge University Press.

Zitelmann, T. 1994. *Nation der Oromo. Kollektive Identitäten, nationale Gruppen, Wir-Gruppenbildung*. Berlin: Das Arabische Buch.

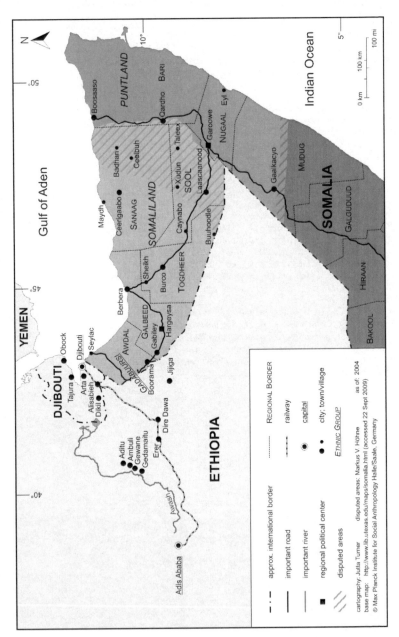

Map 3 *Somali borderlands*

84

Five

Trans-Border Political Alliance in the Horn of Africa
The Case of the Afar-Issa Conflict

YASIN MOHAMMED YASIN

Introduction

This chapter takes a look at the cross-border political alliance in relation to the long-standing conflict between the Issa-Somalis and the Afar along the Ethio-Djibouti border. It argues that Somali governments and the ideology of a 'Greater Somalia' helped the Issa in Djibouti and Ethiopia to dominate the Afar and expand into their territory. The Afar are marginal constituencies in the adjacent states where they live.

The Issa, a section of the Dir clan of the Somali, inhabit the coastal portion of the Awdal region of Somaliland, the southern part of the Republic of Djibouti and the Shinile Zone of the Somali National Regional State in the Federal Democratic Republic of Ethiopia. Around 300,000 Issas live in Djibouti. Another quarter of a million Issas are believed to reside in Somaliland.[1] The land inhabited by the Issa-Somali incorporates border areas between Djibouti and the self-proclaimed state of Somaliland. It also stretches along the Ethio-Djibouti railway where the immediate neighbours of the Issa are the Afar (Lewis 1961: 71).

The Afar people have a distinct cultural and linguistic identity of their own and inhabit a well-defined territory in the African Horn, an area commonly referred to as the Afar Triangle, which is divided between Ethiopia, Eritrea and Djibouti (Abdallah 1993: 1).[2] Afars are estimated to amount to 2.2 million in the three states they inhabit in the Horn, living along the main road that connects the centre of Ethiopia with the harbours of Assab and Djibouti. The main perennial river, the Awash, also traverses the land of the Afar. Furthermore, coastal islands in Eritrea as well as Djibouti where both Afar and Issa co-exist make their land geo-politically strategic. The Afar and Issa-Somali have many cultural features in common. Both are entirely adherents of the faith of Islam, and share similar myths of origins and a pastoral way of life. Simultaneously, and as

85

is often the case with close neighbours in pastoral nomadic settings, they are frequently in conflict.

Dynamics of conflict

In the past, the conflicts between Afar and Issa-Somali have been mainly over water, pastoral land, access routes and cultural values, reminiscent of traditional pastoral conflicts. One of the exceptional features, compared with other conflicts in pastoralist areas, is the confrontation between them even during the rainy seasons, when there is no shortage of water and pasture. In addition, political disputes between the two ethnic groups residing in the four states in the Horn have been very common during the last few decades. According to some Issas interviewed in the Gedamaitu area, 'land is seen as a gift from Allah. All his creatures have the right to access its resources.'[3] Hence, they argue that Somalis should have the right not only to temporarily use but also to possess the land along the Awash River on a par with the Afar. Some Issa elders have claimed the territory as their traditional homeland, which their forefathers had inhabited.

From the perspective of Afar interviewees, and as cited in ABAO (2005: 21–2), the movement of Issa-Somalis to the northern Afar land and their settlement along the main road leaving behind more than thirty perennial rivers, lakes, wells and water springs is nothing but a territorial invasion.[4] Generally, and as will be shown in this chapter, external interventions and cross-border political alliances, especially among the Somalis, and to a lesser extent among the Afar, have played and still continue to play a paramount role in transforming the Afar and Issa conflict. What started as a 'traditional' conflict over resource use in a pastoral nomadic environment has turned into competition over territory and political control in Djibouti.

Several attempts at bringing about peace and reconciliation between the Afar and the Issa-Somali have failed. The traditional conflict settlement strategies became overstrained in this context. A number of previous peace agreements between the two groups were broken, seemingly more often by the Issa than the Afar.[5] In their confrontations both groups, to varying degrees, have been able to muster external support from kinsmen across state-borders. The Issa received political and logistical support from the former Somali Republic. In addition, the newly founded (but not internationally recognized) Republic of Somaliland, Djibouti and the Somali Regional State of Ethiopia provide some help to their kinsmen in Ethiopia and Djibouti. The Afar in Djibouti, on the other hand, are occasionally aided by relatives residing in Ethiopia and Eritrea. These alliances further complicate the conflict. In the following pages, I discuss the various sets of actors and their respective interests along the Ethio-Djibouti border.

Somalia's interventions

The Somali Republic was established in 1960 as a voluntary union of the British and the Italian Somalilands. In spite of internal problems in integrating the different (ex-colonial) administrations, the post-independence Somali political scene was dominated by the vision of incorporating the Somali-inhabited regions in the Horn. This pan-Somali sentiment, expressed in the concept of 'Greater Somalia', was focused on eastern Ethiopia (the so-called Ogaden region, nowadays renamed the Somali Regional State), Djibouti and north-eastern Kenya. These territories were acquired by the different colonial powers through conquest and treaties in the late nineteenth and early twentieth century. The preamble to the Constitution of the Republic of Somalia approved in 1961 included the statement that 'the Somali Republic promotes by legal and peaceful means the union of the territories'. It also stated that all ethnic Somalis, no matter where they resided, were citizens of the Republic. The light blue national flag of Somalia with a central white five-pointed star represented those areas claimed as part of the Somali nation.

This policy led Somalia into military confrontations with Ethiopia and Kenya. As indicated in the Global Security Military Report (n.d.: 1), though the government of Somalia denied any assistance to the Somali guerrilla campaign against the Kenyan police and army between 1960 and 1964, Kenya insisted that the guerrillas were trained in Somalia, equipped there with Soviet arms, and directed from Mogadishu.[6] The first armed conflict with Ethiopia began in the Somali-inhabited Elkere region in Bale province in 1963, in an area inhabited by Somalis.[7] It grew steadily and eventually led to small-scale clashes between Somali and Ethiopian armed forces along the border in early 1964. The second war between Ethiopia and Somalia erupted in 1977. After General Mohamed Siyad Barre had seized power in a military coup in Mogadishu in 1969, he built up the national military forces. Moreover, the new Somali government fostered Somali nationalism, as a means of overcoming internal clan divisions. When Ethiopia was in turmoil after the fall of Emperor Haile Selasse, President Barre took the opportunity to realize the long-standing 'national dream' of many Somalis and to integrate the Somali territories in Ethiopia into Somalia. However, due to the support of the Soviet Union, Cuba and South Yemen for Ethiopia under the revolutionary Derg regime, Somalia lost the so-called Ogaden war in early 1978. This defeat seriously undermined pan-Somalism and in fact marked the beginning of political fragmentation in Somalia (see also the chapter by Hoehne in this volume).

Besides engaging in armed conflicts, the Somali governments used political propaganda to spread their ideas among the Somalis beyond the borders of the state. Of course, government policies in Ethiopia and Kenya also contributed to the wish of Somalis to end marginalization and foreign domination and join their brethren in Somalia. The Ethiopian regimes, in particular, had a long tradition of oppressing Somali pastoral nomads in the peripheries of the empire (Barnes 2000).

The Issa–Somali were among those who were receptive to the project of Greater Somalia. They were expected by other Somalis to incorporate Djibouti, where they were dominant politically, into Somalia.[8] They also saw a chance to expand the western frontier of the Somali-inhabited territory. This brought them into conflict with their neighbours, the Afar. Consequently, with support from the Somali Republic, the well equipped and trained Issa fighters set out to drive away the Afar and expand their territory from the Erer River westward of the Addis–Assab main road and northward to the Obno valley and then to Aditu, a village in the Awash valley basin. Within a few decades, the Issa became able to control approximately one-fifth of the Afar land. Various Ethiopian documents outline that extensive support was flooding to the Issa from the former Somalia Republic.[9] These further list the names of those Issa young men recruited by the Issa clan chief (*Ugaas*) in Ethiopia to be sent to the military camps in different border towns of Somalia. In addition, testimonies recorded by some Issa prisoners in Ethiopia confirmed that firearms and thousands of sealed boxes of bullets had been taken out of the stock that Somalia had provided in order to strengthen the Issa's power.[10]

Moreover, administrators and military officials in eastern Ethiopia briefed the central government in Addis Ababa about Somali towns like Hargeysa, Zeila and Mogadishu that were safe havens for the Issa guerrillas. From the information gathered through interviews, it can be learned that up till recently, prior to the Somali state collapse, Issa fighters who had been injured during clashes with Ethiopian border guards or with the Afar were brought across the border for medical treatment.[11]

After the fall of Siyad Barre in early 1991, the financial and military support for the Issa diminished drastically. More recently, however, the *de facto* state of Somaliland in north-western Somalia continued to provide services for the Issa as a gateway to transfer goods including arms via the new road that connects Somaliland directly to Gadamaitu. Moreover, while Somaliland is not a very powerful player in the Horn, most Ethiopian officials interviewed in both regional and federal government pointed to the Republic of Djibouti as having taken over Somalia's former role in backing up Issa expansionism.[12]

The 'invisible' but strong hand of Djibouti

The Issa-dominated government in Djibouti supports the Issa's territorial expansion campaigns within the Afar region in Ethiopia. Some of the Somali interviewees, particularly in the newly established hamlet of Ambuli, stated that they receive aid, which ranges from flour distribution to financial support from the government of Djibouti.[13] Though it is difficult to verify the accuracy of the information, some informants in Djibouti reported to the Afar regional government in Ethiopia that there is a project being implemented for settling retired Issa army members in the occupied territories within the Afar region.[14]

Djibouti has also become the main station for trafficking arms, providing intensive political and logistical support to the Issa in Ethiopia. Nowadays Issas, straddling the boundary between Ethiopia and Djibouti, have managed to connect Gadamaitu and Undufo (hamlets in Ethiopia) to Asale and Alisabieh towns in Djibouti. Despite the internationally recognized border of Galafi between the states of Ethiopia and Djibouti, Issa on both sides are able to move people and goods freely without checks.

In addition, the government of Djibouti offers a quota for the Issas in Ethiopia to receive military training abroad.[15] When serious armed conflict between the Afar and the Issa erupted on the Ethiopian side of the border, Djibouti repeatedly sent military advisors and commanders to guide the Issa fighters. For instance, when Afar and Issa fought each other in Gala'lu in March 2002, the Afar claimed to have captured Issa fighters with Djibouti identity cards, including those with high military rank in the Djibouti National Army.[16] Arguably, the Afar–Issa conflict even on the Ethiopian side may have repercussions for the domestic political setting in Djibouti. This is an important reason for Djibouti's trans-border interventions.

The Somali National Regional State in Ethiopia as an actor

Among the nine administrative zones in the Somali National Regional State of Ethiopia, Shinile Zone is home to the Issa. For nearly ten years now, Issas have occupied the post of Vice-president in the regional government.[17] In addition, the sole ministerial position reserved as a quota for the ethnic Somali at the federal level in Ethiopia has also been held by an Issa for successive years.[18]

The Issa also dominate political power in Dire Dawa, the only chartered city other than the metropolitan Addis Ababa. Because of the uncontested political power the Issa enjoy at both regional and federal level, they are usually accused of masterminding the conflict between Afar and Issa.[19] The Somali regional administration does not restrain its constituency from incursions deep into the Afar region. Rather, Somali officials argue that, as citizens of Ethiopia, all Somalis have the right to settle anywhere they wish within the country's boundary. Markakis (2002: 451–2) outlined that the Somali regional government has officially demanded that a referendum be held on the contentious territories, expecting that these hamlets will be integrated into Shinile zone.[20]

The Afar National Regional State in Ethiopia as an actor

Even though the Afar people, like the Somali, reside in three adjacent states in the Horn of Africa, they have not been able to benefit from this to strengthen their politico-economic power *vis-à-vis* their neighbours. In Djibouti, as stated above, Afars are dominated by the Issa-Somali who have also held the presidency since the early years of independence. Similarly, as discussed thoroughly by Dahilon (2001), due to their unionist sentiment (aiming at reunification with Ethiopia) and opposition to Eritrean independence, the Afar in Dankalia (the Afar region of Eritrea) are in deadly conflict with the Eritrean government. Let alone establishing strong cross-border coordination among Afars in the Horn region, the Afar in Dankalia are divided into two administrative zones, the north and south Red Sea Regions. Moreover, under the motto 'one nation, one people, one heart', Afars are pressurized to shoulder the ethnic Tigrinnyas' hegemony in terms of politico-economic as well as cultural values.[21]

Most of the interviewees among the Afar argued that, as the majority of the Afar population reside in Ethiopia and are among those who suffered most from the Issa-Somali's intrusion, the Afar National Regional Government in Ethiopia was supposed to play a paramount role in resolving the conflicts with the Issa. Furthermore, Afar argued that the administration of this regional state should coordinate the Afar in the Horn to enable them to strengthen their socio-cultural and politico-economic ties across the artificial political borders imposed on them. To the disappointment of many Afars, the regional government remains silent regarding recently expanding Somali settlements in Adaitu, Gadamaitu and Undufo, as well as the newly created Issa hamlet, Ambuli, just 15km away from Gewane. Afars further accused the regional administration of being negligent when the Issa fighters left them dumbfounded by crossing the Awash River via Mille and continuing their move further into Telalak and Dawe near the border of the Amhara region.

Though the majority of the Afars claimed that the regional government did not play its role as expected, there have in fact been some measures taken by Afar officials. The Vice-President and Secretary General of the regional council lost their posts as a result of having been accused of allowing Ugugumo, an armed Afar organization based in the Danakil Depression, to infiltrate fighters to assist and train Afar youths within the regional state boundary.[22] In addition, under strong pressure from the people, the administration of Zone 3 (southern part of the Afar regional state) moved some district capitals from the vicinity of the Awash River onto the Addis-Djibouti main road.[23] Apart from conducting a series of joint committee peace deals and negotiations, occasional objections by the Afar regional government to the national flags of Somalia and Djibouti, as well as the flag of the Somali National Regional State, being flown over the Issa hamlets within the Afar regional territory could also be considered as major official actions taken by the regional administration. Furthermore, the Afar Region Border Affairs Office (ABAO), established in the region in 2003, focuses mainly on collecting historical documents to enable the regional government to attach them to the usual appeals to the federal government against Issa encroachment. Recently, in spite of the federal government's failure to bring about a long-lasting remedy for this conflict, the office submitted about 900 pages of historical maps, exchanges of letters and other documents to the House of Federation and Ministry of Federal Affairs in Ethiopia. Nevertheless, there is no doubt that the central government's main concern is the security of the road and railway to Djibouti and cherishing the cordial relationship with the Issa government in Djibouti, as its port is the principal sea outlet for landlocked Ethiopia. Also the close ties between Somali illicit traders and the military chiefs stationed in Awash Arba could well be a factor, as many Afar have claimed, in explaining the blind eye the central government has turned towards the danger to the lives of Afars and the stability of the region. In this light, and afraid of being eased out of office, officials at the regional level have definitely not been able to do their best to amend their standstill position regarding the Issa-Somali movement.

Ugugumo as equilibrist

As the Issa's intrusions into Afar territory increase, Ugugumo leaders pay due concern to this 'unbearable repression' of their people.[24] Ugugumo, which means 'uprising' or 'revolution' in the Afar language, is an Afar armed resistance group established in 1981 to oppose the TPLF (Tigray People's Liberation Front) fighters' violent intrusions into northern Afar lands bordering Tigray. Though the federal government of Ethiopia attempted several times to negotiate with the leaders, some factions still remain in their base in the Danakil Depression and claim to be struggling for the Afar cause.

Some Ugugumo fighters had moved from their base in the Danakali Depression in the north to the southern tip of the Afar region in 2001, and they offered military training along with modern arms for Afar youths in the conflict area. After fierce fighting on 23 March 2002, the new Afar trainees succeeded in defeating Issa fighters and established the district capital at Gala'lu. Consequently, senior officials in the Afar regional and local administrations accused of having clandestine linkage with the Ugugumo leaders, were automatically dismissed from their posts.

FRUD's abortive Afar alliance

The political history of Djibouti from the colonial era to the post-independence period has been one of constant friction between the Afar and Issa-Somalis (Shehim and Searing 1980). As French colonial rule imposed the superiority of one ethnic group over the other, jointly with the Somalis' boundless political and economic assistance, Issa-Somalis have been able to secure their dominance in every aspect of life in Djibouti.[25] Their major achievements are territorial extension, population growth, and the gaining of leading political and economic positions.

The Afars' disappointment which had developed over decades turned violent and erupted in 1991 in an armed insurgency by the *Front pour la Restauration de l'Unité et la Démocratie* (FRUD) which attempted to overthrow the reign of President Hassen Gouled. Even though the front had achieved control of about three-fourths of the Republic within a few months, the Issa government managed to prevail, largely due to external support. It had received political and military support from the old colonial master, the French. In addition, weapons and marine fighting boats also arrived in the port of Djibouti from Iraq on the eve of the first Gulf War. Interviewed FRUD fighters asserted that the then newly established EPRDF (Ethiopian People's Revolutionary Democratic Front) government interfered in the Djiboutian civil war by siding with the Issa government. The Eritrean Marine Force also supported the Issa. According to an interview with veteran FRUD fighters EPLF's (Eritrean People's Liberation Front) naval boats were actively blocking the coast bordering Djibouti in order to cut the supply route for the FRUD army.[26]

This campaign, in which the Afar in the Horn collaborated against the Issa-dominated regime in Djibouti that is believed to be the main sponsor for the Issa's intrusion in the Afar region of Ethiopia, was a historic exception. Hence, political and logistical moral support flooded in to the opposition front from all directions of the Afar land. Afar young people including females joined the FRUD in order to end the Issa domination and intrusion, as they claimed.[27] In general, the civil war in Djibouti in the early 1990s was one of the few occasions when the Afar cross-border political alliance was realized.

Conclusion

This case study indicates that cross-border support amongst kin groups facilitated the transformation of traditional pastoral conflict between the Afar and Issa-Somali over access to pasture and water into a modern political dispute over power and territory. The two ethnic groups do their best to take advantage of the cross-border relations with their kin across the adjacent states.

Trans-border political alliance, particularly among fellow Somalis in the Horn region, helped the Issa to strengthen their politico-economic status and to expand their territory by incorporating strategic areas in the region. In particular, Somalia (before 1991) and Djibouti, the two Somali-dominated states in the Horn, are directly and indirectly involved and consider the conflict their internal affair. Apart from providing medical treatment for Issa-Somalis injured in armed conflicts, contributing money, and being a safe haven for irredentist fighters in Ethiopia, the two states further equipped the Issa with modern arms, offered them military training within their countries as well as abroad, and even at times sent their own army officers to command during armed confrontations with the Afar. Apart from channelling illicit goods, unofficial vehicle routes from the Issa-controlled hamlets within the Afar region of Ethiopia to border towns in Djibouti and Somaliland have benefitted the Issa with opportunities of cross-border smuggling and manoeuvring. In the political sphere, Djibouti in particular uses its port as a tool for imposing political influence to discourage the Ethiopian government from taking any strong action against the Issa invaders in the Afar land. Internally, the Issa also receive political support from the Somali National Regional State in Ethiopia, where the Issa hold considerable political power.

Cross-border alliances of the Afar in the Horn enabled them not only to maintain social relationships, but also to defend themselves, to some degree. But this did not halt Somali politico-economic domination in the Republic of Djibouti and deep intrusion into the Afar land in Ethiopia. The formation and fighting of the FRUD in the Djibouti civil war of the early 1990s, and the intervention of Afar armed opposition groups (Ugugumo) in the hostilities between the Afar and Issa–Somali at Gala'lu in March 2002 are instances of cross-border assistance among the Afar. Further Afar engagement is hindered due to the oppression of the Afar in Eritrea by the regime in Asmara. Moreover, given the current political situation in Ethiopia and Eritrea, the Afar in Dankalia have no significant role to play in strengthening the Afar's political standing in the regional power game. Meanwhile, Djiboutian Afars who are politically dominated by the Issa are not able to give any support to fellow Afar across the border.

To sum up: the partition of an ethnic group through state-borders can be recognized as an opportunity particularly in politico-economic terms for those groups that are well established in several neighbouring states. However, divided ethnic groups with little political as well as economic influence in either of the adjacent states in which they reside can not benefit *per se* from their partition through and connections across borders. Hence, groups like the Issa benefit more from social relations across the border by effectively activating their kin networks within different states where they have considerable influence. Trafficking of arms and illicit commodities across the porous borders, financial and manpower assistance (medical and military personnel) from Somali-dominated governments, military training in camps deliberately established in border towns, as well as transportation of injured fighters and fugitives across the border are some of the resources the Issa generate through their social networks which in turn enable them to dominate the Afar politically, economically and militarily.

Notes

1 Demographic statements have to be treated with caution in the Somali context, where many people still live as nomads and, at least on the Somali side of the border, no official census has been undertaken for more than two decades.

2 The Afar Triangle stretches from the northern-most fringes of the Boori peninsula to the vicinity of the Abyssinian highland plateau in the west. The eastern border of the Triangle extends from the city of Djibouti in the South and follows the railway line from Erer to Awash town. And both the west-east borderlines meet at Namale Fan, which is 140 miles north-east of Addis Ababa. The north-south Afar coast line runs along the Red Sea shore for over 800 miles (Aš Šami 1997: 28–9).

3 This position is in fact common among Somali and possibly other pastoral nomads.

4 Between Aledeghi and Asabot, for instance, there are about 14 perennial rivers such as the Ayabut, Keraba, Bekie, Gota, Erer and Hurso.

5 Documents compiled by the Afar Region Border Affairs Office (ABAO) and submitted to the House of Federation and the Ministry of Federal Affairs in Ethiopia testify to the Issa's frequent violation of the peace and border agreements.

6 For further information on this issue access: http://www.globalsecurity.org/military/world/war/somalia1.htm

7 As a result of political and logistical support from the Somalia government the Ethiopian Somalis together with Oromo insurgents staged a revolt in Bale province for several years in the 1960s. General Waqo Gutu (died 3 February 2006) led the rebellion.

8 Mohammud Harbi, a renowned Issa politician during pre-independence in Djibouti, had established the liberation front of the Somali coast, with its headquarters in Mogadishu. This front had aimed at the complete independence of French Somaliland and its union with Somalia. For further reading on the pan-Somali movement in pre-independent Djibouti, see Thompson and Adolf (1968).

9 The ABAO has compiled five volumes of historical documents that include the exchanges of letters among the local administrations, from security, police, military and the interior as well as the foreign affairs office and other institutions. The first volume includes the Republic of Somalia's intervention in Ethiopia's internal affairs among which backing the Issas' westward expansion was the major one.

10 In Volume 5 of the historical documents compiled by ABAO, a confidential letter written to the Harar police chief on 2 August 1960 confirmed that Issa tribesmen, namely, Esuri Sullen, Mohamed Abdi, Ali Beralie and Ali Jama went to Hargeysa to get help from Somalia and distributed about 150 boxes of bullets and bombs to the Issa herders. The same source also speaks of the military training of about 3000 Issa in a camp near Mogadishu.

11 Interview with former Ethiopian military officer, 15 August 2006 at Addis Ababa. The informant had served in Afar and Somali areas for over three decades.

12 Interview with government officials at the Ethiopian Ministry of Federal Affairs on 12 August 2006 and Afar regional state officials, 12 July 2005.

13 The information about aid flowing from Djibouti is gathered through informal discussions with local people at Ambuli, 10 July 2005.

14 Interview with Afar regional state officials, 12 July 2005.

15 This is first-hand information I have got through informal discussions with Somali friends currently residing in Gadamaitu and Undufo. In addition, Afar government officials in the Republic of Djibouti who asked for their names to be withheld confirmed that Issas from Ethiopia, who have never been in Djibouti, have obtained military training opportunities in the Gulf States.

16 Djibouti military identity cards found in the battlefield during the March 2002 Gala'lu armed conflict were handed over to the federal government of Ethiopia by Afar regional administrators.

17 From the early 1990s till now, Abdulqadir Mohamed, Ali Farah, Ahmed Gedi, and Abdu Jebriel have successively held the position of Vice-President in the Somalia Regional Government.

18 Mohammud Derir is an Issa, who has held ministerial position for a decade in the Federal Republic of Ethiopia. After concluding his term as Ethiopian Ambassador in Zimbabwe, he became a minister in the Federal Ministry of Transport and Communications, Mining and Energy and currently he is Minister of Culture and Tourism.

19 Abdul Jibril, who was Vice-President of the Somali Region, lost his post in 2005 after successive charges against him of earmarking the security budget for the Issa's campaign in the Afar region. Moreover, Ambassador Mohammud Derir played a major role in the expansion of Issa settlements within the occupied territories in Afar region while he was Minister of Transport and Communication. Major construction camps, which were later handed over to the Issas, were built in these hamlets.

20 The Somali Regional Government has the experience of using a referendum as the ultimate conflict resolution mechanism. Nevertheless, the referendum which was held in October 2004 in about 420 *kebele* ended up with 80% of the disputed areas falling under Oromia regional administration.

21 For further reading on the 'predicaments of the Afar in Eritrea' see Dahilon (2001).

22 Vice-president Hamedu Ali and Secretary General Mohamed Lale were eased out of their posts by the decision of the Prime Minister in 1994.

23 Such as Adebtoli, Andido and Gala'lu.

24 Interview with a former Ugugumo leader, 24 August 2006, Mekelle.

25 The Mammassan sub-clan of Issa/Somali has held the presidential office since independence. Important ministries like defence, interior, national security, office of nationality affairs, foreign affairs, education, finance and national economy and the army are the stronghold of Issa supremacy. Except for a number of nominal positions, Afar civil servants are insignificant in government employment and there is hardly any Afar contribution in the private sector. For detailed statistical facts, see Adou (1993:100-2).

26 The land and boundary between southern Eritrea and northern Djibouti was used as a military base for FRUD combatants who obtained arms and ammunition from the runaway Ethiopian soldiers during the 1991 regime change in Ethiopia.

27 Field interview with former FRUD members, 13 June 2005, Awash town.

References

ABAO (Afar-Region Border Affairs Office) 2005. *Historical Documents on the Afar–Issa/Somali Conflict compiled and submitted to the House of Federation and Ministry of Federal Affairs.* (Five volumes in Amharic), Samara.

Abdallah A. Adou, 1993. *The Afar: A Nation on Trial.* Stockholm.

Afar Region Border Affairs Office 2005. *Amharic Historical Documents on Afar – Issa-Somali Conflict Compiled in Five Volumes.* Samara: ABAO.

Aš Šami 1997. *Al-manhal fi tariò wa aòbar al-ŸAfar (al-Danakil)* (The Source of the History and the Narratives of the ŸAfar [Al-Danakil]). Cairo.

Barnes, C. 2000. *The Ethiopian State and its Somali Periphery circa 1888–1948.* PhD thesis,

University of Cambridge.

Dahilon, Y. 2001. 'The Predicament of the Afar in Ethiopia and Eritrea'. Unpublished paper presented at 'Peace Building and the Role of the Afar People' Conference. Stockholm December.

Global Security Military Report n.d. Somalia-Ethiopia, Kenya Conflict. <http://www.global security.org/military/world/war/somalia1.htm> Accessed on 7 December 2005.

Lewis, I.M. 1961. 'Notes on the Social Organization of the 'Ise Somali'. *Rassegna di Studi Etiopici* 17(1): 69–82.

Markakis, J. 2002. 'Anatomy of a Conflict: Afar and Ise Ethiopia'. *Review of African Political Economy* 96: 445–53.

Shehim, K. and Searing, J. 1980. 'Djibouti and the Question of Afar Nationalism'. *African Affairs* 79(315): 209–26.

Thompson, V. and R. Adolf 1968. *Djibouti and the Horn of Africa*. Stanford, CA: Stanford University Press.

Six

People & Politics along & across the Somaliland-Puntland Border

MARKUS VIRGIL HOEHNE

Introduction

Somewhere between the towns of Laascaanood and Garoowe, the only tarmac road running through the semi-desert of northern Somalia passes a dusty old bush. This bush, which stands alone within closer range, would normally not be worth mentioning. There are thousands of others along the road. But, when driving past it the second or third time, locals told me that it had a name; it was called Yoocada.[1] My co-passengers added that in colonial times it indicated the border between British and Italian Somaliland. British Somaliland covered the northwest of the Somali peninsula; Italian Somaliland stretched from the northeast to the south of it.

This border was dissolved in July 1960, when both colonial territories became independent and united as the Republic of Somalia. It gained renewed significance in the context of state-collapse in Somalia. In May 1991, Somaliland seceded from the rest of Somalia in line with the borders of the former British Protectorate. Yoocada was claimed as the marker of its eastern border. This territorial rearrangement, however, is contested by Puntland which was established as an autonomous regional state in north-eastern Somalia in August 1998. In contrast to Somaliland, Puntland does not pursue secession but aims at rebuilding a unitary Somali state within its pre-civil war borders. Consequently, its supporters do not accept Somaliland's self-declared independence and ignore the former colonial border. Thus, while not having a strong 'physical' presence, Yoocada divides people in northern Somalia politically, into those endorsing the 'two-state' vision of Somaliland and Somalia, and others, who adhere to the 'one-state' vision of a united Somalia.

The political conflict surrounding this border is of course most visible in the borderlands between the two state-like entities in northern Somalia.

According to Horstmann and Wadley (2006: 3–6), borderlands are located at the margins of states. It is here that (national) identities and politics, which are otherwise taken for granted, are questioned or reinforced. The legitimacy of states can be undermined or strengthened through the agency of borderlanders (ibid.). In the case of Somaliland and Puntland, the borderlanders are Dhulbahante and Warsangeeli who reside in the regions Sool, (eastern) Sanaag, and (southern) Togdheer. These clans and their clan-homelands were part of the British Protectorate. They are claimed as belonging to Somaliland by the government in Hargeysa, which is dominated by members of the Isaaq clan-family. Simultaneously, Dhulbahante and Warsangeeli have a stake in Puntland that politically unites the members of the Harti clan-confederation; these are, among others, the Majeerteen, Dhulbahante and Warsangeeli clans.

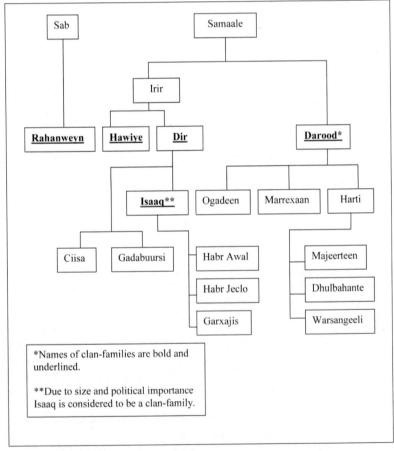

Chart 6.1 *Genealogical divisions, northern Somalia*

This situation brings about certain advantages and disadvantages for the divided borderlanders. On the one hand, the political conflict between Somaliland and Puntland over secession and unification, respectively, renders the contested borderlands virtually 'no go areas' for local and international NGOs and other organizations. They are therefore economically and politically marginalized. Since 2001, several military confrontations between the two sides erupted in the borderlands (Hoehne 2006, 2007a; Roble 2007). On the other hand, Dhulbahante and Warsangeeli try to make arrangements with both sides. Individuals with the necessary skills and political will pursue careers in the centre of Somaliland or Puntland; some even switch and work first for one, then for the other 'employer'. Borderland communities accommodate administrative and military structures from both sides, which secures salaries for a considerable number of locals.

The governments of Somaliland and Puntland also try to profit from the contested and, as will be seen, empirically rather flexible and open border-situation. Their approaches are, of course, mutually exclusive. While Puntland ignores the borderline as a former colonial (and therefore 'arbitrary') border, Somaliland re-claims it, precisely because of its colonial history. Until recently, the governments of both political entities in Hargeysa and Garoowe were less concerned with the empirical realities on the ground than with the international effect of their claims and actions. This afforded the borderlanders a degree of 'freedom' and opportunities, as outlined in this chapter. Nonetheless, when both sides decided to enforce their claims militarily, people in the borderlands suffered.

This chapter is based on extensive field research in northern Somalia, and particularly in the above-mentioned borderlands, between October 2003 and December 2004. It first introduces the setting, before outlining individual and collective strategies of resourcing the (*de facto*) state border in the region.

Colonial partition of the Somali peninsula

The colonial partition of the Horn set in forcefully in the 1880s, when Italy, France and Britain scrambled for territories along the Gulf of Aden and further inland towards the Ethiopian empire. European emissaries concluded various treaties with Somali clans and negotiated with Menelik II after Ethiopia had proved its standing as an independent power in the region by defeating the Italian army at Adwa in 1896. The borders of the British Protectorate of Somaliland were established in the Anglo-French agreement of 1888 (to the west), the Anglo-Italian protocol of 1894 (to the east), and the Anglo-Ethiopian treaty of 1897 (to the south). Between 1889 and 1925 the territory from the northeast to the south of the Somali peninsula came under Italian administration (Lewis 2002: 47–61, 99; Cassanelli 1982: 29–33; Information Service of the Somali Government 1962).

Initially, the colonial administrations in the north of the Somali penin-sula were extremely limited in scope and vigour. Britain established itself in the port of Berbera on the northwest coast, and was mostly interested in the export of livestock to its garrison in Aden, on the other side of the Gulf. Italy, which was concerned with widening its sphere of influence in the Horn, made arrangements with the traditional authorities in the northeast, *Boqor* Cusman and *Suldaan* Yusuf Cali of the Majeerteen clan of the Darood clan-family, who continued to rule their subjects under Italian suzerainty.[2]

The limited influence of the colonial powers in the northern Somali territories became obvious when the Dervishes (*Darawiishta*), a group of nomadic fighters led by the religious leader and poet Maxamed Cabdille Xassan, rose against the colonizers in 1899. The majority of the warriors came from the Dhulbahante clan, the group of Maxamed's mother. Many Somalis perceived the resistance as jihad against Christian invaders. The uprising also included an element of sectarian fighting. Sufi orders which were opposed to the Salihiya, the school of Islamic thought which Maxamed Cabdille Xassan propagandized in northern Somalia, were also targeted. In 1909, for instance, Shaykh Uweys, a famous leader of the Qadiriya *tariqa* in southern Somalia, was assassinated by Dervishes. The Dervish war was also a fight for power in the region between different clans and their leaders. Besides his matrilateral relatives Maxamed Cabdille Xassan mobilized the Ogadeen, his patrilineal kinsmen. Dhulbahante and Ogadeen Dervishes frequently attacked Isaaq groups with whom they were engaged in perennial feuds over water and grazing. Not surprisingly, many Isaaq sided with the British and were equipped with weapons against the Dervishes.[3]

Maxamed Cabdille Xassan managed to establish a firm grip on the Dhulbahante only after some of his followers had killed *Garaad* Cali, the highest-ranking traditional authority of this clan. The relationship between the Majeerteen and the Dervishes was an uneasy one; it oscillated between cooperation and antagonism. On the one hand, *Boqor* Cusman, the head of the north-eastern Majeerteen who controlled the coast and ports along the Gulf of Aden, supported Maxamed Cabdille Xassan's troops with weapons. On the other, he and his cousin, the rival *Suldaan* Yusuf Cali Keenadiid of Hobbiyo further to the southeast, fought against Dervish domination in their territories. They even entered into agreements with the Italian colonial power against the insurgents. The Warsangeeli residing on the northern coast of the British Protectorate had first been supportive to the cause of the Dervishes. Later on, however, after it had become clear that Maxamed Cabdille Xassan would not tolerate political rivals, their war-leader *Suldaan* Maxamuud Cali Shire cooperated with the British in order to strengthen his own power – ultimately against both the Dervishes and the colonizers (Hoehne 2007b: 160). Despite the fact that the Dervishes were militarily inferior to the British they managed to sustain their uprising for two decades and occasionally inflicted serious losses upon

100

the colonial troops. In decisive moments, the insurgents escaped into the 'bush' or across the British-Italian or British-Ethiopian colonial borders. Since the British had to respect these borders, these moves gave the Dervishes time to relax and reorganize. The Dervishes were only defeated in 1920, when the British used aircraft against their enemies. In the aftermath of this war, the British and Italian colonial powers consolidated their administrations in northern Somalia (Lewis 2002: Chap. IV and V; Samatar 1982: 99–121; Sheikh-Abdi 1993; Cassanelli 1982: 250–3; Doornbos 1975: 20–30).

Somali nationalism rose from the 1940s onwards. Political parties were founded and campaigned for independence. The British Protectorate became independent on 26 June 1960. Five days later, on 1 July, the Italian-administered territories followed suit, and both united to establish the Somali Republic on the same day. For the first two post-colonial decades, Somalia was firmly based on Somali nationalism and pan-Somalism. These concepts comprised the idea of uniting all Somali-inhabited territories in the Horn in one 'Greater Somalia' and informed Somalia's often aggressive foreign policy towards its neighbours (Information Service of the Somali Government 1962; Matthies 1977).[4]

State collapse and political reconstruction in northern Somalia

Somalia's statehood reached its zenith under the Somali Revolutionary Council (SRC) led by General Maxamed Siyad Barre which came to power in a bloodless coup in October 1969. 'Scientific socialism' and nationalism formed the ideological foundation of the new government. The SRC launched a number of reforms, the most effective of which was the introduction of a Somali script. It also expanded the state and security apparatus and built a strong national army. This was facilitated by various allies in the East and the West, which supported Somalia because of its geo-strategic position and Barre's political pragmatism. The defeat of the Somali army in the so-called Ogaden war against Ethiopia (1977–8) marked a decisive change in Somali politics.[5] Subsequently, Siyad Barre's rule was increasingly challenged by disgruntled military, political and business elites. With the Somali Salvation Democratic Front (SSDF) and the Somali National Movement (SNM) two guerrilla factions were set up in the early 1980s. Their aim was to overthrow President Barre, whose rule had turned into a clan-dictatorship based on narrow genealogical alliances.[6] The guerrilla factions were also largely based on descent, the SSDF being Majeerteen-dominated while the SNM was mainly supported by Isaaq. The armed opposition operated from Ethiopia, the territory of the 'arch-enemy' and beyond the reach of the Somali national army. In reaction the government resorted to summary punishment of the relatives of the guerrillas in northern Somalia (Abdi 1998: 316-17, 338-39; Prunier

1995). In retrospect, it becomes clear that both Somali guerrilla 'focus points' in the twentieth century, the Dervish uprising as well as the SSDF and SNM struggle, had used state borders and trans-border alliances (of the Ogadeen clan, in the case of the Dervishes, and of Isaaq and Majeerteen relatives in the case of the SNM and the SSDF, respectively) in order to wage their wars.

In January 1991, Siyad Barre was forced to flee the capital Mogadishu and the United Somali Congress (USC), the movement of the Hawiye clan-family, took control of much of the south. Subsequently, southern Somalia plunged into civil war and warlordism, and was subject to multiple external interventions (de Waal 1997: 159–78). In contrast, northern Somalia developed quite differently. The northwest was taken over by the SNM in early 1991. The SNM leadership immediately engaged in peace negotiations with representatives of the Gadabuursi, Ciisa, Dhulbahante and Warsangeeli clans in the region. Most members of these clans had stayed neutral during the previous guerrilla war, or had even sided with Siyad Barre. Peace in the northwest was established in a series of local clan conferences (Somali sing.: *shir*) (Farah and Lewis 1997). In the light of the ongoing fighting in the south and due to the strong feelings of many Isaaq and SNM guerrillas against the southern government, the independence of Somaliland was declared in May 1991. The representatives of most non-Isaaq clans were not in favour of secession but accepted it in order to keep the peace in the region where the SNM was clearly the superior military power.

Over the years, Somaliland has developed from a conflict-ridden and guerrilla-ruled polity into a veritable *de facto* state. It is based on a mixture of Somali traditional and modern government institutions. A constitution underlining the independence of the country was adopted in a referendum in 2001. This paved the way for the recent introduction of a democratic multi-party system (Cabdiraxmaan 2005; Renders 2006). The remaining major problems are a lack of economic resources, the lack of international recognition, and internal and regional tensions related to the independence of Somaliland and the question of Somali statehood.

North-eastern Somalia came under the control of the SSDF in 1991. Politically, the SSDF leadership engaged in a number of peace conferences for Somalia, all of which, however, proved to be futile. After several years without a government, Puntland was established at a *shir* in the city of Garoowe in August 1998. In contrast to Somaliland, it remains part of Somalia. The meeting was attended by representatives of the different Harti clans, including Dhulbahante and Warsangeeli. Members of these clans were given high positions in the new government (Battera 1998; Doornbos 2000). Dhulbahante and Warsangeeli therefore belong simultaneously to Somaliland and Puntland. Yet, only rump administrations consisting of locals paid by one of the two political centres, Hargeysa and Garoowe, were installed in their clan-territories from 1999 onwards.

Undoubtedly, their intermediate location had some negative effects for the inhabitants of the contested borderlands. With very few exceptions, no international NGOs came, and no state development projects were implemented. Few politicians from Hargeysa or Garoowe ever visited Dhulbahante and Warsangeeli lands. Since late 2002, the political conflict between Somaliland and Puntland over the control of the border regions has been escalating on a military level. In December 2002 Dahir Rayaale Kaahin, the President of Somaliland, visited Laascaanood, the capital of Sool region.[7] As a result, Somaliland and Puntland troops clashed in the town. In the aftermath of this event the government in Hargeysa pulled all its official representatives out of Laascaanood. One year later, in December 2003, Puntland police and military forces came to the area and took effective control of Laascaanood. Somaliland reacted and dispatched new troops to Sool region in early 2004. In October that year a fierce battle between Somaliland and Puntland troops erupted. The military confrontation continued, with further clashes throughout 2007 (Hoehne 2006; Hoehne 2007a). Yet, despite the conflict-proneness of the border-lands, being divided also provides some advantages for the locals. It opens up room for individual and collective manoeuvring along and across the border.

Living along the Somaliland-Puntland border

DIMENSIONS OF THE BORDER

The border between Somaliland and Puntland is not just a line on the map or in the sand.[8] It has different spatial, political and social dimensions. Consider this ideal typical journey sometime in 2004: Driving from Hargeysa, the capital of Somaliland, to Laascaanood in the east one usually stopped for a break after around five hours in the town of Burco. There, in the middle of Somaliland, the Somaliland Shillings that were introduced as new currency by the government in Hargeysa in 1994 were exchanged for Somali Shillings, the old Somali currency, which was used in eastern Somaliland, Puntland and southern Somalia. Continuing from Burco, the driver soon exchanged the (white) Somaliland for a (black) Somalia number plate. As far as I could observe in 2003 and 2004, this was a routine operation, and every driver on the road to or from Laascaanood had the two plates and the necessary toolkit. As soon as the car entered the territory inhabited by Dhulbahante in the Sool region, the flags hoisted at the roadblocks were no longer the Somaliland but the Somali flag.

When the destination of Laascaanood was reached one was tempted to think that this was Puntland now. In fact, upon my first arrival the local police officers there demanded that I bought a Puntland visa in their station, which, however, according to the colonial border and the contemporary perspective of the government in Hargeysa, was still part of

Somaliland. Continuing from Laascaanood to the east, to Garoowe, the capital of Puntland, differentiated the 'border-space' further. The next roadblock was 120 kilometres east, just before Garoowe. Here, the passengers coming from Laascaanood were checked carefully. As a foreigner, I had to show my passport and visa for Puntland. Finally, the local police officers in Garoowe demanded that I bought a Puntland visa again. They argued that they could not accept the visa issued in Laascaanood. Only after I insisted that, according to their own government's position, Laascaanood was part of Puntland, and showed my readiness to address their superiors in this matter, did they leave me alone.

These aspects of a journey from Hargeysa to Laascaanood and further to Garoowe show that the border between Somaliland and Puntland is spatially not limited to a clearly demarcated line. One passes Yoocada between Laascaanood and Garoowe. But the border starts already in Burco with regard to currency. It continues somewhere in between with changing the number plates. In many respects, Laascaanood seems to be part of the Puntland state of Somalia, as indicated by the Somali flag hoisted and painted on walls everywhere, and the issuing of Puntland visas in the local police station.[9] In Garoowe it becomes clear that Laascaanood is perceived as the political periphery and people there are not fully trusted by the officials in the capital of Puntland. In this light, the border space between Somaliland and Puntland extends between Burco and Garoowe over a distance of *circa* 300 kilometres.

Moreover, border-crossing involves important social aspects. The border presents itself differently, depending on who is crossing it. Ordinary people without political or military positions pass through the border space between Somaliland and Puntland without problems. At the roadblocks, soldiers mostly check the faces of the passengers only by looking through the windows of the cars. The drivers are usually well acquainted with the soldiers. In exchange for a small sum of money the guards open the barrier and the journey continues. Trade across Somalia is also not hindered by borders. Besides paying taxes in the centres of Somaliland and Puntland and some extra money at checkpoints, trucks transporting goods across northern Somalia pass freely. Smuggling is not a big issue, according to my information. I only occasionally heard of illegal goods such as alcohol or refugees from Ethiopia on their way to the port of Boosaaso (and then further by boat to Yemen) being 'smuggled' through the countryside in order to avoid checkpoints. Pastoral-nomadic movements, particularly in times of drought, are also not restricted by the borders.

Nonetheless, when politicians, soldiers or high-ranking traditional authorities traverse the border-space the situation changes. From the Somaliland side, Yoocada then indeed marks a decisive line; east of it the enemy's land starts. Any official going there without permission is a traitor. For Puntland, treason starts as soon as one of its officials enters the Isaaq-inhabited areas to the west. Yoocada is thus not important from the perspective of the government in Garoowe, but clan-boundaries between Harti and Isaaq are. The presence of officials from Hargeysa or Garoowe in the borderlands causes tensions as demonstrated by the shoot-out between Somaliland and Puntland soldiers following the visit of the President of Somaliland to Laascaanood.

Clearly, the border between Somaliland and Puntland represents less a territorial than a political division. In everyday life, ordinary people move across the extended border-space without any serious restrictions. Only when officials enter the contested borderlands do the centres voice and set out to enforce their mutually exclusive positions. Then the border appears as something 'fixed' – at least temporarily, for a moment of confrontation.

INDIVIDUAL CASES

In northern Somalia, most probably similar to other settings characterized by conflicting claims to borders, individual switching of allegiances and loyalties is advantageous for members of the borderland elites. The first case presented here concerns a high-ranking military officer. Cabdi was in his late fifties when I met him in December 2003 in Garoowe.[10] Genea-logically he belonged to Nuur Axmed, a sub-clan of the Dhulbahante clan, whose members inhabit the Nugaal Valley where the small town of Taleex is also located. The Dervishes had their last and largest headquarters in Taleex, which was destroyed by the British air force in 1920. In November 2003 I visited the still impressive ruins of the Dervish fortress. Many Nuur Axmed men whom I met during my field research were very proud of their Dervish history. It seemed therefore to be perfectly suitable that Cabdi was Vice-Commander of the *Ciidanka Darawiishta*, the Dervish Army, as the Puntland military forces were called.[11] Cabdi told me that the armed forces in Puntland were named *Darawiish* 'not to forget the history of Maxamed Cabdille Xassan.'[12]

Cabdi had joined the Somali army in the 1960s and stayed there until the fall of the government in 1991. His last rank was *Gaashaanle Sare* (Colonel). When the civil war escalated in the south, Cabdi took refuge in the north, in the city of Laascaanood, which is almost exclusively inhabited by Dhulbahante. In early 1991 he had been part of his clan's delegation at the *shir* in Burco, where peace among the clans of the northwest was negotiated and the secession of Somaliland was proclaimed. Even if Cabdi did not personally favour secession, he emphasized that everybody agreed on peace in those days. He argued that the relationship between Dhulbahante and Isaaq was based on 'mutual understanding ... that we [Dhulbahante] do not have with any other people'. Common traditions, common history (colonial history), intermarriage, and going to school together were the building blocks for this understanding. '*Aqoonta aanu Hartiga walaalaha nahay isu lahayn mid ka fiican ayaan Isaaq isu lahayn*' (We know that we are brothers of the Harti but we have a better knowledge of the Isaaq [meaning: we understand the Isaaq better]). Cabdi reiterated

105

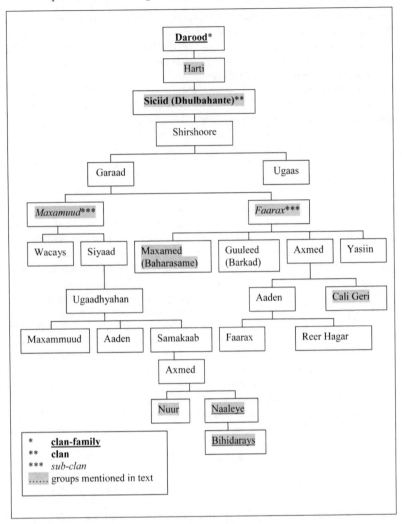

Chart 6.2 *Simplified genealogical outline, Dhulbahante clan*

that the 'Harti brothers' from the Majeerteen clan had been under Italian colonial administration, whereas the Dhulbahante had been under British rule, together with Isaaq and other clans in the northwest. This in fact corresponded to the perspective of many other Dhulbahante about their relations with Isaaq. Elders, politicians and many ordinary people in the Sool region and in the Dhulbahante-inhabited village of Buuhoodle in southern Togdheer told me time and again that 'culturally' they were close to the Isaaq, with whom they also frequently intermarried.

After his flight from Mogadishu, Cabdi was much closer to Isaaq than to Majeerteen. He mentioned that he used to go to Burco, Hargeysa and Berbera, which are Isaaq cities several hundred kilometres west of Laascaanood. In those days he never went to Garoowe, where Majeerteen reside, even if it was much nearer.[13]

In August 1991 Cabdi started to work in Hargeysa, the capital of the newly established Republic of Somaliland. At first he was director of disarmament in the National Demobilization Commission, which co-operated with the German *Gesellschaft für Technische Zusammenarbeit* (GTZ). In 1994 he was appointed chief of staff of the Somaliland armed forces. He held this position until 1996. From my sojourns in Hargeysa I knew that the former SNM guerrillas and other people there usually referred to the members of the former Somali National Army – among them many members of the Darood clan-family, to which Siyad Barre's Marrexaan clan also belonged – as *'faqash'*, which translates as 'dirty or corrupt person; filth' (Hashi 1998). I asked Cabdi if the Somaliland soldiers, most of whom had been in the SNM before, respected him as commander. He answered 'yes', and added: 'even more than an Isaaq colonel.' The reason for this was, according to Cabdi, that the Isaaq knew that 'without us [Dhulba-hante] they cannot be a government'. This again quite accurately sum-marizes a position that was widely spread among Dhulbahante, according to my findings. Being aware that they were a minority in Somaliland, Dhul-bahante would still underline that the dominating Isaaq would need them in order to build a viable and internationally recognized state. This position referred to the fact that the Dhulbahante and their territory were part of the British Protectorate, the borders of which Somaliland still views as valid.

Cabdi was on good terms with the commander of the Somaliland army, who was Isaaq. In 1996, however, Cabdi lost his job, for reasons which he did not reveal immediately.[14] After that he just stayed in Hargeysa, where he had previously married an Isaaq woman. In May 1999 he went to the east, to Laascaanood, and from there he continued to Garoowe at the invitation of a friend. He did some travelling through different regions of Puntland and visited relatives on his mother's side. Cabdi decided to stay in Garoowe, in a hotel that was owned by a man from Dhulbahante/Nuur Axmed. During this time he met several times with Cabdullahi Yusuf, the President of Puntland, who offered him a position in the army, which Cabdi finally accepted.

I asked Cabdi why he chose to join the administration of Puntland. He was silent for a moment; then he answered: 'Actually, I had good experiences with the Somaliland administration; I was just interested in what was going on in Puntland. You have to bear in mind that the Somali society is based on tribalism.[15] When you are in Hargeysa you can feel that you are a minority, but here [in Garoowe] you don't feel anything [negative].' After this statement Cabdi paused; he seemed uncomfortable. Abruptly, he started again, revoked what he had just said about 'being minority' [as Dhulbahante among Isaaq] and explained: 'I never felt inferior when I was in Hargeysa; these people [the Isaaq] were very

generous. It was just a matter of luck.' After that he again paused. Finally
he said: 'I left Hargeysa because of political problems with [President]
Cigaal.' Cabdi was dissatisfied with what he perceived as structural
injustice within the leadership of Somaliland. In his perspective, too many
key positions in the government were held by Isaaq and there was no
proper power-sharing. Again, this accusation against the government in
Hargeysa was very common among Dhulbahante. Many Dhulbahante
had told me that their clan, according to size and 'importance', should be
second after the Isaaq in Somaliland.[16]

In July 2000 Cabdi was appointed Vice-Commander of the *Ciidanka
Darawiishta* in Puntland. The Commander was Majeerteen and a close
relative of Cabdullahi Yusuf.[17] Cabdi mentioned that his wife and children
visited him occasionally in Garoowe, but their home was in Hargeysa,
where the children went to school. He could no longer go there since he
now worked for another government and would possibly be arrested in
Somaliland.

About eight months after this meeting, I spoke to Cabdi again in
Garoowe in August 2004. He had just resigned from his position after a
recent reshuffle in the Puntland army, in which his superior, the
commander in chief of the *Ciidanka Darawiishta*, had been replaced with a
younger Majeerteen officer. Cabdi told me that he could not accept the
new commander, who had been appointed for 'tribal' reasons but was
junior to him according to length of service and experience. Cabdi complained about 'corruption' in the army and the government of Puntland,
which had increased over the years. He had seen this before, but with the
former commander he had been on good terms personally. This had
enhanced his tolerance of injustices according to 'tribalism'. Cabdi also
mentioned that he and the whole military had received no salary for
several months, due to maladministration in Puntland. In addition, he did
not agree with the recent steps the government in Garoowe had taken
against Somaliland. Between our first and second meeting, Puntland police
and military troops had occupied Laascaanood in December 2003 and
January 2004. This had provoked a serious military confrontation with
Somaliland, as mentioned above. In August 2004 Cabdi said that he still
had friends in Hargeysa, and that his priority was the safety and security of
all people in Somaliland and Puntland.

His resignation had not yet been accepted by Cabdullahi Yusuf, the
President of Puntland. The latter spent most of 2004 in Nairobi, where he
was a candidate for the Somali Presidency at the Somali Peace and
Reconciliation Conference hosted by Kenya under the auspices of the
Intergovernmental Authority for Development (IGAD). I asked Cabdi what
he wanted to do in the future and he answered that he had not yet decided.
He could stay in Garoowe and possibly get involved in politics there, or go
to Laascaanood. He also thought about joining his family in Hargeysa.
There, as he emphasized at the end of the interview, 'life would be best'.

In sum, Cabdi's case provides interesting insights into conflicting loyalties and the positioning of individual actors between Somaliland and Puntland. Culturally and socially, Cabdi was clearly more closely related to Hargeysa, where he had a family and old friends, than to Garoowe. In Puntland, however, he was offered a job after he had run into trouble with the Somaliland administration. He was therefore able to pursue his individual career by changing sides. This change was certainly aided by Cabdi's nostalgia about the glorious Dervish history, which was firmly anchored in the collective memory of Nuur Axmed, his sub-sub-clan. The Dervish war had become part of the post-colonial Somali national history, which was upheld and/or revived in Puntland.

The second case deals with precisely the opposite situation: a Dhulbahante politician moving from Garoowe to Hargeysa. Xassan and I met for the first time in Laascaanood in November 2003. He was a Dhulbahante from the sub-clan Bihidarays and had come for a visit from Garoowe, where he worked as Minister for Education in the government of Puntland, despite his relatively young age of around forty years. Xassan invited me to visit him in Garoowe and soon afterwards we met there.[18]

Initially, I was particularly interested to hear more about the events surrounding the visit of the Somaliland President to Laascaanood in December 2002. Xassan told me that he had (co-)organized the attack of some Puntland forces on the delegation of President Dahir Rayaale Kaahin. Xassan's account was confirmed by other sources too. Accordingly, Xassan and some other Dhulbahante politicans in Puntland led two or three 'technicals' (pick-up trucks with heavy machine guns mounted on top) into Laascaanood on 7 December a few hours after the President of Somaliland had entered the town. Following a brief but fierce exchange of fire between Puntland and Somaliland troops inside the town, Dahir Rayaale Kaahin ordered the retreat, despite the superiority of his forces. He allegedly feared a general uprising of the Puntland followers in town.[19] The Puntlanders celebrated the 'flight' of the President as a great victory. In the months following the event the government in Hargeysa ordered its local rump administration to leave Laascaanood.

During my visit to Garoowe, in November 2003, Xassan occasionally mentioned that he did not feel comfortable among Majeerteen. He perceived them as not very welcoming. In his house, where he entertained me for some time, he was surrounded by male and female Dhulbahante relatives, who ran his household and served as drivers and bodyguards. Most of his acquaintances from the Majeerteen clan were fellow politicians working for the Puntland administration.

Besides politics, Xassan was very interested in religion, in the ecology of northern Somalia, and in the history and poetry of Maxamed Cabdille Xassan. He told me that his family, the sub-clan of Bihidarays, had fallen out with the Dervishes, and had even sided with the British against the insurgents. At the same time Xassan repeatedly recited poems composed by the Dervish leader. When I asked him about that, he answered half-jokingly: 'I'm a Dervish.'

The next time I saw Xassan following this visit to Garoowe was in Laascaanood in late January 2004. The Puntland police and military forces had just begun to establish some basic administrative structures in town. Xassan told me that he would remain in Laascaanood as a member of the new Puntland administration. However, to my great surprise, the *Somaliland Times*, one of the independent newspapers in Hargeysa, reported only three weeks later that a 'Senior Puntland Official Defects to Somaliland' (*Somaliland Times*, Issue 109, Saturday, 21.02.2004). The article stated that Xassan, who had been a Puntland Minister and Cabdullahi Yusuf's 'war secretary' for the Laascaanood area, had fled via the town of Ceerigaabo in Sanaag region to Hargeysa, where he had been warmly welcomed by the Somaliland authorities.[20] Xassan's defection was, of course, posted as triumph for Somaliland.

In April I met Xassan in Hargeysa. He told me that his disagreement with the leadership of Puntland about the politics in Sool had motivated his move to Somaliland. In Xassan's view, the occupation of Laascaanood by Puntland forces damaged the local and regional economy and provoked a military confrontation with Somaliland, which predominantly would harm Dhulbahante living in the contested area. Xassan also mentioned that he had not received his salary in Garoowe for several months, and that he felt generally mistreated as a Dhulbahante in Puntland, which was by and large controlled by Majeerteen.

Up until the end of my field research in December 2004 I had several more chances to sit and discuss with Xassan in the capital of Somaliland. During that time he married a Dhulbahante woman working in Hargeysa and rented a house there. He strove to obtain a political position in Somaliland. After I had finished my field research and left for Germany I learned through the internet that Xassan had become a candidate of one of the national parties in the parliamentary elections, which were held in Somaliland in September 2005. The last news was that, after not having succeeded in the elections, he had left the city in order to pursue his political chances in southern Somalia.

There are some striking similarities between Xassan's and Cabdi's stories. Both men obviously felt more comfortable in Hargeysa than in Garoowe. When Xassan and I met in the capital of Somaliland after he had changed sides, Xassan was much more relaxed than when we had seen each other in Puntland. In Hargeysa, he was well integrated into the local Dhulbahante community. On the other hand, I interpreted his admiration for the poetry of Maxamed Cabdille Xassan as an expression of his 'Dhulbahante pride', which usually goes along with the political vision of a strong, unitary Somalia. This attitude was shared by Cabdi.

The last individual case concerns a prominent Dhulbahante politician, who has in fact changed his allegiances three times, so far. Axmed belongs to the Baharasame sub-clan.[21] This is the 'aristocratic' lineage of Dhulbahante, to which *Garaad* Cabdiqani, the highest ranking traditional authority of the clan, belonged.[22] Axmed had made a military career under Siyad Barre. After the collapse of Somalia he returned to his clan-homeland in and around Laascaanood. In 1993 *Garaad* Cabdiqani, who personally had established good relations with the SNM and the Isaaq already in the late 1980s, sent Axmed to Hargeysa as the leading Dhulba-hante politician in Somaliland. For a few years, Axmed served as speaker of the House of Representatives (*Golaha Wakiilada*), until he fell out with President Maxamed Ibraahim Cigaal in 1996/7. Subsequently he turned his back on Somaliland and participated in the establishment of Puntland, where he became Minister of Interior in 1998 (Liban 2005: 14). Recently, in the summer of 2007, Axmed got into open disagreement with Maxamuud Cadde Muuse, who was then President of Puntland, and his Vice-president, Xassan Dahir Afqurac. The former is Majeerteen, while the latter belongs to the Dhulbahante clan, but to another sub-clan than that of Axmed.

Axmed who had been close to the previous President of Puntland, Cabdullahi Yusuf, was personally not on good terms with Maxamuud Cadde Muuse.[23] In addition, Axmed thought the policy of Puntland towards Laascaanood and the Sool region was mistaken and not benefiting the local community. Since early 2004, no stable civil administration had been built up there. Consequently, while visiting some Dhulbahante-inhabited places in September 2007, Axmed initiated the establishment of a local administration which was supposed to be independent from Somaliland *and* Puntland. Behind this step was not only the personal discontent of the minister with the general policy towards the Dhulbahante-inhabited area, but also the looming tensions between two large Dhulbahante sub-clans, Maxamuud Garaad and Faarax Garaad. Many of the Faarax Garaad sub-clan felt that the new Vice-president of Puntland, Xassan Dahir Afqurac, who belongs to the Maxamuud Garaad branch, was distributing important positions under his authority to members of his own group to the exclusion of other Dhulbahante groups. Axmed, who by descent is a member of the Faarax Garaad branch, tried to counter these developments by initiating a kind of local Faarax Garaad administration. President Maxamuud Cadde Muuse reacted by calling Axmed back to Garoowe. The minister delayed his return, allowing the President of Puntland to dismiss him for defying his orders.[24]

Following his dismissal, Axmed went to Laascaanood and its surround-ings to mobilize members of his Dhulbahante/Faarax Garaad sub-clan against Puntland. As well as encouraging local opposition to the adminis-tration in Garoowe, the dismissed minister approached Somaliland, his former employee, for support. The government in Hargeysa was eager to help him, and in early October 2007 Somaliland troops, with the consent and help of some Dhulbahante, advanced towards Laascaanood and pushed the Puntland army out of its positions in and around the town.

For some time in early 2008 Axmed was made Somaliland's 'Special envoy for Sool'. Later, however, he resided in Hargeysa without an official position. The Dhulbahante community was clearly split over the conflict.

While some parts of the clan collaborated with the Somaliland side, and Somaliland troops established themselves in and around Laascaanood, the majority of the Dhulbahante traditional authorities condemned the military occupation of their clan homeland by Somaliland forces (Bo'ame declaration of Dhulbahante clan elders).

To sum up: Axmed's case had the most far reaching consequences, at least with regard to current politics and the ongoing conflict in the borderlands between Somaliland and Puntland. Generally, his repeated switches reveal the same pattern as the previous cases. A certain closeness of Axmed and his influential relative, *Garaad* Cabdiqani, to the Isaaq in central Somaliland initially facilitated Axmed's political career in Hargeysa. When he got into trouble with President Cigaal, Axmed pursued new options in Puntland, establishing himself firmly for almost ten years. Axmed's most recent switch from Puntland back to Somaliland was caused by his personal enmity with the new President of Puntland and a power struggle within the Dhulbahante clan.

In all three cases the actors were borderlanders by descent. As Dhulbahante, they belonged to the borderland community, regardless of their place of birth or residence.[25] Descent also provided the basis for their switching, since Dhulbahante and Warsangeeli are represented in the administrations on both sides of the Somaliland-Puntland border. In addition, the actors described had a particular potential for changing sides. They were well educated, and Cabdi and Axmed in particular belonged to the 'old' Somali elite; they had had their careers already before the collapse of the Somali state. In the civil war many Somali professionals were either killed or fled abroad. This created a strong demand for known and skilled officials in the context of post-war state-building in northern Somalia. The governments in Hargeysa and Garoowe needed capable figures who could represent the different constituencies of their respective polities. Therefore, former military officers such as Cabdi and Axmed, as well as young and well-educated intellectuals like Xassan, were welcomed in both political centres. To some extent, they could choose their allegiances. They can be understood as 'borderland entrepreneurs' who used the competition between the two state-like entities in northern Somalia to their advantage. The question of the 'border' between Somaliland and Puntland is a core issue in this competition, and once the entrepreneurs engaged in their political 'game', they had to reckon with the border – which meant that they could not cross it without partly severe personal and political consequences.

The three individual cases also demonstrated that the actors described felt culturally closer to Isaaq than to Majeerteen, their 'Harti brothers'. Politically, however, Cabdi, Xassan and Axmed were quite sympathetic to Puntland's programme of re-building a unitary Somalia in the borders of 1990. The historical reference point in this regard, at least for Cabdi and Xassan, was the Dervish uprising under the charismatic leader Maxamed Cabdille Xassan. The switching of political loyalty was in all cases driven by personal ambitions and the opportunistic pursuit of positions of power. Finally, Cabdi, Xassan and Axmed also expressed concern about the misguided policy of the Puntland leadership towards Laascaanood and the Sool region.

BORDERLAND COMMUNITIES

Apart from these rather spectacular individual cases, there are examples of the everyday ways in which Harti borderlanders collectively profit from being divided between Somaliland and Puntland. Buuhoodle is a town on the border between northwest Somalia and Ethiopia; Dhulbahnate belonging to the branch of Faarax Garaad reside there. According to the administrative structure of Somaliland, Buuhoodle is a district town in the southeast of Togdheer region next to Sool. In January 2003, however, the government in Garoowe declared Buuhoodle the capital of the newly created Cayn region of Puntland.[26]

Despite this conflict between the two political centres in northern Somalia, Buuhoodle was a stable place when I visited it in March 2004. The town had two civil administrations, as well as two police and military forces. Yet, every resident with whom I talked mentioned that the only effective power lay in the hands of the traditional authorities. The elders coordinated political, civilian and humanitarian affairs between Somaliland and Puntland for the benefit of the local community. Ismaaciil, the Commander of the Somaliland army in Buuhoodle, pointed out: '*Marki dawladdi tagtay waxaa xukumayay waddanka Garaadadda iyo nabadoonadda*' (when the government went away the *Garaad*s and the elders/peace seekers ruled the country).[27] According to Ismaaciil, neither Somaliland nor Puntland had any administration in the town before 1999. Then, however, Puntland military was established in Buuhoodle. A man called Bashiir Jaamac Baydan, a senior officer in the Somali National Army, became the commander. Ismaaciil, who was an experienced soldier himself, joined him. The troops were equipped and paid by the government in Garoowe. Soon afterwards Bashiir and Cabdullahi Yusuf, the President of Puntland, got into personal conflict and in 2002 Bashiir, Ismaaciil and some others went to Hargeysa to talk with the Somaliland government about possible cooperation. After the talks had been concluded successfully, a Somaliland National Army (Somali: *Ciidanka Qaranka Somaliland*) was set up in Buuhoodle supported financially by Hargeysa.[28] I asked about the role of the elders in this political change. Ismaaciil answered that he and Bashiir had talked to the elders and to *Garaad* Cabdullahi Soofe, the leading traditional authority of the locality, before they went to Hargeysa. The local community leaders had approved their plans.

Bashiir died in November 2003, and Ismaaciil succeeded him as commander of the Somaliland forces in Buuhoodle, in consultation with Nuux Ismaaciil Taani, then the Commander in Chief of the Somaliland army. At the same time, Puntland installed a man called Cabdillahi as the

113

new commander of its troops in Buuhoodle. Ismaaciil mentioned that he himself, Cabdillahi, and the late Bashiir were all from the same sub-clan of Reer Hagar. Aaden, an assistant of Ismaaciil, who was present during our interview, emphasized that the ordinary soldiers in both armies came from the same families.[29] To illustrate this point, Aaden said: 'the soldiers get their salary from different sides, but they sit and chew *qaad* together' – a statement which embarrassed Ismaaciil. In reaction, he stressed that the different troops in Buuhoodle would not fight each other but coexisted. They were '*dad isku qabiil ah, dad isku dhalasha ah*' (people of the same clan, people of the same birth-place).[30]

I asked Ismaaciil what he would do if the government in Hargeysa were to order him to mobilize his troops to fight against the Puntland army in the area of Laascaanood, whereas the elders of Buuhoodle would not approve any fighting. The commander replied that he could ignore neither the orders of the Somaliland government nor the decision of the elders. Therefore he possibly would move his troops; however, he would still try to avoid fighting and seek peace.

In this interview and in many other talks with Dhulbahante in Buuhoodle and elsewhere, it became clear that allying with one or the other side is not only a matter of pure opportunism. There were also deeply felt identity issues at stake. Ismaaciil, for example, emphasized at one point that Buuhoodle and Puntland were 'far from each other'. The context of the interview revealed that he meant rather the political and/or cultural distance between Dhulbahante and Majeerteen than the geographical distance. This conformed to the position I heard from a number of elders in Buuhoodle who stressed that the only thing dividing the local community and the Isaaq was the issue of secession. In fact, Buuhoodle is located south of the Isaaq-inhabited area in Togdheer region. Consequently, intermarriage is common between Dhulbahante and their Isaaq neighbours.

Simultaneously, and with regard to Somali politics in general, people in Buuhoodle are clearly Somali nationalists. Again, the reference to Maxamed Cabdille Xassan and the Dervish movement was frequently made by informants to underline this point. The Dervish history had a particular significance in Buuhoodle, since Maxamed Cabdille Xassan was born in the nearby countryside from a Dhulbahante/Cali Geri mother. He had grown up in the area. Dhulbahante from Buuhoodle were among the first and most persistent supporters of the Dervish cause (Samatar 1982: 99–122). Up to the present, this fills many inhabitants of the town with pride.[31]

A few days after the interview session with Ismaaciil and Aaden I had the chance to attend the meeting between the local elders and a delegation of Save the Children/USA and HAVOYOCO (Horn of Africa Volunteer Youth Organization), a local NGO based in Burco and Hargeysa.[32] The elders, the members of the local women's organizations and some other dignitaries welcomed the aid workers. Maxamuud Xaaji Qarshe, the spokesman of the local elders, emphasized that Buuhoodle was peaceful and that here both sides, Puntland and Somaliland, could coexist. Looking at me, he added that even a white man could stay here without any problem. The ensuing speeches emphasized the peacefulness of the place and the need for assistance, particularly for water-trucking in the current drought. The situation changed only briefly when Ismaaciil, the commander of the local Somaliland forces, spoke. He talked about politics and this outraged Maxamuud Xaaji Qarshe, who interrupted him to ask him to stop talking. The commander continued to speak, but after a few minutes he was called to sit down and be silent, which he finally did. Ironically, this was a good demonstration of what Ismaaciil himself had mentioned earlier, namely, that the traditional authorities rule the place. After the reception, the NGO delegation held further talks with the local school-teachers and other people, before leaving in the afternoon. About a week later the first trucks with drinking water sponsored by HAVOYOKO and Save the Children/USA arrived in Buuhoodle. The distribution of the water was observed by elders and their assistants.

Similar examples of parallel administrative structures of Somaliland and Puntland can be found all over the borderland regions of Sool and Sanaag. Until the attack on President Dahir Rayaale Kaahin in December 2002, locals in Laascaanood worked for both sides. In 2003 and 2004 villages and small towns in the Nugaal valley as well as in the east of the Sanaag region, where predominantly Warsangeeli reside, usually had two mayors. The military structures in Sool and Sanaag were also often duplicated. At the 'national' level, influential families among the Dhulba-hante and Warsangeeli had members in leading positions in Hargeysa *and* in Garoowe. At the local level, traditional authorities tried to balance the interests of their people between the two centres.

INTERESTS OF THE CENTRES

Of course, the governments in Hargeysa and Garoowe also have their interests regarding the 'bush-border'. Somaliland strives to validate its claim to independent statehood on the basis of the resolution of the Organization of African Unity (OAU), dating from 1964, to respect the borders existing on the achievement of independence (Herbst 2000: 104).[33] The Foreign Ministry in Hargeysa produced a briefing paper on *The Case for Somaliland's International Recognition as an Independent State* in 2002.[34] It briefly sketches the 'ill-fated' history of Somali unity, and then refers to the colonial treaties between Britain, France, Italy and Ethiopia as markers of Somaliland's borders. Moreover, the booklet addresses the conformity of Somaliland's claim to statehood with the Charter of the African Union, the public support for independence inside the country, and the economic viability of Somaliland. In the appendices, international documents referring to the independence of Somaliland in 1960, as well as a report on and the results of the constitutional referendum in May 2001 are attached (Somaliland Ministry of Foreign Affairs 2002).[35]

After a delegation of British parliamentarians had visited Somaliland in January 2004, President Dahir Rayaale Kaahin was invited to London in March 2004, where he officially addressed the members of the British House of Commons. In his speech, the President emphasized that Somaliland was given independence by Britain, and that several other countries, including Egypt, Ghana and Libya, had recognized the country as an independent state in 1960. Dahir Rayaale Kaahin stressed that Somaliland today possessed a permanent population, a defined territory, a government, and the capacity to enter into relations with other states. He complained that the UN seat of Somalia was given to the ineffective and, from the Somaliland point of view, illegitimate Transitional National Government (TNG) based in Mogadishu.[36] Moreover, he argued that his government had patiently waited for the formation of a representative government of Somalia, with which Somaliland could enter into dialogue. In the main part of his speech, Dahir Rayaale Kaahin outlined the positive developments in Somaliland since 1991. Finally he came to talk about the problems caused by the lack of international recognition, such as the impossibility of travel without recognized documents and the difficulties in attracting foreign investments (Republic of Somaliland 2004).

In contrast, Puntland denies Somaliland's independence and profits from the permeability of the former colonial border. Elsewhere I argue that Puntland in its whole set-up imitates Somaliland – institutionally but also with regard to its political claims (Hoehne 2009). Towards the wider Somali and international community Puntland evokes the impression of being on an equal footing with Somaliland. Consequently, the conflict over the Harti-inhabited territories in Sool, eastern Sanaag and southern Togdheer seems to involve two regional states fighting over their borders. This serves Puntland's actual aim to prevent Somaliland's further development as an independent state. As long as Somaliland is unstable due to the border conflict, external observers may refrain from accepting Hargeysa's claim for international recognition.

It has to be noted that Yoocada as marker of a contemporary border exists only in the view of the government of Somaliland and its supporters. Somaliland, at least in the eyes of its advocates, needs a stable and clearly demarcated state-border in order to enhance its chances of recognition by the international community. Puntland, on the other hand, does not accept Somaliland's secession and therefore does not ascribe any significance to Yoocada. The government in Garoowe undermines Hargeysa's claim for independent statehood by incorporating the Harti-inhabited territories in Sool, eastern Sanaag and southern Togdheer.

Conclusion

This chapter has focused on the Harti borderlanders along the Somaliland-Puntland border who are simultaneously integrated into two emerging states. Culturally and socially, many Dhulbahante and Warsangeeli are closer to the Isaaq who dominate politics in Somaliland. On the other hand, as Harti, they are part of Puntland and oppose the secession of Somaliland. The Dhulbahante in particular refer to the anti-colonial struggle of the Dervishes when talking about contemporary politics in northern Somalia, thereby recalling a heroic episode in which many of their grandfathers were involved. Beyond clan history, the Dervish uprising is also part of the corpus of Somali nationalism, which is, in the absence of a strong Somali state, promulgated by Puntland. This situation illustrates what was mentioned in the introduction to this book, that border regions are zones of socio-political ambivalence.

It was further shown that living in the contested borderlands between Somaliland and Puntland provides opportunities for the local population. Members of the borderland community who possess certain skills and social capital, such as Cabdi, Xassan and Axmed, can pursue political and military careers on both sides. When these actors presented in the individual case studies faced serious problems with their employee – one or the other of the two governments – they switched to the other side and tried to continue there. Motives of gaining and preserving individual power and positions were in the forefront here. However, as the protagonists also pointed out, changing sides was a way of protesting against government policies that they perceived as negative for their local communities.

The borderland communities as a whole also try to gain something by carefully balancing their position between Somaliland and Puntland. In Buuhoodle traditional authorities and members of the local elite managed to accommodate military and administrative structures from both sides. This provided a considerable number of local people with paid jobs. Being divided thus helps people at the margins of the state to survive.

A non-economic motivation for staying divided must also be taken seriously. During my field research, many of the Harti borderlanders expressed the idea that they could mediate between Somaliland and Puntland. Sometimes people even said that, as Dhulbahante or Warsangeeli, they would 'suffer for holding Somalia together'. This shows that identities and politics are questioned and reinforced in the Harti-inhabited borderlands in northern Somalia. The general observation of Horstman and Wadley (2006: 3) that the 'agency [of the borderlanders] moves equally between "resistance" and accommodation' applies to the situation discussed here. Dhulbahante and Warsangeeli resist being completely incorporated into Somaliland or Puntland. They adjust to the situation of being divided by trying to get the most out of it in the form of jobs, positions and political influence on both sides of the border.

The two competing administrations in northern Somalia have precisely opposite attitudes towards the border represented by the bush called Yoocada. Somaliland strives to make it a 'real' border in order to substantiate its claim to independent statehood. By contrast, Puntland takes concrete military steps to show the fictitiousness of the colonial border claimed by Somaliland. In this sense, Yoocada denotes at the same time a flexible (for most of the people residing along it), a fixed (for Somaliland), and a non-existent, merely historical border (for Puntland).

Notes

1 Somali place and personal names in this text follow the Somali orthography (with the exception of Mogadishu, which is so well established in English and the names of some Somali authors who adopted an anglicised version of their names). The Latin 'c' stands for a sound close to the Arabic 'ع' (ayn); 'x' denotes 'ح' (ha), as in, e.g., Laascaanood or in Faarax.

2 The Darood clan-family consists, among other subgroups, of the already mentioned Harti clan-federation, the Marrexaan clan and the Ogadeen clan (see Chart 6.1).

3 Political position and descent did not, of course, converge 100 per cent. Some Isaaq, at least initially, supported the anti-colonial cause of the Dervishes. Similarly, some of Maxamed Cabdille Xassan's relatives were repulsed by his authoritarian style of leadership and joined the British against him, or retreated into the 'bush' in order to stay neutral.

4 As a result of colonialism Somalis were divided between Somalia, Djibouti, Ethiopia and Kenya.

5 Between 1974 and 1977, Somalia was most strongly allied with the USSR, but when it attacked Ethiopia under the socialist rule of Mengistu Haile Mariam, Moscow severed its ties with the country. From 1982 onwards Somalia enjoyed the strong support of the United States but this support vanished with the end of the Cold War and when Somalia's appalling human rights record became unbearable towards the end of the 1980s.

6 Beneath the façade of socialism and nationalism, Barre was a skilled 'clan-politician' who shared resources and power among a few selected followers and his own Marrexaan clan.

7 Dahir Rayaale Kaahin was Vice-president of Somaliland from 1997. When President Maxamed Ibraahim Cigaal died in May 2002, Kaahin took over as President according to Somaliland's constitution. Cigaal had never visited Laascaanood during his time as President (1993-2002).

8 Similarly, in colonial times, the border between British and Italian Somaliland was only a single line on colonial maps. In everyday life it was quite permeable for nomads and even the first Somali 'guerrillas' – the Dervishes around Maxamed Cabdille Xassan. However, between the Italians and the British the existence of this border was not contested.

9 This was the situation in 2004. Since the town was retaken by Somaliland forces in October 2007, the situation has changed.

10 The names in the section are *not* fictitious. The cases discussed here are all well-known in northern Somalia and concern public figures. Therefore it is impossible to completely anonymize the actors' identities. I believe that my outline will not do harm as the described events are part of the local history.

11 Interview with Cabdi, Garoowe, December 2003. At the beginning of this very first interview, Cabdi told me that he only agreed to meet me because he had heard that I had been in the Nuugaal Valley and Taleex before and that I was on good terms with the people living there. Between December 2003 and August 2004 Cabdi and I met three times. The interviews were conducted in a mixture of English and Somali.

12 I found it astonishing that the Puntland army, which is dominated by Majeerteen, is called after Maxamed Cabdille Xassan's movement. Historically, the relationship between Majeerteen and the Dervishes was rather problematic, as outlined above.

Therefore, I interpret the name *Ciidanka Darawiishta* for the Puntland armed forces first, as reference to Somali nationalism, and secondly, as provocation towards the Isaaq in Somaliland, many of whose forefathers had been allied with the British against the Dervishes in the early twentieth century.

13 The distance between Laascaanood and Garoowe is about 130 kilometers.

14 As it turned out later during the interview, he had had a fallout with President Cigaal of Somaliland, who in the mid-1990s restructured his administration. In this context, Dhulbahante became marginalized.

15 'Tribalism' is an English loanword in Somali. The Somali term (which comes from Arabic *qabiilat*) is *qabyaalad*, which can be translated as 'clanism'.

16 In the absence of any recent and clan-specific census, this argument of size remains absolutely subjective.

17 Roughly, the system of power-sharing in both Somaliland and Puntland follows estimations about clan size. In Somaliland, the Isaaq dominate, whereas in Puntland Majeerteen take the lead. Yet, while in Somaliland political reforms have been introduced and the country is functioning, officially at least, as a multi-party democracy, politics and military in Puntland are strictly controlled by Majeerteen.

18 The interviews took place during one week in Garoowe in November 2003 and at several other occasions in Laascaanood and Hargeysa in 2004. Xassan and I spoke partly in English, partly in Somali.

19 Some people in Laascaanood argued that Dahir Rayaale Kaahin had acted very responsibly and wanted to avoid bloodshed among civilians.

20 Ceerigaabo is inhabited by Isaaq and Harti clans and is located on the clan-border between them (west of which Isaaq reside, east of which Harti). The administration of the town is dominated by Isaaq, so Ceerigaabo belongs to Somaliland.

21 I met Axmed briefly in Garoowe in August 2004. In contrast to the two cases presented earlier, Axmed and I did not talk much about his personal history. Rather, I gathered the details of his political biography from various sources throughout my field research. I was, for instance, particularly close to some of Axmed's relatives in Laascaanood. For information on his most recent political moves I conducted a number of telephone interviews with people in Garoowe and Buuhoodle in October and November 2007.

22 *Garaad* Cabdiqaani died in February 2006. He was a grandson of *Garaad* Cali who had been killed by the Dervishes.

23 In mid-2001 the term of office ended for President Cabdullahi Yusuf; but he refused to step down. A counter-president was elected by the opposition and supported militarily by General Maxamuud Cadde Muuse. Fighting between the adversaries and their followers continued throughout 2002. Axmed had been on the side of Cabdullahi Yusuf. Finally, peace was negotiated and Maxamuud Cadde Muuse and his forces were integrated into the Puntland army. After Cabdullahi Yusuf had been elected Somali President at the peace and reconciliation conference in Kenya in October 2004, Maxamuud Cadde Muuse succeeded him as President of Puntland in January 2005.

24 Personal communication with informants in Garoowe and Buuhoodle, October 2007.

25 Even if a Dhulbahante or Warsangeeli person had been born in the south, e.g., in Mogadishu, and had stayed there most of her/his life, she/he was considered as belonging to either Sool or Sanaag. This was a result of the 'clan cleansing' during the Somali civil war. These regions are the clan-homelands of both groups.

26 The government in Garoowe claimed henceforth that Puntland consisted of the regions Bari, Nuugaal, Mudug, Sanaag, Sool and Cayn. According to the government in Hargeysa, Somaliland consisted of the regions Awdal, Saaxil, Sanaag, Sool, Togdheer and Waqooyi Galbeed. For Hargeysa, the region Cayn simply does not exist; it is part of southern Togdheer.

27 Interview Buuhoodle, 8 March 2004, conducted in Somali.

28 The monthly salary of an ordinary soldier in the Somaliland forces was said to be about $40; a Puntland soldier supposedly earned $10 more. About half of the salary was paid in food rations.

29 Later I heard that even one of Ismaaciil's own brothers was a Puntland soldier.

30 In August 2004, during the second interview with Cabdi in Garoowe, I mentioned that I had been in Buuhoodle before and had seen the two armies of Somaliland and Puntland sitting together under two flags (Somaliland and Puntland/Somalia), 'chewing their salary'. Cabdi, who had recently resigned as Vice-Commander of the Puntland army, simply commented that 'they follow their interest, they want to eat something'.

31 This history is kept alive in orally transmitted poems composed by the Dervish leader, his followers and his adversaries, many of which can be found in Buuhoodle.

32 Meeting with community representatives and NGO in Buuhoodle, 13.03.2004; language: Somali.

33 The African Union (AU) succeeded the OAU in 1999. The principle of the sanctity of the colonial borders was sustained.

34 I can only assume that the addressees of the briefing paper are international organizations working in Somaliland, as well as Somaliland supporters and lobbyists in the diaspora.

35 In this referendum the Constitution of Somaliland was approved by the majority of the population. However, it was boycotted in most of the Harti inhabited territories of Somaliland.

36 The TNG was established at the end of the Arta peace conference hosted by Djibouti in 2000. It was later replaced by the Transitional Federal Government (TFG), which was created in Kenya at the end of the Somali Peace and Reconciliation Conference from October 2002 to January 2005. The TFG is perceived as equally illegitimate by the government in Hargeysa.

References

Abdi Hassan Jimale 1998. *Dhacdooyinka Maddeganayaasha Geeska Afrika (Soomaaliya)*. Norresundby: Horn of Africa Books.

Battera, F. 1998. 'Remarks on the 1998 charter of the Puntland State of Somalia', Working Paper, United Nations Development Office for Somalia (UNDOS). '

Bo'ame declaration of Dhulbahante clan elders. Garooweonline. <http://www.Garoowe online.com/artman2/publish/Features_34/Somalia_The_Bo_ame_Declaration_of_Dhu lbahante_Clan_Elders.shtml> (24.11.2007).

Cabdiraxmaan, J. 2005. 'Consolidation and decentralization of government institutions', in WSP (Wartorn Societies Project) International (ed.), *Rebuilding Somaliland. Issues and possibilities*. Lawrenceville, NJ: Red Sea Press, pp. 49–121.

Cassanelli, L.V. 1982. *The Shaping of Somali Society. Reconstructing the history of a pastoral people, 1600-1900*. Philadelphia, PA: University of Pennsylvania Press.

De Waal, Alex. 1997. *Famine Crimes. Politics and the disaster relief industry in Africa*. Oxford: James Currey.

Doornbos, M. 1975. 'The Shehu and the Mullah: The jihads of Usuman Dan Fodio and Muhammed Abd-Allah Hassan in Comparative perspective'. *Jeune Afrique* 14(2): 7–31.

—— 2000. 'When is a state a state? Exploring Puntland', in P. Konings, W. van Binsbergen and G. Hesseling (eds), *Trajectoires de libération en Afrique contemporaine*. Paris: Karthala, pp. 125–39.

Farah, A.Y. and I.M. Lewis. 1997. 'Making Peace in Somaliland', *Cahiers d'etudes africaines* 37(146): 349–77.

Hashi, A.A. 1998. *Essential Somali English Dictionary*. Addis Ababa: Fiqi Educational Materials.

Herbst, J. 2000. *States and Power in Africa. Comparative lessons in authority and control*. Princeton, NJ: Princeton University Press.

Hoehne, M.V. 2006. 'Political Identity, Emerging State Structures and Conflict in Northern Somalia'. *Journal of Modern African Studies* 44(3): 397–414.

—— 2007a: 'Puntland and Somaliland clashing in northern Somalia: Who cuts the Gordian knot'. [online] http://hornofafrica.ssrc.org/Hoehne/printable.html>, accessed 06.03.2008.

—— 2007b. 'From pastoral to state politics: Traditional authorities in Northern Somalia', in L. Buur and H.M. Kyed (eds), *State Recognition and Democratisation in Sub-Saharan Africa: A new dawn for traditional authorities?* New York: Palgrave, pp. 155–82.

—— 2009: 'Mimicry and mimesis in dynamics of state and identity formation in northern Somalia'. *Africa* 79 (2): 252–81.

Horstmann, A. and R.L. Wadley 2006. 'Centering the margins in Southeast Asia: Introduction', in A. Horstmann and R.L. Wadley (eds), *Centering the Margin. Agency and narrative in southeast Asian borderlands*. New York and Oxford: Berghahn, pp. 1–24.

Information Service of the Somali Government 1962. *The Somali Peninsula. A New Light on Imperial Motives*. Mogadishu.

Lewis, I.M. 1961. *A Pastoral Democracy: A study of pastoralism and politics among the Northern Somali of the Horn of Africa*. London: Oxford University Press (npr. [1982] 1999 London: James Currey).

—— 2002. *A Modern History of the Somali*. Oxford: James Currey.

Liban, Ahmad, 2005. *A Map of Confusion: Somaliland, Puntland and people of Sool region in Somalia*. Manchester: Hilin Publishing.

Matthies, V. 1977. *Der Grenzkonflikt Somalias mit Äthiopien und Kenya. Analyse eines zwischenstaatlichen Konflikts in der Dritten Welt*. Hamburg: Institut für Afrikakunde.

Prunier, G. 1995. *Somalia: Civil War, Intervention and Withdrawal 1990–1995*. online: <www.asylumlaw.org/docs/somalia/country_conditions/prunier.pdf>, accessed 30.01. 2006.

Renders, M. 2006. *Traditional Leaders and Institutions in the Building of the Muslim Republic of Somaliland*. PhD dissertation, University of Ghent.

Republic of Somaliland. 2004. 'Speech by the President to Members of the British House of Commons', 17 March 2004 (unpublished).

Roble, F. 2007. 'Somaliland: Is Invading Las Anod Part of Creating 'New Reality on the Ground?'' Wardheernews homepage. <http://wardheernews/articles_07/october/21_Somaliland_Faisal_ Roble.html> accessed 31.10.2007.

Samatar, S.S. 1982. *Oral Poetry and Somali Nationalism: The case of Sayyid Mahammad 'Abdille Hasan*. Cambridge: Cambridge University Press.

Sheikh-Abdi, Abdi. 1993. *Divine Madness: Mohammed 'Abdulle Hassan (1856–1920)*. London: Zed Books.

Somaliland Ministry of Foreign Affairs. 2002. *The Case of Somaliland's international recognition as a state* (Briefing Paper). Hargeysa: Ministry of Foreign Affairs.

Somaliland Times, Issue 109, Saturday, 21 February 2004.

Seven

The Ethiopian-British
Somaliland Boundary

CEDRIC BARNES

Introduction

This chapter examines the history of the Ethiopian-(colonial) British Somaliland border, through the lens of local society. It is clear that the territorial claims and administrative ambitions of the respective governments provided both problems and opportunities for borderland Somali subjects. In the British Colonial Office archives the local Somalis are portrayed as the victims of Ethiopian manipulation, but the colonial voice does not allow for the Somalis' astute manipulation of the border in their individual, local and group interests. Yet careful reading of British Foreign Office records detailing events at the eastern Ethiopian periphery, reveals various repertoires employed by the trans-border Somali communities and the affordances of state boundaries in the first half of the twentieth century.

The background

The borderland area dividing the Somali-inhabited territory of northeast Africa has a complex administrative history. Large parts of the northwestern Somali peninsula were claimed as part of the British Somaliland Protectorate. The Ethiopian victory at Adwa in 1896 and Ethiopia's effective occupation of large tracts of Somali-inhabited areas at its eastern periphery, forced the British to relinquish their original territorial claims in 1897 (Marcus 1965). The British colonial administration in Somaliland, along with many of its Somali subjects, bitterly regretted this cession. In fact, shortly after the British government reduced its territorial claims, the administration of what became the British Somaliland Protectorate desperately sought a solution that would reintegrate the lost areas back into the Protectorate territory (Silberman 1961; Drysdale 1964). It was not until the Second World War reached the region in the 1940s that a momentary solution arose.

During the 1930s the whole of northeast Africa (Ethiopia, Eritrea, British and Italian Somaliland) was militarily annexed by Italy. Following Italy's declaration of war in 1940, by 1941 British and Commonwealth forces, in alliance with Ethiopian patriots, had attacked and defeated the Italian East African Empire. The defeat of Italy brought the whole of the Somali-speaking lands in northeast Africa (apart from French Somaliland/ Djibouti) under British Military Administration, including the previously Ethiopian-ruled Somali territories. Therefore, with the defeat of the Italian East African Empire and the establishment of the British Military Administration (BMA), the Protectorate government temporarily achieved the recovery of its lost areas by default, though Ethiopian sovereignty of the area was never denied. Once in possession of the lost areas, the Protectorate administration was loath to relinquish the territory once more.

It had been a constantly regretted fact that the 1897 cession of some of the British Protectorate's claims 'lost' some prime grazing lands to Ethiopian control. The 'loss' had made securing grazing rights for their subjects a priority for the British Somaliland administration. By the 1950s – fuelled by fifty years of changes to the economy of the region – the situation had become acute. Though the differing impacts of imperial Ethiopian rule on the Somaliland protectorate and the British rule of the Somaliland Protectorate on the adjacent Ethiopian administered Somali territory have not been fully investigated, nevertheless archival records note the extent of change that the Protectorate government and economy had on the Ethiopian Somali borderlands.

One such record is a Foreign Office reply to a memorandum by the Governor of the Somaliland Protectorate pressing for the retention of lost Protectorate territory under British administration. The Foreign Office representative took the opportunity for a long and detailed rejoinder to the Protectorate's claims:

> The kernel of this thesis [the retention of Ethiopian 'Haud' borderland territory under British Administration] is the statement that the pasturage of the British Somaliland Protectorate is deteriorating and thus rendering the Protectorate unable to support its population. ... But it is pertinent to ask what the deterioration is due to ... The truth seems to be that because the country is being over grazed by an ever increasing population, and that the increase in population is due chiefly to the fact that the British administration has reduced infant mortality, animal mortality and the mortality due to tribal warfare, it appears, in fact, that the *pax Britannica* is in the process of creating, or at least helping to create a situation in which the choice lies between territorial expansion and starvation.

The document continues in ever more critical tones:

The idea is prevalent that we have some sort of moral right to demand the cession by Ethiopia of the Haud because such a cession by Ethiopia provides the only means of 'preserving the tribal *status quo*'. When analysed this convenient form of words is seen to mean that in the past we treated a certain area of Ethiopia as our own for all practical purposes, the Ethiopians being unable to prevent it, and that we wish, now that they are able to prevent it, to regularise the position by advancing our frontier to cover the area in question.

Finally the Foreign Office tears down a dearly held myth at the heart of the British Somaliland colonial administrative history:

> We cannot even contend with any plausibility that the original frontier was incorrectly drawn in the light of the tribal distribution: the Haud is not a vacuum into which British tribes pour at seasonal intervals, but a region inhabited for the greater part by tribes which do not belong to us. ... The fact of the matter is that by preserving the *status quo* we really mean preserving a situation which is constantly evolving to the detriment of the Ethiopian element in the shared area (Lascelles 1948).

This withering reply certainly underlines the fact that by the late 1940s – if not before – the British Somaliland Protectorate had outgrown itself, though the Protectorate could not very well admit this fact.

The 1954 Border Agreement

By the 1950s, with a weakened Britain in the first stages of imperial retreat in Africa, the Protectorate was finally forced to return parts of borderland territory it had retained after the war, back to Ethiopia. However, for a time there was an attempt to preserve a dual British-Ethiopian authority in the borderland area in a 1954 agreement that recognized the 'rights' of British subjects in Ethiopian territory. The 1954 agreement attempted to regularize the relationship between the cross-cutting interests of Ethiopian and British Somaliland administrations of their common borderlands and trans-national subjects. Yet, rather than simplifying matters, the agreement gave full vent to myriad affordances that the borderland had enjoyed and endured over the previous half-century.

The 1954 agreement foundered on the conflicting interpretations, not to say divergent *governmentalities*, of the British colonial and Ethiopian imperial states. The divergence of governmental practice is revealed in the minutes (Stebbing 1956) of a series of conferences between the two governments held in Harar, Ethiopia, between 1955 and 1956, to iron out problems arising from the 1954 agreement. These reveal that each territorial administration refused to admit that their policies would have an impact across the frontier, despite the constant (and contradictory) complaints of the depredations of the other's policies on their respective administrations.

There was a great deal of suspicion between the two governments. A letter from the Chief Secretary to the Government of British Somaliland, J. R. Stebbing, listed what he saw as Ethiopia's 'real' agenda:

i) to reduce grazing rights by cultivation and to encourage settlement by Ethiopian tribes, or persons they claim as Ethiopians, wherever rainfall and soil conditions are suitable;

ii) to claim as sedentary peoples, and therefore outside the 1954 agreement, any nomadic people who cultivate land, even in the rudimentary and temporary fashion;

iii) to claim as Ethiopian subjects any fully nomadic peoples who spend the greater part of the year in the territories;

iv) to appoint Ethiopian tribal leaders (*akils* and elders) over any tribes or tribal sections to which they can ... lay claim, or over which they can fabricate a claim for Ethiopian jurisdiction ...;

v) to split the potential alliances of Somali peoples against them, by fostering the traditional antipathy between Isaq and Darod groups of tribes and the fear of the Darod over Isaq expansion into their country (Stebbing 1956).

Without a hint of irony, given the Protectorate's own historical designs on Ethiopian sovereign territory, Stebbing added for the record:

The Somaliland Protectorate members of the delegation were also agreed that Ethiopian policy towards Somaliland is undoubtedly expansive and imperialistic and ... that at some later date the Ethiopian government will claim right under the 1954 agreement of reciprocal facilities, so that they may set up their own liaison organisations within the Protectorate, and so, very greatly expand their influence.

But this increase of Ethiopian-claimed Somali subjects was not merely Ethiopian imperialism. Indeed, of the many hundreds of specific cases that find their way into the historical record, the common theme is *which* jurisdiction Somali individuals or sections of clans *chose* to claim. More often than not they claimed both. Moreover, as John Drysdale (one of the original participants in the 1956 Harar conferences) later reflected about the period of dual administration in the borderlands: '[A]s a clan aligned itself with one government, and then with the other, shifting according to the expediency of the moment, each government would be provoked into action to preserve its dignity, and would intensify the competitive struggle for the nationality of the clan in question' (Drysdale 1964: 82).

It is also striking – given the benefit of historical hindsight – how many of the cases recorded in the 1955–56 Harar conferences showed continuities of local strategies towards the boundary since the outset of Ethiopian and British rule over the region in the late nineteenth century. While much of the discourse on the Somali-Ethiopian borderlands has concentrated on the 'pastoral' (herding) Somali sections, agro-pastoralists are also a significant presence in the borderlands. Agricultural Somalis were as astute in making use of the affordances of the borderlands as their pastoral cousins.

A Gadabuursi case study

The agricultural or agro-pastoral transformation of the north-western Somalilands is an important but little studied process, and the trans-border dimension to it has received even less scholarly attention. The two acknowledged experts on the region, Abdi Samatar and Ioan Lewis, have both written on the rural transformation of the British Somaliland Protectorate (Samatar 1989; Lewis 1961), but neither author has taken into account the impact of the agricultural transition across the Ethiopian border, and specifically, the fact that the transition to agriculture added further dimensions to the question of the border 'dividing' Somali populations.

The increase in sedentary agriculture certainly began in the late nineteenth century in the north-western Somali lands, though some Somali clans – especially those inhabiting the Harar highlands – were already well-established farmers by then. Agriculture began to increase on both sides of the border in earnest from the 1920s onwards. Work on the Somaliland Protectorate has shown that the transition to agriculture in the Protectorate, and the accompanying registration and enclosure of lands, put pressure on the wells and grazing of the Protectorate clans in the higher and well-watered areas of the Protectorate (Kakwenzire 1976).

During this period the Protectorate government followed a policy of minimizing social change after the experience of the disastrously expensive and socially disruptive rebellion led by Mohamed 'Abdille Hassan (better known to non-Somali audiences as the 'Mad Mullah'). Though the Protectorate government was attracted by the increased revenues that farming Somalis generated, it nevertheless found agriculture an added headache. In the Protectorate the agricultural transition was above all an 'administrative' issue to be dealt with carefully for the overall good of all sections of the population.

On the other side of the border, however, the Ethiopian government positively welcomed and pushed the transformation of pastoralists to tax-paying ox-plough farmers. Grain-growing farmers were vital for Ethiopia's agrarian-based taxation system. Therefore while the British attempted to closely regulate and circumscribe the agricultural activities within what they perceived as the 'customary institutions of their Somalis', the Ethiopians energetically encouraged farming by local Somali clans, and introduced highland settler-farmers for good measure.

Indeed, thirty years after the transition to farming began in earnest – as the documentation of the 1955–56 Harar conferences shows – one of the main problems identified by the British was the fact that the guarantee of trans-border grazing rights for pastoralists in the original border treaties

126

was adversely affected by the increase in cultivation on the Ethiopian side (Stebbing 1956). But it was also the case that the increase in pressure on trans-border grazing rights – that is, British clans' grazing rights in Ethiopia – was undoubtedly increased by the Protectorate's own enclosure of grazing land for agriculture at the heart of its territory. The complaints made in Stebbing's list against the Ethiopian policy of settling Somalis into agriculture were doubly disingenuous since cultivation on the Ethiopian side had vastly expanded under the British Military Administration of the reserved areas in the 1940s in response to a boom in grain prices (Barnes 2004).

In the 1920s as part of the consolidation of rule in the Somali periphery, the local Ethiopian government based in the eastern garrison town of Jigjiga had attempted to reform and regularize the collection of revenues. The Ethiopian administration took advantage of the expansion of farming already undertaken by some sections of Somali clans since the late nineteenth century. In 1917 the then (sub) Governor of Jigjiga, and one of Ethiopia's early 'modernizers', Takla-Hawaryat, began to formalize the previously erratic collection of agricultural revenue (grain) from the increasing numbers of farming Somalis. Inevitably, the more regular demands for tax either in cash or in kind brought resistance from some quarters, not least the Gadabuursi clan, who had begun profitable sorghum gardens on the well-watered hills that made up the northern section of the border between Ethiopia and the Somaliland Protectorate.

In a sub-province still dominated by camel herders, cultivating clans like the Gadabuursi were especially valuable tax-payers – tax which was primarily paid in grain. Ethiopian officials pointed out that, like any civilized power, their provincial administration needed regular revenues to ensure good administration (Archer 1918; Summers 1923). In 1920 Takla-Hawaryat was replaced as Governor of Jigjiga by *Qagnazmach* Gadla-Giyorgis, whom the colonial officials in Somaliland saw as 'unscrupulous, determined and tyrannical, but clear-headed and remarkably plausible'. For the nascent modernizing regime in Ethiopia, Gadla-Giyorgis was an ideal governor, extracting the 'last ounce of tribute' from the district and remitting valuable revenues to Addis Ababa 'without misappropriating much for his own use' (Plowman 1927a). Like Takla-Hawaryat, Gadla-Giyorgis paid particular attention to the Gadabuursi cultivating on the border with the Protectorate.

The Ethiopian tax demands should also be seen within the context of British administrative withdrawal (*circa* 1909–13) from the Somaliland interior to a mere coastal presence as Mohamed 'Abdille Hassan's rebellion raged in the Protectorate. During the period of British withdrawal, the Gadabuursi clan had received 'protection' and wages from the Ethiopian government. When the British administration eventually returned it did not tax subjects directly for fear of prompting another revolt. But the Protectorate's tax-breaks were directly corrosive of attempts at good 'provincial' governance by the Ethiopian administration. Instead the British encouraged trade with the coast, thereby gaining indirect taxes from import and export tariffs, and established a customs post close to the Ethiopian border around which the district of Borama evolved. Many Gadabuursi clans welcomed the British presence which would counteract the advance of Ethiopian administration and their incessant demands for taxation along the yet to be demarcated border (Walsh 1942).

During the 1920s harvests improved, and markets stayed healthy. The Gadabuursi enjoyed good revenues from their grain harvests which they sold in the Protectorate where tax was light and indirect. Indeed, after the British re-established themselves in the Gadabuursi areas of the Protectorate there was an abrupt decline in trade between the Ethiopian centre of Somali trade in Jigjiga and the Protectorate. Customs receipts at one of the Protectorate customs posts at Gabileh fell from 27,000 Rupees in 1920 to 12,000 Rupees in 1922, with official imports of grain falling from 1,625 tons to 832 tons. The decline in revenues was partly due to increased cultivation in the Protectorate itself, but the figures hid the increasing instances of grain being smuggled from Ethiopia across the border to markets in the Protectorate avoiding Ethiopian taxes at Jigjiga (Monthly Intelligence Report 1923).

In spite of Ethiopian efforts to collect taxes and establish effective administration on their side of the border, the British rather churlishly accused Gadla-Giyorgis of 'maladministration', reporting that he had reduced the once-prosperous town of Jigjiga 'to a half-deserted weed-grown ruin' (Monthly Intelligence Report 1924). They appeared to be blind to the effects that their timid indirect taxation was having in the Jigjiga region. Nevertheless the Ethiopian government continued to bolster its claim to the Gadabuursi through the recognition of individual ambitions to the 'chieftaincy' (known as the *Ugaas*) of the Gadabuursi.

Early on in the Protectorate's history, the government recognized a certain *Ugaas* Robleh as hereditary chief of the Gadabuursi, before their temporary withdrawal from the Protectorate in 1909. On their reoccupation, the Protectorate government discovered that Robleh had taken money from the Ethiopian administration in their absence (not unreasonably, it would seem, given the abandonment of the interior by the protecting government). The Protectorate replaced him with another man who failed to gain clan-wide recognition among the Gadabuursi, so the British appointed *Ugaas* Robleh's son, Daudi, supported by other important Gadabuursi personalities. These adjuncts to Daudi were revealingly called 'trade agents' by the British, and their appointed task was to attract Gadabuursi goods and grain away from Ethiopian jurisdiction into the Protectorate.

Meanwhile, Daudi's father, *Ugaas* Robleh, continued to work for the Ethiopian government who maintained their claim to the Gadabuursi as an 'Ethiopian' clan. However, under the more stringent conditions of Gadla-Giyorgis's rule and the evident economic and agricultural success among the Gadabuursi of the Protectorate, *Ugaas* Robleh became disgruntled and returned to British territory. In the meantime his son Daudi went over to the Ethiopians and Governor Gadla-Giyorgis, helping to collect tax and registering sections of Gadabuursi as 'Ethiopians'. Daudi eventually earned himself the Ethiopian title of *Grazmach* (Kittermaster 1926a; Plowman1926).

The struggle to claim Gadabuursi became intense. In November 1923 a British Gadabuursi was killed by an Ethiopian party trying to collect taxes from a village at the frontier (Kittermaster 1925). In another instance the Ethiopian police arrested a trading caravan for smuggling grain to the Protectorate, but local (presumably Gadabuursi) Somalis killed the police and the caravan escaped to the Protectorate (Plowman 1925). When Gadla-Giyorgis proceeded to levy a camel tax on all caravans of grain going out of Jigjiga district, many Somalis were roused, and by 1925 five Ethiopian tax collectors had been murdered (Summary of Intelligence Reports 1925).

In an attempt to stop the leakage of grain and revenue from trade from Jigjiga to the Protectorate, Gadla-Giyorgis resorted to more forceful measures. He put Daudi Robleh in charge of armed bodies of irregular Somali police whose role was to collect customs dues at the border and grain taxes, and to register sections of the Gadabuursi as Ethiopian. The methods the Somali irregulars used were often violent, and levies of customs dues quickly escalated into the plunder of entire caravans, with some of these gains being sent back to Gadla-Giyorgis and some being kept for themselves (Kittermaster 1926b).

The Ethiopian border administration under Gadla-Giyorgis was exposed to continued British criticism throughout the 1920s. Many of the incidents came about through Gadla-Giyorgis' vigilance in the collection of revenue which the British saw as 'maladministration'. Finally in June 1927 the British were given real cause for complaint when the zealous Gadla-Giyorgis attacked a Somali caravan for 'taxes', not realizing, however, that the caravan was carrying the property of the ex-Governor of Somaliland, Archer, who was accompanying the Maharajah of Kutch on a shooting expedition in southern Ethiopia (Plowman 1927b). On account of this unfortunate incident, the Ethiopian government was obliged to remove Gadla-Giyorgis, much to the satisfaction of the British (Archer 1927).

Nevertheless, the Gadabuursi continued to exploit their ambiguous status and the affordances of boundary administration, a situation that had suited the British up to a point. However, by 1930 the situation had changed. The then Governor of the Protectorate, Harold Kittermaster, wrote:

The question of the border tribes is becoming increasingly urgent. His Imperial Majesty Haile Selassie is apparently making genuine attempts to improve the administration of the border districts and naturally the indefinite procedure of the past must be improved. Cases are being constantly filed in the Buramo [Borama] court against Gadabursi who have always been regarded as British but who are now living in Abyssinia and if application is made to the Abyssinian authorities for the execution of the judgements they challenge the validity of the British courts to try the case at all. ... In view of the closer administration of the district by the Abyssinians I now withdraw the opinion I expressed two years ago that the demarcation of the border should be postponed as long as possible. I think it should be undertaken at once. (Kittermaster 1930)

Later that year there was an ugly incident during a dispute over the Ethiopian right to tax certain sections of the Gadabuursi clan. During a meeting at the border between the new Governor of Jigjiga, *Fitawrari* Taffassa, and his British counterpart in Borama, District Officer Walsh, to resolve taxation rights and dues, tensions escalated and shots were fired. A number of Ethiopians were killed (Walsh 1942).

Problems continued to bedevil Gadabuursi country near the border with the British Protectorate's Borama district, since Ethiopian soldiers regularly prevented grain and other produce from being taken across the border for sale (Addis Ababa Intelligence Report 1931). Later in 1934 when the Ethiopian government introduced a 'poll tax' to their side of the border, it immediately provoked the old problem of the dual nationality of Gadabuursi when, as in the past, the local officials at Jigjiga taxed all the Gadabuursi present in Ethiopia regardless of their 'nationality' (Somaliland Protectorate Intelligence Report1934).

The intervention of the Italian invasion of Ethiopia and British Somaliland, the Italian defeat and the subsequent administration of the eastern Ethiopian periphery by the British Military Administration 'solved' the borderland problems for a time. However, in the post-war period the division of the Gadabuursi clan on either side of the border was the most perennial of the 'borderland' problems, and many Gadabursi cases were included in the deliberations of the Harar conferences in the 1950s.

Conclusion

Though it is not always explicit in the written records, it is evident that Gadabuursi 'agricultural' clans were actively engaged in using the affordances of the border to full effect. For some, the less stringent fiscal demands of the early British colonial regime made an Ethiopian nationality less attractive. However, it is also clear that some elements preferred being Ethiopian for various reasons, for example to evade court cases in the Protectorate. The divide in the Gadabuursi ruling family hints at a wider Gadabuursi agency in the exploitation of borderland affordances. The choice between territorial administrations was a complex calculation of short-term 'household' interests – rational economic decisions – as well as wider questions of the relative strengths of other Somali clans, past experience and future ambitions.

References

(Abbreviations: PRO – Public Records Office, Kew, UK; FO – Foreign Office, BSP – British Somaliland Protectorate)

Addis Ababa Intelligence Report, 1931 (Barton to Henderson, Addis Ababa, 3 February 1931, PRO: FO 371/15389/J571).

Archer, 1918 (Enclosure No. 1, Archer to Long, Sheikh, [BSP], 6 November 1918, in Colonial Office to Foreign Office, 22 January 1919, PRO: FO 371/3497/12877)

Archer, 1927 (Archer to Plowman, Jigjiga, 21 July 1927, PRO, FO 371/12351/J2286/1446/1).

Barnes, C. 2004. 'The Political Economy of Somali Nationalism in Eastern Ethiopia *circa* 1941–48', in A. Kusow (ed.), *Putting the Cart before the Horse: Inverted Nationalism and the Crisis of Identity in Somalia*. Trenton, NJ: Red Sea Press, pp. 33–57.

Drysdale, J. 1964. *The Somali Dispute*. London: Pall Mall Press.

Kakwenzire, P. 1976. 'Colonial Rule in the British Somaliland Protectorate, 1905–39'. (Unpub. PhD dissertation, London University.)

Kittermaster, Harold. 1925 (Kittermaster to Amery, Sheikh [BSP], 15 August 1925), PRO:FO371/10875/J2691/897/1.

—— 1926a (Kittermaster to Bentinck, Sheikh [BSP], 20 February 1926, PRO: FO 371/11559/J805/8/1).

—— 1926b (Kittermaster to Bentinck, Sheikh [BSP], 18 February 1926, PRO: FO 371/11559/J827/8/1).

—— 1930, (Kittermaster to Passfield, Sheikh [BSP], 16 May 1930, PRO: FO 371/14593/J2099).

Lascelles, 1948. 'Observations concerning the problem of the Hawd' (Lascelles to Bevin, British Legation, Addis Ababa, 16 October 1948, PRO: FO 371/69294/J6841).

Lewis, I. M. 1961. *A Pastoral Democracy: A Study of Pastoralism and Politics among the Northern Somali of the Horn of Africa*. Oxford: Oxford University Press.

Marcus, H. G. 1965. 'The Rodd Mission of 1897'. *Journal of Ethiopian Studies* 3(2): 25–36.

Monthly Intelligence Report, 1923 ('Monthly Intelligence Report for March', Addis Ababa, April 1923, PRO: FO 371/8408/A2436/2276/1).

—— 1924 ('Monthly Intelligence Report, Addis Ababa for October', November 1924, PRO:FO 371/9994/E11310/173/1).

Plowman, 1925 (Plowman to Assistant Secretary, Berbera [BSP], Harar, 15 March 1925, PRO: FO 371/10874/J3565/681/1).

—— 1926 (Plowman to Bentinck, Harar, 30 December 1926, PRO: FO 371/12344/J229/54/1).

—— 1927a (Report on Harar Province, C. H. F. Plowman', Harar, 13 August 1927, PRO: FO 371/12353/J2925/1).

—— 1927b (Plowman to Bentinck, Harar, 23 July 1927, PRO: FO 371/12351/J2284/1446/1).

Samatar, A. I. 1989. *The State and Rural Transformation in Northern Somalia 1884–1986*. Madison, WI: University of Wisconsin Press.

Silberman, L. 1961 'Why the Haud was Ceded'. *Cahiers d'Etudes Africaines*, 5(2): 37–83.

Somaliland Protectorate Intelligence Report. 1934. ('Somaliland Protectorate Intelligence Report' Major C. V. Bennet, Burao [BSP], 31 December 1934, PRO: FO 371/19104/J758).

Stebbing, J. 1956. 'Minutes of the Harar Conference between Representatives of the Somaliland Protectorate Government and the Imperial Ethiopian Government, 12 December 1955 – 21 January 1956', Mss. Afr.s.2109, Rhodes House Library, University of Oxford.

Summary of Intelligence Reports. 1925 ('Summary of Intelligence Reports for 1925', Addis Ababa, 10 October 1925, PRO: FO 371/10878/J3349/2480/1).

Summers, 1923. (Summers to Russell, Sheikh [BSP], 10 October 1923, PRO: FO 371/9986/E3447/363/1).

Walsh, D.C. 1942. 'History of Borama station in Zeila District of British Somaliland Protectorate' – (written from memory in 1942 after the original record was lost during the evacuation of BSP in 1940), Mss. Afr.s.605, Rhodes House Library, Oxford.

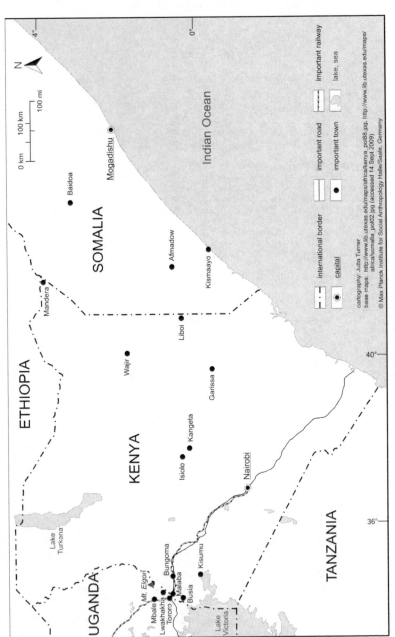

Map 4 *Kenyan borderlands*

cartography: Jutta Turner
base maps: http://www.lib.utexas.edu/maps/africa/kenya_pol88.jpg, http://www.lib.utexas.edu/maps/
             africa/somalia_pol02.jpg (accessed 14 Sept 2009)
© Max Planck Institute for Social Anthropology Halle/Saale, Germany

Legend:
- international border
- ⊙ capital
- important road
- ● important town
- important railway
- lake, sea

Places labelled on map:
ETHIOPIA
SOMALIA
KENYA
UGANDA
TANZANIA
Indian Ocean
Lake Turkana
Lake Victoria
Mt. Elgon

Mogadishu
Baidoa
Afmadow
Kismaayo
Mandera
Liboi
Wajir
Garissa
Isiolo
Kangeta
Nairobi
Bungoma
Mbale
Lwakhakha
Tororo
Malaba
Busia
Kisumu

Scale: 0 km 100 km / 100 mi

Eight

~~~~~~

The Opportunistic Economics
of the Kenya-Somali Borderland
in Historical Perspective

LEE CASSANELLI

Introduction

The history of the Somalia-Kenya borderland over the past century offers a classic example of the ways international boundaries can create opportunities as well as hardships for the peoples who live along and across them. This borderland has long been a site of contact among various ethnic/linguistic communities, among sedentary and mobile populations, and among competing political authorities with different concepts of sovereignty and legitimacy (see, e.g., Schlee 1989; Menkhaus 2005). Over time, these interacting groups constructed a series of cross-border alliances, financial networks and commercial mechanisms which came to constitute a distinct and dynamic frontier economy. While operating largely outside the 'official' economies of colonial and independent Kenya and Somalia, borderland traders contributed substantially to the growth of several sectors of both national economies in the past and have more recently become important actors in the emergence of a wider regional economy in the Horn of Africa.

While the topic of cross-border trade has not been completely ignored in the historical literature, most contemporary scholarship on the Kenya-Somalia frontier has been preoccupied with issues of ethnic conflict, political instability and criminal activity, giving the impression that the borderlands were at best a costly nuisance and at worst a serious security threat to states in the region. It is certainly the case that many economic activities associated with the border areas such as livestock raiding, banditry, smuggling, gun-running and the like were and still are considered illegal by state authorities, and as such have required policing and occasional military intervention by those authorities. Other forms of quasi-legal business that crossed the border, such as the long-standing commerce in *miraa* (a mild plant stimulant used widely in the Horn of Africa) or

133

livestock, usually fall into the category of informal or second economies, which by definition are difficult to document and not readily susceptible to formal economic analysis. The result is that borderland economies have not been systematically analyzed as historical systems in their own right.[1]

In keeping with this book's theme, I want to reframe the discussion by placing cross-border trade at the centre of the analysis rather than at the periphery, so as to emphasize the agency of its economic actors. The recent explosion of transnational studies (in disciplines ranging from history and geography to anthropology and sociology) has begun to reveal the extent and impact of cross-border commodity, currency and refugee flows in many parts of contemporary Africa. The Kenya-Somalia case reminds us that cross-border transactions often have a history reaching back to the early colonial era, and that the seemingly marginal traders of the borderland have in fact been important agents of economic change well beyond their own frontier communities for more than a century.[2]

Emphasizing the dynamic role of borderlands trade in the modern economic histories of Kenya and Somalia does not mean ignoring the frequently disruptive or dysfunctional aspects of that trade, nor does it deny the very real dangers that conflict over scarce resources, emerging economic inequalities, brigandage and trafficking in illicit goods along the frontier have posed to national governments in the Horn (see, for example, Murunga 2005). It is simply to shift our angle of vision away from state-centred narratives and to look at the borderlands trade on its own terrain, with its own historical trajectory.

To take the argument one step further, I want to suggest that beyond simply affording its inhabitants the freedom to trade, migrate and manage their affairs in their own way, the borderland economy has been a catalyst for the Kenyan and Somali economies more broadly. It may even offer us a glimpse of what a future trans-regional economy in the Horn will look like. The kinds of commercial innovations described here as characteristic of the Kenya–Somalia borderland have also begun to emerge along the Berbera corridor which links the self-proclaimed Republic of Somaliland with eastern Ethiopia. Communities on both sides of that border have experienced booms in the transport, construction, and service industries, which have in turn stimulated commercial agreements between the two governments and investments from overseas Ethiopians and Somalis. The proliferation of consumer goods made available via the duty-free shop of a stateless Somalia (Hagmann 2005) is not simply a borderlands phenomenon but one that is linked to and has repercussions for the entire Horn. The cross-border networks established by frontier traders in east and northeast Africa during the colonial era have actually grown in scale and substance since the collapse of the Somali state, as illustrated, for example, by the diffusion of *hawala* (money transfer systems) which first gained attention in the early days of Somalia's civil war. Peter Little has recently even suggested that a 'Greater Somalia' of trade and finance networks has expanded beyond the Horn of Africa to encompass parts of the Middle East and to link numerous international cities to Somalia (Little 2005: 9–10).

Brief administrative history of the Kenya-Somalia borderlands

Nineteenth-century European travellers frequently noted the vitality of the inland caravan trade in the Horn of Africa. Numerous sources described the long-distance routes across the region that would later become the Kenya-Somalia borderlands, and stressed their future commercial potential.[3] However, once the colonial boundaries were firmly established, European officials came to regard the area between the Juba and Tana rivers more as a geographical buffer zone than as a target of economic opportunity. There were good reasons for their attitudes. The vast plains between British Kenya and Italian Somaliland included some of the most arid districts in the new colonies, suitable only for the pursuit of nomadic pastoralism. Colonial planners saw the future in commercial agriculture, and so invested in the fertile highlands of Kenya and the irrigable lands along the Shabelle and Juba river valleys in Italian Somaliland. They effectively left the sparsely populated and inaccessible frontier zones to fend for themselves. Indeed, part of the process of constructing colonial states and economies in the Horn involved the construction of their borderlands, not only as geographical spaces to be administered separately from the core agricultural districts, but also as conceptual spaces whose residents and resources were thought of as outliers in every sense. Even colonial nomenclature reflected this categorical remoteness: in Kenya, the 'Northern Frontier Province'; in Italian Somaliland, 'Oltre-Giuba', or the land beyond the Juba.

When the state paid any attention at all to the frontier, it was mainly to halt raids by unruly pastoralists into the settled districts, or to prevent them from displacing more tranquil livestock-keepers like the Oromo.[4] Kenyan authorities sought to confine the pastoral populations of the remote northeast to a series of tribal territories, or blocks. The Northern Frontier District (NFD) was administered separately under a series of special ordinances which revealed the government's official attitude towards the region.[5] The NFD's administrative border also constituted a boundary between different levels of state investment in infrastructure and social services, reflecting the different futures envisioned for the colony's core and periphery. While Kenya's peasant farmers and white settlers were to provide the 'platform for upcountry Kenya's European-style modernization,' its north-eastern pastoralists were left to pursue their traditional ways of subsistence (Goldsmith 1997: 15).

Containment and neglect also characterized the frontier policy of the Italians in Somalia. The lower Juba valley, which formed part of the initial boundary with British Kenya, was the site of Somalia's earliest colonial experiments in European plantation agriculture. The Italian authorities were chiefly concerned to safeguard the Italian concessions from raids by the pastoral clans resident in adjacent British Jubaland. After acquiring the Jubaland province from the British in 1924 as a reward for joining the Allies in World War I, the Italians continued their predecessors' policy of paying local *askaris* (chiefly Harti clansmen from the Kismaayo district) to maintain security in the border regions. The Italians invested few resources in the trans-Juba area, turning their energies instead to the frontier with Ethiopia in the build-up to the Fascist invasion of that country in 1935.[6]

Following the collapse of the Italian East African empire in 1941, ex-Italian Somaliland came under the control of a British Military Administration (BMA), which brought many northern Somalis from the British Protectorate to the south as soldiers and civil servants. British rule also brought the borderlands between Somalia and Kenya under the same European power for the first time; in retrospect, this arrangement seems to have offered the single best opportunity in the region's history to create a legal, officially sanctioned 'open border'. But British Foreign Minister Bevin's proposal to establish a Greater Somalia in the Horn (with its potential for closer economic ties to Kenya) was thwarted when the United Nations Four-Power Commission opted to return southern Somalia to the Italians as a Trust Territory. From 1950 to 1960, the Italian Trusteeship Administration (AFIS) put considerable planning and resources into their mandate, but did little in the trans-Juba area apart from sinking a few wells. During the same period, British Kenya's resources were being drained by the Mau Mau rebellion in the Central Province, leaving little for the remote NFD.

Only as the colonial era came to an end did the Kenya-Somalia border become an international issue. While economic interest in the borderlands remained negligible, the political concerns of the departing European powers proved to be well-founded. The contentious history of the NFD in the early independence era is well known (Lewis 1963; Drysdale 1964; Mburu 2005). The 1962 referendum which found that the majority of Kenya's Somalis wished to join the newly independent Somali Republic was rejected by the outgoing British and the incoming Kenyatta administrations. Kenya's repudiation of the referendum's results prompted a series of skirmishes known as the *shifta* wars between Kenyan authorities and small bands of armed Somalis in the NFD who enjoyed considerable support from the Republic next door. Unrest in the region remained a source of political anxiety for the independent government of Kenya throughout the 1960s and reinforced the image of the frontier district as a source of chronic violence and insecurity.

Only in the 1970s did the borderlands, particularly their southern half, begin to attract serious economic interest from state authorities. On the Somali side, the authoritarian regime of Mohamed Siyad Barre sought to turn Kismaayo, the chief seaport for the region, into a major livestock-export centre for southern Somalia and hence a source of foreign-exchange earnings for the state. With assistance from the World Bank (the Trans-Juba Livestock Project) and USAID (Kismaayo Port Project), the Somali government sank a number of mechanized boreholes along inland stock routes and began to modernize the livestock holding facilities and infrastructure at the Kismaayo port (Little 2003: 34, 39-42).[7] On the Kenyan side, the prolonged drought of the early 1970s raised fears of growing desertification and called attention to the fragile ecology of the borderlands which appeared to be deteriorating. National and international agencies launched relief and resettlement projects and commissioned studies of local environmental practices in many districts of north-eastern Kenya.[8] The Kenyan borderlands received even greater global exposure with the influx of refugees from Ethiopia and Somalia, beginning in the 1970s and reaching massive proportions following the collapse of the Somali state in 1991. The UNHCR and countless NGOs poured money and manpower into refugee camps and rehabilitation projects. When Kenya chose to relocate its burgeoning refugee camps to remote sites close to the Somali border, international relief aid flowed to these areas. Ironically, Kenya's long-standing strategy of containing its Somali population in the frontier districts led in this instance to the injection of vast amounts of money, construction materials, and salaried personnel into the NFD. The subsequent economic boom which the refugee industry brought to the borderlands – in the form of jobs, school construction, medical services, and new markets for consumer goods – soon spread far beyond the camps (Hyndman 1997, 1999). What Menkhaus (2005) calls the globalization of the borderland economy was reflected in the appearance of new shops, the construction of small airstrips, and the introduction of a regular bus service between the NFD and Nairobi.

Borderland trade in the pre-colonial and early colonial era

Since 1990, the economic vitality of the borderland districts has become visible to the outside world. But the residents of the borderlands had long been involved in the wider economy of the region. As noted above, camel caravans were traversing the area for at least half a century before the European partition of Africa. This pre-colonial commerce involved the transport of high-value products like ivory, rhinoceros horn, ostrich feathers and rare animal skins from points as far inland as Lake Turkana and the upper Juba river to ports along the Somali and Swahili coasts. Because of the foreign demand for these products, they were frequently mentioned in European travel accounts of the time as well as in commercial surveys conducted by early colonial administrators. In contrast, commodities destined for African consumption (such as natron salt, medicinal plants, meat and farm products, etc.) received scant attention in the written sources, even where they moved over long distances. Until quite recently, trade which served African consumers and generated no revenues for the state was of little interest to administrators and policy-makers. This pattern helps to explain why much of the important cross-border commerce discussed below was virtually undocumented before contemporary times.

One form of early cross-border trade which did draw the attention of colonial officials was the continuing traffic in ivory and animal trophies. As early as 1897 Kenya's colonial government enacted game laws that enabled it to collect revenue on ivory exports at official stations and to impose sanctions on violators. This was one of the earliest attempts by the Nairobi authorities to undercut the independent caravan trade through the borderlands; it was the start of a policy which promoted commerce based on townships and licensed shopkeepers (predominantly Asian immigrants) whom the state could regulate and tax. The notion that unlicensed itinerant traders were parasitic, unproductive, and resistant to modern monetary transactions was typical of administrative attitudes throughout much of the colonial era.

Somali ivory traders responded by refusing to register under the trophy laws –after 1927, there were no Somali names on the lists of licensed rhino and elephant hunters – and by redirecting some of the traffic in ivory and skins away from the British-controlled port of Kismaayo to markets in Ethiopia, where there were no export restrictions and prices were higher. Following the transfer of British Jubaland to Italy in 1925, the British attempted to lure the trade away from Kismaayo (now under Italian control) to alternative ports in Kenya, chiefly by improving roads and introducing lorries to the towns of the north-eastern province. However, Somali traders from the NFD ignored the new boundary and continued to take their ivory by camel caravan to established dealers in Kismaayo. British authorities accused the Harti traders in Kismaayo of exercising a practical monopoly as middlemen in the illicit ivory trade (Dalleo 1979). From the perspective of the Kenya Somali traders, the commerce was not illicit but simply a continuation of what they had been doing for at least three generations. At the same time, the higher costs of doing business on the Kenya side gave them further incentive to 'transgress' the border and to continue to direct their business to Kismaayo.

Other Somali entrepreneurs, however, found commercial opportunities in the British colony. Colonial records report that several alien Somalis – the term was used by British authorities to designate Harti and Isaaq Somalis who had come into Kenya from the Somalilands – had set up *dukas* (shops) in the new townships of Wajir, Garissa, Isiolo and several smaller NFD settlements. British authorities often mistrusted these immigrants from across the border because of their tendencies to evade taxation and to traffick in livestock without licensing; nevertheless, they reluctantly accepted the alien Somalis because of their active contribution to the growth of the new township economies in Kenya (Dalleo 1975: Ch. 3).

Social networks, not colonial boundaries, provided the grid upon which the frontier traders operated. Clan ties cut across all of the Horn's artificially created boundaries, enabling traders to readjust their routes when necessary and to circumvent the regulatory regimes imposed by the colonial states. Even in wartime, when colonial authorities were especially vigilant, cross-border trade flourished. A good example comes from the 1930s, as the Fascist administration in Italian Somaliland began to mobilize the colony's resources for the expected invasion of Ethiopia. In an effort to stockpile supplies within its colony, the Mogadishu government prohibited all exports in kind, including livestock, initially permitting only the export of Italian currency (lira) for the purchase of trucks and military material from suppliers in Kenya. By 1936 the occupation of Ethiopia had begun, Italian soldiers were confiscating Ethiopian cattle, and the export of lira beyond the Italian-controlled areas was prohibited. Nonetheless, in the first half of 1936 more than 2.5 million lira were reportedly exchanged in the Kenya frontier town of Wajir, where Kenyan Somalis purchased livestock trekked in from Ethiopia and then smuggled them into Somalia through kinsmen who resold them to the Italian authorities at a substantial profit.[9] As a footnote, in late September 1936, when news reached Kenya that the devaluation of the lira was imminent, trade stopped with a suddenness that no policy controls could have produced (Smith 1969).

What these few examples reveal is that smuggling and illicit trade were labels imposed by colonial policemen on transactions among African traders whose networks straddled political boundaries and in most cases actually predated the establishment of those boundaries. The labels stigmatized an African commerce which was simply following the logic of supply and demand across a fluid economic region, rather than adhering to the logic of colonial autarky which sought to confine trade within static political boundaries.[10] As Smith observed in the wartime example noted above, 'the British and Italian Governments both applied policies designed to reduce their imports without any reference to either the established pre-colonial trade routes or the practical demonstration that the Africans of the least developed Province in Kenya were able to trade effectively in unrestricted markets with fluctuating currencies' (Smith 1969: 42).

THE *MIRAA* TRADE

While specialists on the Horn are familiar with the importance of *miraa* (khat) in the contemporary economies of Kenya and Somalia, the colonial history of the *miraa* trade is not so well known. The rise of *miraa* to its current status as the most successful indigenous cash crop in Kenya began in the years before World War II (Cassanelli 1986; Goldsmith 1997). Though its use today is widely associated with the Somalis, *miraa* has a long cultural history among the Meru as well, who cultivated it in the Nyambene Mountains of central Kenya. For generations, the Meru chewed *miraa* leaves during initiation ceremonies and at important meetings of the elders' councils (*njuru*). The product eventually made its way from Meru to Nairobi during the interwar period, where it found a small market among African Muslims, notably Swahilis and the few Somalis who resided in the town. As British colonial authorities relaxed their restrictions on African urban settlement during World War II, *miraa*'s popularity among town residents increased, though it continued to be associated with Swahili ghettoes and with the urban underclass more generally (Goldsmith 1997: 16).

The role of Kenya's Somalis as major consumers and traders of *miraa* also clearly predates World War II, although the evidence is rather sparse.[11] As Goldsmith notes, the Nyambene range in northern Meru was unique among the highland areas of Kenya in its connections with the pastoral populations of northern Kenya. These included the Somalis, many of whom settled in Isiolo following their service as soldiers with the British army in World War I. At the same time, the growth of Nairobi's population stimulated the demand for meat, leading highland traders to seek out new sources of livestock from rangelands in the NFD. Isiolo town soon became the terminus for animals supplied by Somali traders to buyers from Nairobi. It appears that 'the formal *miraa* trade [also] dates back to this time as Igembe [Meru] began making the long day's walk from Kangeta to Isiolo in order to supply the growing numbers of Isiolo-based Somalis with the product' (Goldsmith 1997: 17). As most of the ex-Somali soldiers and policemen living in Kenya were Isaaq and Dhulba-hante from northern Somaliland, they were probably already familiar with Ethiopian khat. As they steadily fanned out across Kenya, northern Tanzania, and eastern Zaire to start small businesses and to enter the long-distance transport sector, these Somalis helped spread the use of *miraa* throughout East Africa.

Increased *miraa* consumption in Somalia itself was probably associated with the growing purchasing power of Somali civil servants and ex-soldiers, many of whom found salaried employment with the BMA[12] during World War II and later with the AFIS administration. Evidence of the growing use of khat can be found even earlier in government attempts to regulate it. As early as 1921, authorities in British Somaliland had restricted licences for the import of Ethiopian khat to four Somali dealers, in an effort to raise the price to the point where ordinary Somalis could not afford it.[13] The ban was re-imposed in 1939 on the eve of Britain's war with Italy over control of the Horn, for fear that cross-border khat traders from Ethiopia might be spies for the Italian administration. After the war, the BMA continued to prohibit the import of the plant apparently because it was being used by political organizers to attract Somalis into meetings of the fledgling Somali Youth League, which was demanding immediate self-government for Somalia.

The Kenya Colony government imposed a similar ban in 1945, following a series of articles in the *East Africa Medical Journal* purportedly providing scientific evidence that *miraa* induced mental illness. (Apparently, only one case was cited to prove the claim!) The point here is that recurrent colonial legislation against *miraa* seems to indicate the existence of an active regional commerce in the commodity which operated outside the official network of licensed traders and shopkeepers. While we can infer that the *miraa* trade was continuous, it seemed to draw official attention and condemnation particularly at times of wartime anxiety or political unrest.

Miraa's transformation from a localized cultural commodity to a highly profitable commercial crop has recently made news in the outside world because of its growing use within African (primarily Somali) émigré communities in Europe and North America. Yet the economic factors working in its favour were well known to East African producers, consumers, and traders long before outsiders took notice. During the twentieth century, *miraa* cultivation was able to expand in highland Kenya 'unencumbered by the formal production and marketing institutions governing other smallholder crops'. Unlike coffee, for example, *miraa*'s use reinforced indigenous institutions (such as Meru life-cycle rituals) and 'remained anchored in local agroforestry systems, generating fodder and fuel wood as well as food'. It provided income for women as distributors and retailers and supported household self-sufficiency (Goldsmith 1997: 17-18). Moreover, because *miraa* consumption was a non-western social activity, the marketing network expanded ties between Nyambene hills growers and other African communities like the Somali and the Swahili.[14]

We have already noted how *miraa*'s expansion into Kenya's Isiolo district was tied to the growing Somali cattle trade between the northern frontier rangelands and urban Nairobi. Somalis with cross-border clan ties also pioneered the *miraa* trade from Kenya to southern Somalia and more recently to markets in Europe and North America. The ripple effects of their enterprise reached other parts of Kenya and East Africa as well. Since World War II, commercial *miraa* production has spread from its traditional niche in the Njia area of Igembe to become the main cash crop in the Nyambene Range's fertile and densely populated interior valleys. After independence, the Igembe continued to play a dominant role in the regional marketing network, and the ever-expanding industry produced a long-running (though highly localized) economic boom in northern Nyambene. The need for Land Rovers refitted with heavy-duty suspension systems to carry fresh *miraa* leaves rapidly across the border into Somalia brought drivers, mechanics, and construction workers directly and indirectly into the *miraa* business. In the past two decades, the introduction of small airplanes to reach more remote towns in central Somalia has added a new chapter to *miraa*'s remarkable economic success story.

'Because *miraa* is a profitable crop which generates high formal revenues (e.g. airfreight charges) and considerable informal ones (e.g., pay-offs at police roadblocks), the Kenya Government has quietly been revising its negative-to-neutral stance vis-à-vis the commodity in recognition of the foreign exchange and tax revenues it generates' (Goldsmith 1997: 17). In addition, its spreading social legitimacy and increasing use by elite consumers both in the Horn and overseas enable the authorities to ignore the criticisms that appear periodically in the popular press with regard to the negative effects of *miraa* consumption.[15]

Meanwhile, the cross-border trade in *miraa* has evolved in response to political transitions. For example, even after Somalia's President Mohamed Siyad Barre in 1984 banned khat ostensibly on the grounds that its widespread consumption was hindering national development and draining the country's hard currency, Kenyan *miraa* continued to flow into Somalia. The reasons were clear: Siyad's ban was intended to take the lucrative *miraa* commerce away from the Isaaq (who had been using some of the revenues to fund resistance to the Barre regime) and transfer it to his own political allies. As Goldsmith (1997: 20, n.18) reports, 'after the ban *miraa* destined for Somalia was delivered to a special depot in Kaelo (several kilometers below Laare), flown to Mandera, shipped across the border [into Somalia] on camels, and picked up by army landrovers who sped it to Mogadishu and Kismayu [sic]'. Meanwhile, Isaaq exporters who had been pushed out of the Mogadishu *miraa* trade began to supply it to consumers in the growing Somali refugee camps in Kenya and to Somali communities abroad, notably in the UK.

While catalyzing several sectors of Kenya's economy, the expanding *miraa* trade invariably generated new economic and ethnic tensions as well. Kenyan Somalis who had grown rich by supplying growing markets for *miraa* in Somalia, the UK, and Eastleigh (Nairobi) began to penetrate Meru supply networks and replace traditional Igembe middlemen with their own agents. When Somali traders began to use their accumulated capital to acquire *miraa* plots in the Nyambene hills, the Igembe responded by pressuring the Kenya government to ban Somali agents from the Meru reserve and launched a short-lived strike on *miraa* exports at the start of Ramadan in 1995. Protracted negotiations mediated by the local administration helped resolve the crisis (Goldsmith 1997: 21-23). While Goldsmith may have been excessively optimistic in suggesting that the resolution of the crisis 'may mark the rise of a new kind of synthetic local institution harmonizing differences among ethnic groups operating within what has been an informal economic sector guided by internal cultural structures,' the episode does point up how the success of the trans-border (and transnational) *miraa* trade has impacted many areas of Kenya's economy, from casual employment to markets in land.

The trans-border livestock trade

The history of the livestock trade between Somalia and Kenya has many parallels with the *miraa* story. Cross-border activity in livestock expanded steadily (if not as dramatically as *miraa*) over the past century. The major commodity has been cattle on the hoof, along with sheep and goats, which typically moved from pastures on the Somalia side of the border to urban markets in Kenya, though occasionally the flow was reversed, as we shall see. The main engines driving the trade since 1950 have been the ever-growing demand for meat among consumers with increased purchasing power in Kenya, and the demand for live Somali sheep and goats in Saudi Arabia, especially during the pilgrimage season. More recently, borderland livestock traders not only survived the collapse of the Somali state but appear to have turned the stateless condition to their advantage. In the absence of any regulatory mechanisms on the Somalia side of the border after 1991, whatever pressures may have existed to restrict the commerce came from interests on the Kenya side, primarily from Kenya's own livestock sector. Here again, however, the economic benefits of the cross-border trade have diffused widely enough in Kenya to relieve the pressure for government regulation.[16]

As in the case of *miraa*, the contemporary cross-border trade in livestock is rooted in a much longer history of economic and social relations among the region's diverse populations. That history reveals the opportunistic character of the borderlands trade, which depended on the mobility and husbandry skills of the local pastoralists. The early development of Kismaayo's animal export trade is a case in point. Kismaayo's importance in the livestock trade resulted from the convergence of two distinct Somali migratory movements in the second half of the nineteenth century: the Ogaden pastoral migrations into the Afmadow area (whence they displaced the southern Oromo), and the arrival of Harti traders from northeast Somalia looking for commercial opportunities along the southern Somali coast. As we have already seen, the enterprising Harti used British restrictions on animal trophy exports from Kenya to build up a lucrative cross-border business in Kismaayo; they subsequently came to play a key role as middlemen in the livestock export trade as well.

Livestock exported through Kismaayo came primarily from the herds of the Mohamed Zubeir and Aulihan, part of the Somali Ogaden clan, which had occupied the rich pastures west of the Juba in the mid-nineteenth century. The Ogaden soon controlled the major stock routes from the interior and became the dominant suppliers of cattle and hides to the planters of the French Mascarene islands and the leather merchants representing the shoe industries of Europe and the US. This modest nineteenth-century trade provided the pastoral clans of Somalia's borderlands with their first link to international markets and anticipated their later involvement in the boom in livestock exports to Saudi Arabia after 1950.

Interestingly, the Ogaden pastoralists generally were not big cattle merchants. That role fell to the aforementioned Harti, who had emigrated from the north to Kismaayo in the 1870s (and. as we saw, later appeared as livestock dealers in the townships of the NFD). The division of labour between Ogaden suppliers and Harti dealers required the two clans to forge a variety of personal, business and marital alliances over the years to ensure the steady flow of cattle through Wajir for export at Kismaayo.[17]

Their partnership permitted the Ogaden, whose grazing lands straddled the border between Somalia and Kenya, to supply both the Kenya and Kismaayo markets with cattle during the colonial period. Whenever excessive conflict, localized droughts, colonial quarantines, or currency restrictions limited their access to markets in one of the colonies, they could redirect their trade to markets in the other territory.

Over the course of the twentieth century, reversals in the flow of cattle between Kenya and Somalia occurred quite regularly, depending on political conditions and market prices (Little 2003, esp. Ch. 5). As we saw earlier, for example, cattle from Kenya's NFD tended to move to Somalia when Italian wartime preparations in the 1920s and 1930s raised demand and market prices there. A similar pattern occurred from the 1970s to the early 1980s, when Mogadishu's urban population was growing rapidly and Saudi purchases of Somali stock for slaughter during the hajj were at their peak. On the other hand, Kenyan markets were generally more attractive to livestock producers on both sides of the border as Nairobi grew during the 1950s and 1960s, and again following the quarantines on Somali livestock by the Saudi government in 1983 and 1999, which drastically lowered animal prices for exporters in Kismaayo and Mogadishu.

These fluctuations remind us that borders afford opportunities for traders and herders who straddle them precisely because the 'national' markets on each side of the border are subject to their own demographic and regulatory trends; these trends, along with variable weather conditions, can affect the forces of supply and demand to the temporary advantage of one market or the other. Those actors with a foot in both economies are well positioned to take advantage of these price differentials, but the affordances are neither automatic nor invariably beneficial for borderlanders. Cross-border trade involves competition as well as co-operation, and new opportunities on one side of the border can easily produce conflict even as they hold out the prospect of windfall profits. While analysts are often prone to emphasize either the integrative (and functional) aspects of cross-border trade or their disruptive (and dysfunctional) tendencies, an historical perspective reveals that both have been an inherent part of the borderland dynamic.

The collapse of the Somali state in 1991 provided a major test of the viability of the cross-border livestock trade. As we saw previously, when civil strife strained relations between Harti and Ogaden and broke the livestock chain to Kismaayo, cross-border cattle trade into Kenya not only survived but actually increased. In part, this was because Kenya's borderland traders were able to maintain their links with Ogaden suppliers in Somalia; in part, it was simply that livestock prices were higher in the Kenyan markets. Between 1991 and 1998, the aggregate value of cattle sales in Garissa, Kenya (which received most of its goods from cross-border suppliers in Somalia) grew by a remarkable 500 per cent; and prices at the Kenya border town of Liboi doubled between 1987–88 and 1996 (ibid.: 5–7). On the other hand, the national cattle market in

Mogadishu was negatively affected by the post-1991 civil war: prices were actually lower in 1998 than in 1987 (Little 2005: 7). One consequence of these price differentials[18] was the extension of the catchment area – i.e., the territory from which cattle destined for the Kenya market are drawn – much deeper into southern Somalia. Whereas in 1986 the eastern boundary of the catchment area was the Juba River, by 1998 it had reached the Doy pasturelands south-east of Baidoa (see the map in Little 2003: 102). In other words, the area affected by the trans-border trade had expanded substantially: pasturelands in Somalia's inter-river region were feeding cattle that in some instances ended up in Kenya, even though the trekking distances might be as long as 550 kilometers.

Further evidence of the adaptability of the cross-border cattle trade can be found in the fact that the costs of transport and brokerage remained relatively stable even after the collapse of law and order in Somalia. Despite increased insecurity resulting from the ready availability of modern weapons and the growing incidence of banditry in many of the border regions, Little discovered that transport costs for livestock moving from Somalia to Kenya did not rise dramatically after 1991; and brokers' fees changed very little between 1988 and 2001 (Little 2005: 15-16). This suggests either that the perceived risks of trans-border cattle trading had not increased substantially, or that efficiencies of scale and increased competition from new middlemen entering the business succeeded in keeping transport and transaction costs low. In either case, the situation testifies to the continued resilience of a business that has received no government support and few inputs from international development agencies over the years.

The capacity of borderland pastoralists and traders to survive and sometimes even prosper under the volatile conditions of the past twenty years depended not only on kinship ties and negotiated partnerships which straddled national boundaries. It also required the adoption of sophisticated business tools and financial mechanisms that helped keep transaction costs under control. Among these tools were informal credit networks; money transfer systems (*hawala*) and methods for foreign-exchange arbitrage; the use of revenues from livestock trade to finance a variety of other imports;[19] and reliance on informally certified brokers (*dilaalo*) to provide advance market information, match buyers with sellers, and facilitate and legitimize commercial transactions (Little 2003, 2005).

While Little observed these institutions and practices during his field work in the 1990s, not all are modern innovations. Many have their origins in the long-distance caravan trade of pre-colonial times, or in the cross-border *miraa* and livestock commerce of the colonial era. Modern transportation and communication technologies did not create the borderlands economies; rather they helped perpetuate and enlarge them. Even as trucking has replaced trekking along some segments of livestock supply routes, and cell-phones have streamlined the flow of information on local market prices and international exchange rates, cross-border traders continue to rely on kin networks and commercial alliances built up over

145

the years. The traders still depend on seasoned trekkers, flexible routes, and experienced middlemen to manage risk and conduct commerce under continually changing local circumstances.[20] There have unquestionably been striking changes over the course of the past century in the composition of the mercantile community, the means of transport and communication, and the markets being targeted in the trans-border trade between Somalia and Kenya. What has been constant is the utility of the border as a frontier of economic opportunity: a border which was legally demarcated and officially regulated but practically porous and regularly transgressed by borderlanders and their business partners in pursuit of the differential opportunities which two distinct national economies provided.

Conclusion

The efforts of colonial governments to contain the African populations of their frontier regions failed to prevent the latter from participating in the wider regional economies of the Horn. To begin with, some African long-distance traders were already providing export commodities for international markets (ivory and animal trophies, cattle and hides) prior to the European takeover of Africa. After the establishment of colonial rule, these experienced traders were well-positioned to circumvent colonial attempts to restrict or divert their commerce within the new, artificially constructed boundaries. Like the pastoral populations whose products they sold and whose services they utilized for transport and security, the borderland traders relied on cross-territorial mobility to evade government taxation, registration and quarantines, and to move their animals and other assets to the most advantageous markets on either side of the border.

By essentially neglecting the frontier districts, colonial bureaucrats and their African successors in both Kenya and Somalia afforded borderlanders the economic space to develop more extensive supply and market networks. While administrative maps and official ordinances suggested that the states exercised sovereignty along the frontiers, the NFD and Jubaland were simply too remote from the economic and political centres of those states to warrant zealous enforcement of the boundary between them. As late as 1960 one British colonial officer commented that the Kenya-Somalia border was arbitrary and meaningless, running as it does 'through the middle of nowhere for a hell of a long way' (quoted in Dalleo 1975: 248). While the central authorities did occasionally attempt to project their power into the borderland areas in response to surges of armed banditry or inter-ethnic conflict, such interventions were typically short-lived and frequently manipulated by frontier politicos eager to gain leverage over local rivals (for examples, see Menkhaus 2005). Political corruption and abuse of authority were no less common on the frontier than elsewhere in colonial and post-colonial Africa, and monitoring by customs officers and policemen even more difficult.

When state officials posted to the frontier were negligent, overbearing or corrupt, borderland residents responded by evasion, resistance or bribery. This gave local entrepreneurs a decided edge in their efforts to maintain their economic and political autonomy. Indeed, the adaptability of borderland traders to shifting state policies has been demonstrated time and again in recent decades. When Siyad Barre pushed the Isaaq out of their dominant position in Somalia's domestic *miraa* trade, the widely-dispersed Isaaq were able to move their operations into trans-national markets in East Africa and overseas. When Kenya relocated its refugee camps to the fringes of the country, opportunistic merchants in the NFD as well as refugees from Somalia reaped the benefits of an international aid industry which had previously centred on the Coast Province. And Kenya's continuing reluctance to extend permanent refugee status to immigrants from war-torn Somalia has in recent years driven many of the latter to take up unofficial residence in the unregulated Eastleigh quarter of Nairobi, where they have helped transform the consumer economy of Kenya by turning that enclave into a bustling marketplace for low- and middle-income shoppers from throughout East Africa (Little 2005: 18–19). Neglect by the centre has thus afforded the frontier populations of Kenya and Somalia the opportunity to pursue a wide range of economic initiatives for themselves, their kinsmen, and their neighbours in the Horn.

Throughout this Chapter, I have argued that the interconnections between the borderland economies and the adjoining parts of Kenya and Somalia are not simply post-1991 developments, but have historical roots in the *miraa* and livestock trades of the colonial era. This history suggests that even as the growth of cross-border and frontier-metropolitan trade helped reinforce established ties of kin and clan among geographically dispersed groups like the Somalis, it also forged new bonds and business partnerships with members of other ethnic communities. While such cross-ethnic alliances were typically opportunistic and hence fragile, some have over time generated precedents and practices that serve to regulate competition, manage conflict, and mediate economic interests which frequently straddle national boundaries. It would be premature to contend that these borderland enterprises will provide the foundation for greater economic integration (much less political cooperation) across the Horn, given the persistent class, ethnic and religious tensions that currently plague all the countries of the region. But if history is any indicator, it may well be the cross-border traders – augmented nowadays by sizable numbers of the urban business classes from all the countries involved – who will spearhead the move towards wider regional cooperation in the Horn. Even as politicians in Mogadishu, Nairobi and Addis Ababa clash over power-sharing formulas and periodically threaten to make war on their neighbours, cross-border entrepreneurs are generating new business opportunities at the local level as they expand linkages with the global economy. As in the past, these opportunistic traders continue to supply national markets with trans-national commodities, ignoring political boundaries in the process and threatening to leave their squabbling politicians far behind.

Notes

1 The work of Peter D. Little and his associates are a valuable exception, and I have relied extensively on their data for the contemporary period.

2 Even some of the excellent research on livestock production, land use and ecology in Kenya's arid lands in the 1970s and '80s, which highlighted the distinctive strategies of the region's inhabitants, tended to reinforce the popular image of the Somalia-Kenya frontier as a circumscribed, isolated and marginal economic space.

3 Many of these sources are noted in Cassanelli 1982: 147–61 and Dalleo 1975: 44–120.

4 In 1912, for example, the British created the so-called Somali-Galla line in an effort to halt continued Somali expansion into Galla (Oromo) pasturelands and to keep the former from reaching the Tana river with their herds. This reminds us that other kinds of borders – in this case the unofficial ones that separated one nomadic population from another – were also being continually contested during the colonial era. For other examples, see Dalleo 1975, 235 ff.

5 These were the Outlying District Ordinance of 1902, the Closed District Ordinance of 1926, and the Special District Administrative Ordinances of 1934; see Mburu 2005, esp. chap. 3.

6 Italian Somaliland's neglect of the colony's border with Kenya stood in marked contrast to its preoccupation with conditions along the Somalia-Ethiopia boundary. Years before the Wal-Wal incident of 1934 which provided the pretext for the Fascist invasion, Italian administrators posted near the Ethiopian border were instructed to gather intelligence about pastoral movements, trade networks, kinship ties and political alliances along and across the frontier. This intelligence was intended to identify potential Somali allies in anticipation of Italy's invasion of Ethiopia, as well as to support Italian propaganda about the desirability of incorporating the Ogaden's residents into a larger Italian empire and to create 'la Grande Somalia'.

7 One consequence of these projects (which was certainly intended by the Marehan-led government of Siyad Barre) was to attract Marehan pastoralists and businessmen from the Geedo region into the Afmadow/Kismaayo area. With government backing, the newcomers began to privatize the water ponds and boreholes in anticipation of future profits from the commercial sales of livestock through Kismaayo. The result was an intensification of conflict with the local Ogaden herders and the military intervention of the regime on behalf of their Marehan kinsmen. This was one of the major reasons for the Ogaden's joining the alliance that brought Barre's government down in 1991.

8 See, for example, the numerous studies conducted between 1976 and 1987 by the Integrated Project on Arid Lands (IPAL) with the cooperation of UNESCO and the Federal Republic of Germany. Though virtually forgotten today, these technical reports can be consulted in the UN Library and the US Library of Congress.

9 In fact, it appears that cross-border wartime trading became so attractive to inhabitants of the border towns that they no longer were available for recruitment as porters by the Kenyan and Italian Somaliland governments.

10 Ironically, the wartime efforts of colonial states to prohibit cross-border trade in certain commodities raised the potential profitability of selling those commodities even as it increased the political risks to the traders. Colonial closure, in other words, made cross-border transactions more profitable for local speculators.

11 One reason is that, unlike the trafficking in ivory and game trophies, which was

encouraged by an international market in India, China, and Europe with agents in East Africa, *miraa* or khat was exclusively consumed and traded by Africans, and so remained largely below the radar screen.

12 The BMA brought many Somalis from the Protectorate to work in the south, and it was these northern Somalis who were popularly regarded as the largest consumers of khat. Only after 1970 did khat consumption become common in the south; see Cassanelli 1986.

13 The reason, we learn from official correspondence, was that khat consumption was associated with the liturgical practices of certain Somali Sufi religious orders which had preached resistance to British rule (Cassanelli 1986)

14 According to Goldsmith (1997: 20), '*miraa* marketing generates fluctuating networks of micro economic organization that has mitigated [*sic*] against the emergence of internal economic diversification including the rise of a patron class. Individual traders have accumulated considerable resources, but until recently a host of factors encouraged Igembe investment in property and businesses outside the Nyambenes, and the diversification of agriculture for the most part into tea and lower zone farms in their home areas.'

15 Over the years, most condemnations of *miraa* have come from communities or countries where it is consumed rather than produced. For the consumers, *miraa* can be a drain on family incomes or on a country's foreign exchange. For the producers, in contrast, it is a reliable alternative to cash crops like coffee whose prices on the world market fluctuate unpredictably. There always appears to be an expanding market for freshly harvested *miraa*; and the continued existence of borders adds value to the transactions for local suppliers and distributors on both sides of the border.

16 During the colonial era, in contrast, European ranchers in the highlands successfully pressured Kenyan authorities to quarantine livestock coming from the NFD to Isiolo and other transit points, ostensibly to prevent the spread of rinderpest and bovine pleuropneumonia from cattle they believed to originate in Italian Somaliland (see, e.g., Dalleo 1975: 104–5, 158–64).

17 Despite occasional rifts, these alliances survived until the collapse of the Somali state, when fierce competition between Harti and Ogaden warlords for control of Kismaayo and its revenues shattered the partnership. Then, unable to cross territories controlled by the Ogaden, the Harti were effectively cut out of the cross-border trade to Kenya, while the Ogaden were excluded from the overseas export markets through Kismaayo.

18 According to Little, cattle prices are generally 20–25 per cent higher in Kenya than in neighbouring countries.

19 While cattle were the primary import into Kenya, traders also carried such commodities as cooking oil, pasta, clothes and small electronics from the Somalia side of the border, providing critical items at reasonable prices to low-income Kenya consumers.

20 Little gives an example of how, during a local drought in the Garissa district in 1996, Somali herders negotiated an arrangement with local elders in a disputed region near Kismaayo to move their herds temporarily into that area, the condition being that the migant herders could not carry weapons with them (Little 2003: 31).

References

Cassanelli, L. 1982. *The Shaping of Somali Society*. Philadelphia, PA: University of Pennsylvania Press.

—— 1986. 'Qat: changes in the production and consumption of a quasilegal commodity in northeast Africa', in A. Appadurai (ed.), *The Social Life of Things: Commodities in cultural perspective*. Cambridge: Cambridge University Press, pp. 236–57.

Dalleo, T. 1975. 'Trade and Pastoralism: Economic Factors in the History of the Somali of

Northeastern Kenya, 1892–1948'. Ph.D. dissertation, Syracuse University.

—— 1979. 'The Somali Role in Organized Poaching in Northeastern Kenya, c. 1909–1939'. *The International Journal of African Historical Studies* 12(3): 472–82.

Drysdale, J. 1964. *The Somali Dispute*. London: Pall Mall Press.

Goldsmith, P. 1997. *Cattle, Khat, and Guns: Trade, Conflict, and Security on northern Kenya's Highland-Lowland Interface*. Nairobi: APPEAL-KENYA. Draft version.

Hagmann, T. 2005. 'From State Collapse to Duty-Free Shop: Somalia's Path to Modernity' (Review article). *African Affairs* 104(416): 525–35.

Hyndman, J. 1997. 'Border Crossings'. *Antipode* 29(2): 149-176.

—— 1999. 'A Post-Cold War Geography of Forced Migration in Kenya and Somalia'. *Professional Geographer* 51(1): 104–14.

Lewis, I. M. 1963. 'The Problem of the Northern Frontier District of Kenya'. *Race:* 48-60.

Little, P. D. 2003. *Somalia: Economy without State*. Oxford: James Currey.

—— 2005. *Unofficial Trade when States are Weak. The Case of Cross-Border Commerce in the Horn of Africa*. EGDI (Expert Group on Development Issues) Research Paper No. 2005/13 (UNU-WIDER).

Mburu, N. 2005. *Bandits on the Border. The Last Frontier in the Search for Somali Unity*. Trenton, NJ: Red Sea Press.

Menkhaus, K. 2005. 'Kenya-Somalia Border Conflict Analysis'. Paper prepared for USAID through contract with Development Alternatives Inc. Nairobi: USAID.

Murunga, G.R. 2005. 'Conflict in Somalia and Crime in Kenya: Understanding the Trans-Territoriality of Crime'. *African and Asian Studies* 4(1–2): 137–61.

Schlee, G. 1989. *Identities on the Move. Clanship and Pastoralism in Northern Kenya*. Manchester: Manchester University Press.

Smith, A. 1969. 'The Open Market. The Economy of Kenya's Northern Frontier Province and the Italo-Abysinnian War'. *East Africa Journal* (Nov.): 34–44.

Nine

{{decorative band}}

Magendo & *Survivalism*
Babukusu-Bagisu Relations & Economic Ingenuity
on the Kenya-Uganda Border 1962-1980

PETER WAFULA WEKESA

Introduction

The issue of community relations across the Kenya-Uganda border can only be underscored within the specificity that appreciates both the international and domestic state-society dynamics defining its functionality. In regard to the specific relations between the Babukusu and the Bagisu peoples, it is not possible to restrict our analysis to conflicts. Both the Babukusu and the Bagisu communities who occupy western Kenya and eastern Uganda respectively have enjoyed a corporate past whose history transcends the current common Kenya-Uganda border. This past is manifested in the peoples' common history of origin, migration and settlement in their present areas (La Fontaine 1960; Were 1967; Makila 1978; Wafula 2000, 2007). Besides similarities in language, semblances among these communities are found in such cultural aspects as codes of conduct, marriage customs, circumcision traditions and even folklore.

The historical dynamics defining the relations between the Babukusu and Bagisu have influenced the nature of their social, economic and political interactions between themselves and with other neighbouring communities that include the Bantu, Nilotic and Cushitic groups. As Makila (1978: 46) has aptly argued, in relation to the Babukusu, 'if they are the Abaluyia[1] by virtue of their geographical circumstance, they are first and foremost members of a duplex community incorporating the Bagisu by virtue of a historical circumstance.' Throughout the pre-colonial, colonial and post-independence periods, the Babukusu and the Bagisu peoples have maintained a fluid cultural zone along the common Kenya-Uganda border that is mainly informed by their strong historical ties. This cultural zone has continually been maintained through shared practices like circumcision rituals, common worship traditions and sometimes common political traditions that transcend the common border. Various degrees of cultural and linguistic closeness as well as geographical proximity between the two groups are symbolized by the closeness of putative genealogical links as far as the founding ancestors of the groups are concerned.

Although the majority of the Babukusu and Bagisu are found in western Kenya and eastern Uganda respectively, substantial numbers of both groups straddle the common border thus not only enhancing its fluidity but equally emphasizing its meaninglessness in the daily activities of the two peoples. As an international line delineating the two communities and nation-states, therefore, the Kenya-Uganda border has stimulated the development of various cross-border transactions, which, though seeming to undercut the states' policies, can be clearly understood within the context of the two communities' long history. This history is characterized not only by various forms of co-existence and interdependence arising from the peoples' common origins but also by the historical process of encounter and change occasioned by the realities surrounding the colonial delineation and transformation of activities around their common border.

The purpose of this chapter is to reflect on how the imposition of the Kenya-Uganda border and its attendant national management strategies have facilitated the emergence of vibrant informal economic activities described as *Magendo* between the two socio-cultural and historically related groups of the Babukusu and the Bagisu.[2] The point is to demonstrate how political patterns of inter-state policy, tension and conflict facilitated the emergence of *Magendo* as a viable survival option among the two related border communities.

Independence, state power and cross-border community dynamics 1962–7

In independent Kenya and Uganda, as elsewhere in Africa, the legitimacy of the colonial partition lines has remained one of the most enduring colonial legacies. Colonialism not only left behind a patchwork of sovereign states in Africa, but the states spawned by this process were also themselves artificial entities. The case of the border communities of the Babukusu and Bagisu illustrates not only the artificiality inherent in the colonial partition, but also the constant challenge posed by trans-border cultural relations to the state-model institution introduced by the colonial rulers. By the time Uganda and Kenya attained their political independence in 1962 and 1963 respectively, they were by no means nations but rather they represented the shells of territorial independence in which different ethnic communities co-existed with each other. The major task of the two new East African governments was to provide the soil in which the seed of their national sovereignty could grow. The process of political consolidation required territorial stability as the most viable means of maintaining national integrity and engendering nation- and state-building.

The attainment of independence, therefore, marked an important watershed in the evolution of the history of border community relations between the Babukusu and Bagisu peoples. Unlike in the colonial period, the leaders of the new East African states, like those in other parts of Africa, readily acknowledged the disastrous effects of the colonial partition of the continent and their countries specifically, but were reluctant, if not totally unwilling, to support policies likely to restrain state sovereignty and consequently their own power. The problems and constraints of officially encouraging harmonious border community relations during the early independence period seemed many and intractable. Specifically, in terms of the border dynamics and the challenges posed by the partition of similar cultural groups by a common boundary, the impact on the national consciousness, as well as the social, economic and political effects taking place at the local, national and regional levels, were important concerns.

Independence meant that both Kenya and Uganda acquired exclusive sovereign rights in the international system to act within their territories without being subjected to any legal control by another sovereign state. Possession of sovereignty conferred upon each of their governments total jurisdiction over the utilization of the strength of its people and resources in whatever manner it wished, without regard to any other political authority inside or outside the national territory (Ojo 1985; Okoth 2002). Each was to make and enforce the laws of the state, decide and carry out the state's policies, both domestic and international, and conduct official relations with other states operating in the international system. Looked at from a purely state-centric perspective, in which the Kenya-Uganda border needed to define patterns of territory and facilitate control from the centre, the border and the activities generated across it were, then, domestically viewed as challenging the stability of the administrations and their quests for hegemony, control and nation-building. Such activities, including the day-to-day informal economic transactions and movements of persons across the border were to be monitored and generally controlled within the formulated state policies and apparatuses.

The common border was thus central to the process of creating national sovereignty since it played a key role in defining and differentiating national groups from 'outsiders'. As Anderson (1983) has argued, such national groups or 'imagined political communities' had to be moulded from the various ethnic groups. To Anderson, they are imagined because, on the one hand, the members of even the smallest nation will never encounter most of their fellow members face to face and have direct contact with them, yet in the mind of each lives the image of their communion. On the other hand, even the largest nation has finite albeit elastic boundaries beyond which lie other nations. The relevance of Anderson's observations to the context of the two new East African states lies in the challenge posed to the new leaders in their effort to weave together a national as opposed to a trans-national community or consciousness. In this context, the common border became an important component in instituting patterns of territorial control and delineating the distinct nationalities of Kenya from those of Uganda and vice versa.

What is perhaps more important in our context is the relevance of this transformation to the nature of relations and to the various social, economic and political activities between the Babukusu and the Bagisu peoples during the independence period. As ethnic entities within different geopolitical states, the two peoples became subject to the social, economic and political transformations in their respective countries. The nature of their relations across the border reflected each state's primary active role in the diplomatic, political and military affairs of its people (Okoth 2002: 281). Thus, in as much as such relations constituted inter-community relations, they were inter-state relations characterized by both conflict and cooperation. In the context of the Babukusu and the Bagisu border peoples, our point of departure is to examine the role played by the new independent states of Kenya and Uganda in influencing border issues and policy, and how these efforts ran into conflict with their daily activities.

Anxious to encourage national sovereignty, the new national leaders were compelled to look inward and rank as their first priority the political, economic and social development of their own polities. The immediate concern, then, was to build viable national groups based on their own traditions and customs. The more national consolidation received high priority, the less the attention paid to informal relations especially between communities with strong inter-state cultural bonds. As pointed out by Nugent and Asiwaju, this situation arose out of the fact that

> at the time of independence, African governments inherited citizens where there had once been colonial subjects. Formally at least, the new rulers imagined that the ensembles of citizens added up to nations – or at the very least nations in the making. But there was an inherent tension between the new ideology of 'nationalism', which assumed that people belonged to one nation or another, and the reality of borderlands where communities merged into each other in spite of official lines of demarcation (Nugent and Asiwaju 1996: 9).

From the outset, therefore, the new political leaders did not display much willingness to sacrifice perceived national interests in favour of trans-border activities. The latter were generally perceived as a threat to the national unity and consolidation that the new leaders directly needed. Thus, the commitment of the leaders to cross-border activities was generally minimal and mainly geared towards control. As Asante (1999: 732) has argued, such cross-border activities only succeeded in contexts where they were not in conflict with considerations of national security, prestige or economic advantage.

Understandably, then, one issue on which there was consensus among the new leaders was the maintenance of the individual state borders through the institutional framework of the Organization of African Unity (OAU). Established on 25 May 1963, the OAU's intended purpose was to promote the unity and solidarity of the African states and to act as a collective voice for the continent. As an organization that sought to unite the African states, the OAU was committed to peaceful relations between them by emphasizing

154

in its Charter respect for the territorial integrity and political independence of each. The relevance of the OAU to the cross-border community activities and inter-state relations between Kenya and Uganda specifically needs to be emphasized. As signatories of the OAU resolutions, the two Presidents, Jomo Kenyatta and Milton Obote respectively, supported the status quo in regard to the sanctity of their common border. In terms of the Babukusu and the Bagisu peoples, this meant that the two peoples were to remain in the new national entities of Kenya and Uganda respectively.

By sanctioning the continuity of the colonial boundaries, the OAU became an important institution in the new states' quest for internal ethnic consolidation. Yet this did not signify an end to the cross-border activities between the two culturally related border communities, or to their cultural consciousness across the common border. Thus, although Bach (1999: 8) could be right in observing that trans-state interactions cannot be associated with an institutionalized process and that they are totally dependent on state policies, the specific case of the Babukusu and Bagisu puts in question the view that their activities are totally dependent on state policies. While residing in different countries, their common identities, characterized by similarities in language, customs, values and symbols among others, persisted across the border. These processes of trans-state or cross-border interactions between the two peoples, though countering the institutional claims of the OAU and the national state in regard to the sanctity of the border, translated into other numerous social, economic and political permutations.

The rise and fall of economic regionalism 1967–80

In both Kenya and Uganda, the early independent leaders adopted different developmental strategies to respond to the challenges posed by the cross-border activities between the different national groups in general, and the border communities specifically. Having defined their national priorities and emphasized the sanctity of the common border, the new leaders became increasingly confronted by the central challenge posed by cross-border activities to their objectives of national consolidation. Based on the colonial federal experience, the political leaders in both Kenya and Uganda embarked on a series of economic programmes geared towards regionalism in an effort to address issues of common interest between the two states.[3] By 6 June 1967 when the treaty establishing the East African Community (EAC) was signed in Kampala, it was clear that the countries of the entire region could not meet their national objectives socially, economically or politically without actively incorporating inter-state integration arrangements within their development agendas. Such arrangements were prompted not only by the nature of the colonial federal institutions, but even more so by the interlocking cultural nature of their geopolitical entities.

155

As in the colonial period, therefore, the EAC arrangements dealt mainly with economic matters of the production of goods and exchange of services. During the colonial period, as Ochwada (2004: 63) notes, the different countries had specialized in the production and export of particular goods and services that served the British colonial system well. While Kenya increasingly specialized in food manufacturing, Uganda produced electricity and processed raw minerals. The different colonies also developed specialized forms of transport and communication as well as services such as reinsurance and tourism (ibid.: 64). These colonial integration arrangements were, together with the associated institutional arrangements, inherited by the independent states. Though replete with various deficiencies, the colonial-based structures were eagerly adopted by the new leaders keen to further their integration efforts.

Both colonial and early independent formal initiatives at integration shared a common feature of being mainly economic in objectives and state-driven. The economic justification for regionalism was overwhelmingly emphasized almost to the exclusion of other possible intervening variables. The economic arguments insisted that, by joining together, states were in a position to exploit larger scale economies and at the same time restructure the regional economy in a way that benefitted the production base of a given region (Clapham et al. 2001). Imbued with western developmental arguments and dreamed up within theoretical assumptions of modernization, regional integration was conceptualized as a mechanism that would ensure economic development. With the signing of the EAC treaty, therefore, it was obvious that the new leaders would continue to pursue a common agenda through integration.

Both Jomo Kenyatta and Milton Obote embraced the ideals of integration envisaged through the EAC and viewed regional integration as a way of liberating their respective states from the throes of economic malaise. By encouraging regional integration, the two leaders together with their Tanzanian counterpart, Julius Nyerere, hoped to create common markets that would allow the free movement of people, capital, services and goods within and between their respective countries to avoid their chronic dependence on the North. As Mazrui (1977) has argued, regional integration efforts were seen as a struggle against the dependency situation imposed upon the continent by its colonial experience. Thus, East African regionalism was acknowledged as a viable strategy through which the different countries in the region would adapt to combat foreign dependency and underdevelopment.

Used rather loosely, regional integration came to characterize various broad social, economic and political initiatives that it was hoped would increase the bargaining power of the respective countries within the international political economy. As Clapham et al. (2001: 59) have argued, the uniting strand within such initiatives was the sense that, as individual states, they could not readily achieve their goals in isolation from their neighbours. This explains why integration schemes were particularly characteristic of groups of states that were aware of both their common identities and their relatively small size and individual weaknesses. Since the East African countries, like those elsewhere in Africa, were seen as being exceptionally small and weak, at least in comparison with those in the North, regional integration was seen as the panacea for their numerous problems. Again, the realities in the region, characterized by shared histories among its people and a strong sense of continental solidarity expressed through pan-Africanism, made the need for East African integration sacrosanct.

The launching of the EAC signalled a major development in inter-state relations in the region. From a state-centric point of view, the member states committed themselves to an economic course that was destined to benefit the peoples of the region and especially the border populations. Though mired in economic as well as political problems, the period 1967–77 saw major economic cooperation facilitated through the EAC between the states of the region generally, and Kenya and Uganda specifically. This was a period characterized by broad national experiences in Kenya and Uganda fostered by the political leadership of three presidencies, Jomo Kenyatta in Kenya and Milton Obote and Idi Amin in Uganda. While Kenya experienced relatively consistent political and economic development by the standards of most African states, Uganda was seriously undermined by the political collapse in the 1970s that came to be manifested in military dictatorship and an authoritarian regime.

Uganda's political problems began with Milton Obote who from 1967 onwards violently suppressed those opposed to his misuse of power. These problems, among other factors, explain Kenya's dominance in the economic fortunes of the region generally and those of the EAC specifically. By 1969, Obote had banned political parties and on May Day 1970 made the so-called 'Nakivubo Pronouncements', nationalizing private business holdings. Within this political atmosphere that was also associated with economic problems that eroded investor confidence, Idi Amin, Obote's army commander, used a disgruntled section of the army to overthrow the government on 25 January 1971. This coup effectively brought Uganda under Amin's military dictatorship that was to last till April 1979. During this regime, Uganda experienced tyrannical economic and political turmoil that caused serious disruptions and led to the eventual collapse of the economy.

This disaster, among other things, intensified the reliance of the Ugandan people on Kenya especially through the provisions of the EAC and other informal economic networks. For example, following the expulsion in the early 1970s of the Indian community that controlled a major part of the country's economy, the sharp decline in Uganda's manufacturing sector was mainly cushioned by Kenyan business people. Consumer goods and other imports from Kenya increased in markets in Uganda. Mamdani (1983: 97) has observed, for instance, that in 1971 imports of animal oil and fats, cotton fabric and sugar valued at Uganda

Shs. 24 million, 12.3 million and 11 million respectively streamed into Uganda from Kenya. Ochwada (2004: 68) has further observed that, by 1976, Uganda imported from Kenya products valued at Uganda Shs 94.99 million. Concomitantly, multinational corporations operating in Kenya extended their commercial undertakings into Uganda. These included Cooper Motors, Leyland Motors, East African Industries, Robbialac Paints and Shell Chemical Company.

The foregoing economic links between Kenya and Uganda, though not wholly credited to the EAC, succeeded within the greater spirit of Pan-East Africanism championed by the political elites in the two countries. Yet this spirit, and the EAC treaty in general, merely mirrored the inherent contradictions that dictated the nature of the commitment of the leaders to the EAC as a supranational body. Essentially, their unwilling-ness to forfeit their political and economic sovereignty posed a major threat to the survival of the EAC. Its broad impact on the lives of most ordinary Kenyans and Ugandans was therefore limited by the deep involvement of the governments and its over-emphasis on economic aspects. In terms of the people inhabiting border areas specifically, the failure of the EAC to consider the close historical and socio-cultural links among them as important elements in the success of regional integration provided a series of reasons for its dismal performance and collapse in 1977.

The reduction of the EAC's integration goals to strictly economic matters militated against their relevance to border communities. The state-centred economic arguments paid little attention to the particular social and political histories that informed the two countries whose peoples were meant to benefit from the EAC's initiatives. Integration, as Adetula (2004: 21) argues, represents much broader and more detailed arrangements which require states to make certain social, political and economic sacrifices and commitments. It also demonstrates their will to redefine their individual and collective participation in the international economy. The EAC became merely an avenue through which infrastructures were created for the exchange of commodities. Human agency was lacking in these initiatives since exchange and markets facilitating the movement of goods were the only ones that were emphasized.

In terms of human agency and specifically the activities of the border communities of the Babukusu and the Bagisu, the EAC meant little without a transformation of their social, economic and political inter-actions in real terms. While the official rhetoric emphasized its economic gains, other dimensions were conflated within the individual political and ideological rivalries of the power elites in Kenya and Uganda. To the ordinary peoples within the different national sovereignties, the boundary between them continued to define their insertion into the power interests at play. For instance, it was easy, from the perspective of the governments in the respective countries, to view cross-border activities and interactions between the various communities as constituting alliances against central authority. In this regard, the Kenya-Uganda border basically remained a line of contact between two sovereign states jealous of each other's territorial integrity and national autonomy. In a sense therefore, contacts in the borderlands remained more often than not contacts of conflict rather than harmony (Asiwaju 1985).

Clearly, the relations between the Babukusu and Bagisu peoples were, within the state-centred economic imperatives, modified by the inhibitive and restrictive tendencies of the two states. The crossing of the border by the population of either country was a challenge that needed to be monitored within the context of each state's policies and interests. This was especially important for the cross-border movements of those with close historical and socio-cultural ties and who continued to view the border as a serious impediment to their daily interactions. As Baubock and Rundell (1998: 8) observe, the crossing of the border by these people blurred three kinds of boundaries: the territorial borders of the states, the political boundaries of citizenship and the cultural boundaries of national communities. When such persons moved from one international location to another, as individuals or in groups, their activities affected the immediate and future development prospects at the source of their move-ment, their place of origin and also the place of destination.

The main regulating mechanism in the participation of the two com-munities in each other's political economies remained the Identity Card or *Kipande* that defined their distinct nationalities. However, the use of the identity card did not translate into much success as far as the control of cross-border movements and relations between the two communities was concerned. This was because of their presence on both sides of the border and their ability to speak both Lubukusu and Lumasaaba[4] and also Kiswahili, the regional language. The common languages have thus provided the two communities with a powerful means of interpersonal communication that has served as social cement during their various trans-actions. Moreover, the identity card could only be issued to those who had attained the age of eighteen. With the increasing participation of the young in the various cross-border transactions, the ineffective system of policing and the insufficient data to determine those who had attained the identity card age, its use as a means of controlling movement and inter-actions between the peoples was an abysmal failure.

The period between 1971 and 1980 was particularly critical in the border relations between the two countries and between the Babukusu and Bagisu specifically. On top of the economic collapse in Uganda, Amin's military dictatorship worsened the security situation there and this continued to have an impact on the border dynamics and relations. By 1975, for instance, thousands of Ugandans including Bagisu had fled into exile in Kenya using the border as their escape route. For most of the Bagisu, the proximity of the border and the presence of their kith and kin in Kenya facilitated their incorporation in that country. This mass exodus continued to cause alarm in the Amin administration of the mid-1970s. As

Okoth (1992: 77) observed, Amin was clearly in difficulties and to get out of them he decided to embark on a confrontation course with Kenya. In February 1976, he announced in a radio broadcast that large tracts of land in Kenya (mainly western Kenya) were originally Ugandan territory and he wondered whether the people in those areas still wanted to remain part of Kenya. He then went on to announce that he would fight any neighbouring country that interfered with Uganda's import-export routes. The Kenyan response to this provocation was to close the border on 23 February 1976, stop the handling of Ugandan goods and give Amin 48 hours to apologize (ibid.). Although Amin climbed down almost immediately, Kenya's subsequent trade embargo, including blocking the entire oil supply to Uganda for a short time in 1976, almost broke the Amin regime before Uganda finally agreed to withdraw its claims.

The tension generated by Amin's territorial claims on Kenya was just one of the many ways in which Kenya-Uganda inter-state relations were consummated in the mid-1970s. From 1976 to April 1979, when Amin was finally ousted from power, the intense suspicions between Jomo Kenyatta[5] and Idi Amin occasionally threatened to bring the two countries to war, with resultant implications for the ordinary people in the two countries and especially those occupying the border areas. For instance, following the humiliation that Amin faced in his failed territorial claims to Kenya territory, deliberate harassment of Kenyans started in Uganda (Okoth 2002: 288), culminating in the death of a Kenyan female student at Makerere University and the 'disappearance' of another in March 1976 (ibid.). This was followed in April by a raid by Ugandan troops in the Kapenguria border area inside Kenya and the killing of five Kenyans. Thereafter, a series of accusations and counter accusations led to steadily rising tempers between the two leaders. It is no wonder that when the Israeli government raided Entebbe in July 1976, Uganda quickly suspected Kenya of complicity. Indeed, this accusation of conspiracy was not only forwarded to the UN and the OAU but also led to the mobilization of troops at the common border by both countries.

That inter-state relations between Kenya and Uganda in the face of mounting tensions were significant in shaping community relations across the common border cannot be gainsaid. More often than not, it was during such periods that the border and indeed the border communities became relevant in the ensuing power play. Stringent economic and political measures, including border closures and enhanced border policing, became important policy options for the national leaders. In such contexts, cross-border relations between the Babukusu and the Bagisu were greatly strained by deliberate government decisions to control or completely curtail movements across the border. Such national decisions, though obviously aimed at meeting the political leaders' aspirations, contradicted the historical realities of cross-border interaction between the two communities. It was within this context that there emerged a strong informal economy at the border.

The informal economy, *Magendo* and the border: Bukusu-Bagisu relations to 1980

The manner in which Kenyan and Ugandan national interests ignored trans-border community relations and the activities they generated led to the emergence of various informal responses, to the border restrictions. These responses continued to define the nature of the border's evolution and transformation over time. As Nugent (2002: 231) argues, borders are shaped as much by the everyday activities of ordinary people as by state politics. While the informal activities along and across borders sometimes undermine, they may at other times also tend to reinforce the formal structures of politics. The nature of the response generated by both the Babukusu and the Bagisu through their regular interaction across the border worked against the logic of national integration and tended to reinforce a transnational sense of commonality between the two peoples.

Two cultural activities among them can perhaps suffice to illustrate the way in which various items and goods were transacted and transmitted across the border oblivious of the two governments' strictures, namely, the elaborate male circumcision rituals and traditional religious practices involving intense visitations and common activities among the two groups leading to sharing of grain, manufactured products and other goods across the common border. Apart from the fact that the rituals associated with these practices involve the participation of peoples from the two groups, there are also common circumcision and worship sites on either side of the border that necessitate the movement of goods and people.

On the other hand, both peoples, in collaboration with others in similar situations, sought to take advantage of their unique location as border peoples to participate in daily cross-border activities that challenged the national restrictions espoused by the incumbent leadership. Oral sources (Wakiro 2005; Kolia 2005), for instance, confirmed that both Babukusu and Bagisu men were the main porters facilitating the transportation of several industrial products including sugar and cooking oil on behalf of other non-local persons across the Lwakhakha border point. The two groups took advantage of their familiarity with the border point to earn commissions by ensuring the smooth flow of goods. The emergence of the informal economy along the border and the increasing direct and indirect participation of the two peoples in its activities need to be conceptualized within broad dynamics.

The proliferation of the informal activities of *Magendo* was due to cross-border interactions that had their own distinctive features but which, as Bach (1999: 8) observes, combined elements of inter-state and transnational regionalism. Although *Magendo* activities manifested themselves in different forms and known by different names, their main characterization is that they were not entered in the national accounts. Since *Magendo* operated

outside the official national networks, its activities challenged the restrictions and tax policy frameworks put in place by the two national states. Its
participants, on the other hand, were viewed as people who operated in
opposition to established norms. Even if *Magendo* activities may not be
interpreted as acts of overt opposition, they may still be seen as acts of what
James Scott called 'everyday forms of peasant resistance', comprising part
of the hidden transcript of power relations. According to Scott (1990: 200):

> the official transcript of power relations seldom elicits explicit challenges
> from subordinated groups, except during moments of systemic crisis when
> the mask will finally be permitted to drop. At other times, when the
> structures of power are secure, the response of the subordinate is to circulate
> their own knowing and hidden transcript among themselves, traces of which
> may seep into the public arena and thus destabilize the official transcript.

The above observation by Scott can only be correct to the extent that
we treat *Magendo* activities not just as open acts of resistance but also keep
an eye on the alternative constructions of reality embedded in the words
and deeds of the ordinary people. In this respect, *Magendo* activities, far
from providing a source of resistance to official state strictures, also and
more importantly open up economic options for the survival of ordinary
peoples living across the common border. Between the Babukusu and
Bagisu peoples therefore, such *Magendo* activities at the border have laid
the common ground for interaction that goes beyond the economic realm
into other social-historical and political interactions. For instance, grain
products traded across the border have facilitated common cultural
activities that have in turn reinforced the unity between the two groups.

The existence of *Magendo* economic activities at the border and its
various categorizations unmasks the constant reality of the ordinary
people's struggle to make a living outside the formal state-defined economic
networks. The context of whether these activities are legal or illegal is
arguably dependent on what Nugent (2002: 259) has distinctly categorized
as the divide between the national and local discourses of morality. Within
the national, most of the activities may be seen as illegal since the states
have historically arrogated to themselves the right to distinguish legitimate
from illegal activities. From the local point of view, on the other hand,
Magendo activities, or what is often described as smuggling, remained
basically an exchange of goods and services across the common boundary.
It was merely an exchange that was consummated within the various
socio-cultural and historical activities between the two peoples but which
continued to be hampered by the various national border management
strategies and policies of the two independent states. One source (Wakiro
2005) clearly wondered: 'since our people are only sharing grain and not
guns, what threat does this pose to the security of the two countries?' This
question raises the possibility of differing perspectives between the local
participants in the *Magendo* trade and the national agents aimed at
controlling it. In essence, the definition of *Magendo* and indeed other

informal cross-border activities boils down to whose point of view, between the national and local, has arrogated the morality issues.

There is no gainsaying the fact that the restrictive policies followed by both Kenya and Uganda created the incentives for the rise of *Magendo* and other informal cross-border economic activities. Restrictions such as import tariffs, quotas, exchange controls, state trading monopolies and export restrictions created incentives whereby the local border peoples could beat the systems in place and gain advantage in the process. Together with the restrictive national policies, past historical linkages and the semi-convertibility of currencies in border areas facilitated the operations of the *Magendo* traders. On the other hand, import licensing, often a response to an overvalued currency, restricted the supply of imports and raised their domestic price which in turn provided incentives for a parallel market in smuggled goods (Ackello-Ogutu 1997: 3). Relative price differentials between countries and shortages in a particular country also encouraged border informal trade. Scarcity and shortages in some of the neighbouring countries created effective demand and high profits, thus making it extremely difficult to control *Magendo*. All these conditions obtained for both Kenya and Uganda and were particularly exacerbated in the 1970s by the civil strife and political instability in the region, as we observed earlier. Unlike the non-border populations therefore, the border communities were in an advantageous position to harness the benefits linked to price differentials and in turn also to minimize the risks occurring from shortages in either country.

The restrictive nature of the state at the borders coupled with the uncertain political climate that disrupted the traditional forms of inter-action between the Babukusu and the Bagisu was mainly responsible for the rise of *Magendo* activities within their common Kenya-Uganda border-land. By 1980 most of the economic gains that had developed across the border during the first decade of independence and before had come to a standstill. These gains had been a product of not only the long cultural interaction but also a flourishing cross-border trade that saw the emergence of major border trading centres and market places like Chepkube, Suam, Lwakhakha and Malaba. The Amin regime in Uganda, the constant border restrictions and the ever-mounting border insecurity, due to the inter-state tensions especially in the 1970s, accounted for the transformation of this trade into a more discrete and contraband nature. The range of commodities that passed through the Kenya-Uganda border includes agricultural commodities (coffee, maize, maize meal, sugar, milk, rice, wheat flour, beans, groundnuts, simsim, bananas, etc.), industrial goods (cooking fats and oils, petroleum products), fish and forest resources, including charcoal and timber.

Although the above list of items that exchanged hands between the Babukusu and the Bagisu is far from exhaustive, a number of observations on the nature of the transactions can be identified. Given the strong industrial base in Kenya, most of the processed items including cooking fats/oils, wheat flour, petroleum products, maize meal, sugar and bread were produced there and sold across the border to Uganda. On the other hand, most agricultural commodities including un-milled maize meal, beans, groundnuts, bananas, rice, and charcoal that were locally produced in Bugisu and elsewhere in Uganda were traded across the border into Kenya. Most of these import/export transactions exploited the old unofficial networks that had historic and cultural links. In the 1970s, however, the transactions became more complicated as the political climate in the two countries and the border restrictions heightened price differentials, greatly affecting the production of certain items leading to scarcity in several areas. This was exacerbated by the entry of other market functionaries, including rich businessmen, multinational organizations and others that had both direct and indirect influence on the local cross-border trade.

By far, the most intricate of the informal transactions between the Babukusu and the Bagisu involved cash crops, mainly coffee and cotton. Although the nature and direction of their transaction were a function of the price differentials in Kenya and Uganda, other intervening variables were identified by my oral sources. With respect to coffee, Wakiro (2005) and Kolia (2005) pointed out that although there were overwhelming income variations arising from the coffee supplied to Kenyan factories as compared with that supplied to Ugandan factories, the mode of payment also influenced the manner in which the coffee was smuggled into Uganda. The failure by Kenyan factories to pay producers on time and the better accessibility to certain Ugandan factories were also important considerations in the decision to sell coffee to Ugandan factories in the 1970s. The issue of accessibility was perhaps more significant than price in the trans-border transactions involving cotton. Ugandan cotton farmers reportedly delivered their lint to Kenyan ginneries located close to the border rather than face the trouble of having to cover many kilometres to deliver it to the ginneries located in Mbale (Munyanda 2005). One thing that seems strikingly similar was the fact that, in whichever direction the products moved, there was an overwhelming consideration of the risk of border crossing and the added advantages of accessing additional scarce items and enhancing kin relations with the respective areas visited.

Whether it was coffee, cotton or the other agricultural and industrial commodities, there was a clear effort through this *Magendo* trade, on the part of both the Babukusu and the Bagisu, to mould the border into something that benefited them. There were certainly various categories within such informal participants in the *Magendo* trade. They could broadly be classified into three: first, the small-timers or what Nugent (2002) has identified elsewhere as armpit traders, second, the commission workers and third, the rich bulk traders. The first and second categories comprise mainly the local Babukusu and Bagisu and are distinguished by the nature of their transactions and the volume of goods traded. While armpit traders dealt in petty or small quantity items, the commission workers, whether on foot or on bicycles, worked for the rich, smuggling bulk goods across the border in order to earn a commission. Their success depended on the discrete nature of the operations and on their ability to develop good working relations with the police and border personnel. The bulk traders involved many rich merchants and companies from Kenya and Uganda and beyond.

The active participation of the Babukusu and the Bagisu in these *Magendo* activities stretched into the 1980s and beyond and is responsible, as observed above, for the rise of prominent trading centres such as Lwakhakha, Suam and Chepkube. Although these border centres appear neglected, they have actually remained active in terms of *Magendo* activities. Malaba town seemed to be the busiest centre owing to the availability of infrastructural facilities including roads, telecommunications, power lines and supporting institutions such as banks. However, within the context of the 1970s and early 1980s Chepkube was perhaps the most active in the entire East Africa region, having earned itself the name *Soko ya Magendo* (the smuggling market). Apart from the local Babukusu and Bagisu peoples, numerous other traders from all over East Africa moved into Chepkube and turned it into an economic hub.

It is also important to note that the discrete and contraband nature of this trade always allowed for the infiltration of criminal elements. With the deteriorating security situation in the region and the lack of appropriate border policing mechanisms, arms found their way into civilian hands and were equally traded across the border. Also important was the issue of women's engagement in prostitution in the main border trading centres. The poor security situation was also reflected in the increase in the number of refugees, especially those fleeing the tyranny of Amin's misrule (Ochwada 2004: 69).

Whereas the networks which the two communities exploited during the *Magendo* activities reflected long established historic and cultural links, it is also not difficult to see their activities as being a resistance to the embodiment of state power which the border represented. As the Kenyan and Ugandan governments began to embrace the renewed mood for regionalism, coupled with the more stable political environment and strong local Pan-East African initiatives from the 1980s onwards, the fluidity within which these informal activities thrived began to wane. Deliberate policy decisions on the part of the political leadership meant that such informal trans-border activities came less into conflict with national state policy interests or were perhaps even more irrelevant within the evolving social, economic and political dynamics.

Conclusion

This chapter has examined the role played by the independent Kenya and Uganda governments in influencing the nature of trans-border community relations between the Babukusu and the Bagisu from the early independence period to 1980. It has been argued that, unlike in the colonial period, the new independent leaders readily acknowledged the negative effects arising from the inherited colonial boundaries but were reluctant, if not totally unwilling, to support policies that would restrain state sovereignty and their power. In terms of borders generally, the leaders, through the OAU, supported the persistence of the status quo in so far as the control of borders was concerned. This meant that both the Babukusu and the Bagisu, as was the case with other African communities, remained within the former colonially defined geopolitical spaces. Having accepted this situation, the challenge the new political leaders faced was to weave together a national community through which it could face the many social, economic and political challenges.

As the chapter has demonstrated, however, the construction of a national community in both Kenya and Uganda was embedded in the intractable debates on regionalism that sought to give power to certain regions and communities. The failure of the nationalist project, coupled with the economic attempts at a broader regionalism, saw the emergence of inter-state tensions and civil strife in Kenya and Uganda that greatly undermined border community relations. While this was happening at the state level, however, a vibrant informal economy characterized by *Magendo* activities was evolving within the Bukusu-Bugisu borderland and challenging the statist restrictions at the economic level. By 1980, the volatile scenario generated by the inter-state rivalries and the deteriorating economic performance of the two countries had transformed *Magendo* into a livelihood strategy for the border communities of the Babukusu and the Bagisu. This strategy no doubt exploited the *primordial* networks whose history stretched beyond the colonial and post-colonial periods.

Notes

1 Abaluyia is a grouping of the various Bantu-speaking peoples living in western Kenya. It is both a cultural and political category that has worked to foment not only a cultural nationalism but also a political programme.
2 *Magendo* is a Kiswahili word meaning smuggling or specifically contraband trade.
3 During the colonial period, the British in East Africa had embarked on a programme of systematic integration of the region within a federal arrangement. In this regard, they established the Court of Appeal of East Africa in 1902, the East African Currency Board in 1905, the Postal Union of Kenya and Uganda in 1911 and a Customs Union in 1917 among other institutions (see Rothchild 1968; Ochwada 2004)
4 Lubukusu is the language spoken by Babukusu while Lumasaaba (sometimes referred to as Lugisu) is spoken by Bagisu. These languages are closely related and mutually intelligible.
5 Jomo Kenyatta died in 1978 and was succeeded by Daniel Arap Moi. Within the short transition period after Moi took over until Amin was ousted from power in 1979 there was no major policy shift in Kenya–Uganda relations.

References

Ackello-Ogutu, C. 1997. *Unrecorded Cross-Border Trade Between Kenya and Uganda: Implications for Food Security.* Nairobi: AFR/SD and REDSO/ESA.

Adetula, A. 2004. 'Regional Integration in Africa: Prospect for Closer Cooperation Between West, East and Southern Africa'. Paper presented at the IDASA/FREDSKORPSET Meeting, Johannesburg, South Africa.

Anderson, B. 1983. *Imagined Communities: Reflections on the Origins and Spread of Nationalism.* London: Verso.

Asante, S. 1999. 'Pan Africanism and Regional Integration', in A.A. Mazrui (ed.), *Unesco General History of Africa Vol VIII: Africa Since 1935.* Oxford: James Currey.

Asiwaju, A.I (ed.) 1985. *Partitioned Africans: Ethnic Relations across Africa's International Boundaries.* London: C. Hurst.

Bach, D. 1999. *Regionalisation in Africa: Integration and Disintegration.* Oxford: James Currey.

Baubock, R. and J. Rundell (eds) 1998. *Blurred Boundaries: Migration, Ethnicity, Citizenship.* Aldershot: Ashgate Publishing Limited.

Clapham, C., G. Mills, A. Morner and E. Sidiropoulos. 2001. *Regional Integration in Southern Africa: Comparative International Perspectives.* Pretoria: SAIIA.

Kolia, S. 2005. Oral Interview. Lwandanyi, Bungoma District.

La Fontaine, J. 1960. 'Gisu'. in A. I. Richards (ed.), *East African Chiefs.* London: Faber, pp. 260–77.

Makila, F. 1978. *An Outline History of Babukusu.*, Nairobi: East African Publishing House.

Mamdani, M. 1983. *Imperialism and Fascism in Uganda.* Nairobi: Heinemann.

Mazrui, A.A. 1977. *Africa's International Relations.* London: Heinemann and Boulder, CO: Westview Press.

Munyanda, S. 2005. Oral Interview, Mbale district.

Nugent, P. 2002. *Smugglers, Secessionists and Loyal Citizens on the Ghana-Togo Frontiers: The Life of the Borderlands since 1914.* Athens, OH: Ohio University Press; Oxford: James Currey.

Nugent, P. and A.I. Asiwaju (eds.) 1996. *African Boundaries: Barriers, Conduits and Opportunities.* London: Frances Printer.

Ochwada, H. 2004. 'Rethinking East African Integration: From economic to political and from state to civil society'. *Africa Development* 39(2): 53-79.

Ojo Olatunde, J.C.B. 1985. 'International Actors', in J. C. B. Ojo Olatunde, D. K. Orwa and C. M. B. Utete (eds), *African International Relations.* Lagos and London: Longman Group.

Okoth, G.P. 1992. 'Intermittent Tensions in Uganda-Kenya Relations: Historical Perspectives'. *Transafrican Journal of History* 21: 132–49.

—— 2002. 'International Relations Between Western Kenya and Eastern Uganda', in W.R. Ochieng (ed.), *Historical Studies and Social Change in Western Kenya: Essays in Memory of Professor G.S Were.* Nairobi: East African Publishing House, pp. 279–92.

Rothchild, D. 1968. *Politics of Integration: An East African Documentary.* Nairobi: East African Publishing House.

Scott, J. 1990. *Domination and the Arts of Resistance: Hidden Transcripts.* New Haven, CT and London: Yale University Press.

Wafula, P. W. 2000. *Politics and Nationalism in Colonial Kenya: The Case of Babukusu of Bungoma District, C. 1894–1963.* M. A. Thesis, Kenyatta University.

—— 2007. *The History of Community Relations Across the Kenya Uganda Border: The Case of the Babukusu and the Bagisu, C.1884–1997.* PhD Thesis, Kenyatta University.

Wakiro, C. 2005. Oral Interview, Mbale district.

Were, G. S. 1967. *History of the Abaluyia of Western Kenya 1500-1930.* Nairobi: East Africa Publishing House.

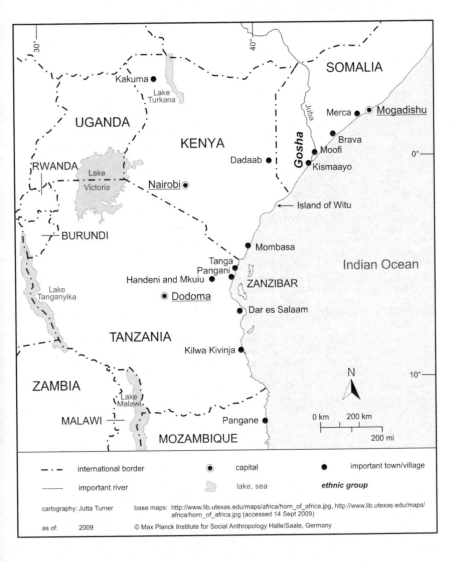

Map 5 *Somalia, Kenya, Uganda, Tanzania borderlands*

Ten

Can Boundaries not Border on One Another?
The Zigula (Somali Bantu) between Somalia & Tanzania

FRANCESCA DECLICH

Introduction

A contemporary map of Africa shows clear-cut state borders all across the continent. We all know, however, that before the colonial scramble for Africa national frontiers and geographic boundaries were much less codified. Nowadays the perceptions of colonial boundaries of the people living in frontier areas are diversified; borders are subject to interpretation and cultural negotiation. Separations created by such colonial borders may not be perceived as permanent, people may feel linked beyond national frontiers, and boundaries may be created through the construction of cultural categories beyond geographical borders. Moreover, the very lines created by national frontiers may foster groupings of ethnic identity markers aggregated differently on each side, so that people can use opposite frontier areas to improve positively their own self-perception and self-esteem.

The Somali Zigula of the Juba River are one example of people who ignored modern national frontiers and regarded cultural similarities as more relevant to their identity.[1] Language and kinship criteria in particular could be manipulated and adapted for this purpose. This chapter describes some ways in which boundaries may not border on one another and can be culturally constructed. It understands frontier areas as locations where branches of 'positive identity' (Epstein 1983: 185) can be experienced and lived. Refugee camps and the status of refugee may be considered frontier areas both in geographical and in metaphorical terms.

During the 1980s, when I met the Somali Zigula along the Juba River in Somalia, it was quite common among them to be careful to maintain their own Bantu-based Zigula language which they regarded as a 'passport'. They were convinced that they would need to use it in case of emergency, should their situation become worse and, in their view, closer to the slavery they had escaped more than a century earlier. In fact, they perceived the increasing marginalization they had been suffering in Somalia since the mid-1970s, which was reversing the early positive integration following the 1969 revolution, as a process leading them towards a sort of renewed slavery. This fear was a consequence of the social stratification related to the slavery system of social organization and production which existed in Somalia whereby slaves were considered inferior to other individuals. Many former slaves and their descendants assimilated quickly to Somali society. They learned some Somali and adopted cultural features of the former 'masters' such as Islamic names and clan-belonging. Nonetheless, physical and cultural features such as curly hair (denominated *jareer*) and the 'broken' Somali spoken by many 'ex-slaves' (the Zigula term for this version of Somali is Mahaway) inevitably pointed to a past of slavery. People displaying these features were marginalized by most other Somalis. They were frequently insulted as *addoon* (i.e. slave) in daily interactions. For some ex-slaves and their descendants who kept their ancestors' language – Kizigula (a Bantu language) – it remained a memory (and reminder) of their 'free origin'. Those who could not trace such origins were considered 'lost people' who had no land to return to.

Language as a marker of freedom

Indeed, a number of slaves escaped or were freed at the turn of the twentieth century and went to live in Gosha area, a territory covered by forests stretching north along the Juba River starting approximately 70 kilometres from its estuary. At that time, the population in Gosha area ranged from 30,000 to 40,000 individuals who claimed a derivation of this kind (Crauford 1897: 57; Dundas 1893; Perducchi 1901). Many people, especially those who had been kidnapped when they were children or were born in slave's houses, did not speak any native Bantu language nor could they trace their genealogical trees to any communities of free groups either in Somalia or outside. These people were considered irrefutably slave descendants as they had lost all memory of their origins; the fact that they could not speak their original language was regarded as a proof of this. Frequently, these individuals were only able to trace their genealogies to the name of the families in which their ancestors served as slaves. They did not recall the names of earlier forefathers.

In this context knowing a language other than Somali was a marker of difference the Zigula of the Juba River were proud of showing. Having kept their Bantu language became an important sign of freedom in the light of the historical vicissitudes of the territories of the Juba River. Language as an important sign of freedom is stressed through the memories recalled in the performance of one ritual song of the Zigula's female initiation ritual *buinda*. The song refers to the Makua chief Mabuluko, who headed the Makua of the Juba River at the end of the nineteenth century and is remembered for not having sufficiently stressed the fact that the Makua people should continue speaking their own Bantu language. The song runs as follows (Declich, 2000: 103; 2002: 63–4): *Mabuluku tulia ikalamahali isingua iamuenye* (Mabuluko you must stop it, this country already has its master).

Whenever asked for an explanation of the words of the song, elders would say that the song reminds the audience not to act like Mabuluko. Abandoning their own Bantu language made the Makua 'slaves' of the Somali and no longer able to prove their origins. Interpretations of ritual songs are difficult since their meanings cannot be translated literally and are hidden in so-called *kufunda*, i.e. metaphorical verses. Yet, the historical events behind this song refer to the chief Maburuc Moro. He was one of the key people with whom the Italians signed agreements in Gosha.[2] Maburuc Moro progressively conveyed power to Somali speakers who, in this case, were the slavers or masters of slaves. At the time, concretely enforced national boundaries did not exist and colonial forces were basically trying to establish some sort of control of the territories in order to collect taxes from the people. The colonizers were mainly interested in controlling local trade, and their presence in the territory was not sufficient to maintain territorial boundaries. In such a framework, neglecting his own language, Mabuluko, was giving Somali speakers power over the territory and over his own Makua people. That is why the song states that the 'country already has its master' and that the chief should have stopped his policy.[3]

When I was in the field in Somalia in the mid-1980s discussions were still being held about the importance of preventing women from marrying outside the Zigula villages as their children would soon lose the Zigula language by living in neighbourhoods where only Mahaway was spoken. One case illustrates the negotiations which were ongoing at the time. A woman living in the village of Mugambo became fed up with her Zigula husband and started an affair with a man who spoke Mahaway and lived in a village some 25 kilometres from her own, near the little town of Jilib. She wanted to divorce her Zigula husband and marry her lover. The entire affair was seriously hampered when somebody informed the woman's father of her plans, which caused a sudden veto from the father, a veto that she could not break openly once it had been formally stated. Her plan was to get everything organized before her father could know what was about to happen and to face him with a divorce and remarriage which had already taken place. She had made many efforts to gain her brother's support for the entire operation. For his part, her brother did not agree with her decision and was worried about his sister marrying outside the Zigula-speaking area because, he said, 'once children are born in Mahaway-speaking villages they lose their origins.'

Boundaries within groups were therefore traced according to the ability to speak one or the other language. The resilience of the Kizigula-speakers was considered a good barrier against dissolution. Although such boundaries existed, they could be blurred in some cases: people, especially Mahaway-speakers who also had curly hair, could cross social boundaries and be included in the Zigula group if they had learnt Kizigula and lived among the Zigula for a long time. When such children were born in a Zigula-speaking context and, therefore, were well integrated in a Zigula village, they could easily be considered Zigula. There was great surprise and resentment against the Somali pastoral women who, having lived for decades in the Zigula community of Mugambo, betrayed the villagers when the war started in 1990/91. As the women knew the Somali language, they informed the Somali army and bandits about who were the rich Zigula and where they had escaped.

Claiming primacy through territorial ownership or by tracing genealogies?

Despite the importance of the spoken language as a sign of distinction, being able to attest one's own genealogy is regarded as a sort of basic identity card in the country which was called Somalia until 1990. Descendants of slaves, although they speak Somali as their first language, usually cannot prove long patrilineal genealogies as free people can. They are mistreated due to their origin. In fact, descendants and alleged descendants of slaves are among the most disregarded people in Somalia, together with individuals belonging to groups considered outcast (Midgaan, Ybir, etc.). This kind of social stratification has existed in Somalia for centuries.

The need to exhibit a consistent patrilineal genealogy to prove descent from free people seemed to embarrass the Zigula who also claimed a past as fierce warriors and later became trustworthy allies of the Somali during the struggle for independence of the Somali nation. They stated that they escaped from slavery, that they fought against slavers, that they constructed a community of free runaways along the Juba River and, finally, that they participated in the political movements which brought Somalia to independence in the 1960s as well as in the multi-party system set up in post-independence Somalia. Their wish to be freed from the stigma of slavery conflated in the construction of the then new Somali independent nation. A number of Zigula were members of the Somali Youth League (SYL) and participated in its election campaigns. One Zigula man, Mze Juma Mganga Mwaleni, was also elected. Yet, his administrative position in Jamaame town lasted only a short while; the 1969 army-led socialist revolution erased the democratically elected institutions.[4]

Besides preserving their language, the Zigula did know the place – Handeni – from where they had originated and where their relatives lived freely in so-called Uzigua, i.e. 'Zigulaland' (central-eastern Tanzania) until today. Zigula was spoken there as dominant language. Conscious of their heritage, many Zigula in Somalia tried to balance the need to prove their

Somali-ness by exhibiting a patrilineal genealogy etc. with their wish to keep their distinct culture as people who were not originally Somalis (Declich 2002: 64). For them their history and heritage testified to a past of victories in battles, brought to mind a hard-won freedom and clarified the fact that they had been able to reside in a territory over which they got control through their strength in battle.

Patrilineal genealogies versus matri-kin ritual naming system

The Zigula's embarrassment regarding the need to present long patrilineal genealogies in order to be considered free in Somalia was also related to a different system of naming used by the matrilineal Zigula people, which was not easy to understand in a context where the usual paradigm is patrilinearity. The naming system among the Zigula in Somalia includes an individual marker for the name of the mother's *kolwa*, i.e. mother's matrilineal ritual descent group. The Zigula of Tanzania also use their *isi* names, which point to the place where the kin grouping came from originally. This designation was rarely used in Somalia and in the 1980s not many people knew its meaning.

A Zigula person in Somalia is called by the name of her/his mother's *kolwa* – which is her/his own *kolwa* – the *kolwa* of the father in addition to his/her personal name, for instance, Mahmud or Khadija. In the first case, he/she would be called <*kolwa*> + Mahmud/Khadija and in the second case his/her name Mahmud/Khadija + <father's *kolwa*>. Another way of addressing an individual is to call him/her by <own name>+<father's own name>+<grandfather's *kolwa*>+<grand father's own name>. The first way of naming given here focuses on the matrilineal group and must be used when addressing an individual especially in front of his/her children. An important aspect of this naming system is that some individuals ended up being called mainly by the name of their *kolwa*, i.e. the *kolwa* of their maternal descent and remembered by it after death. Thus they left a memory of their matrilineal descent group rather than of themselves as individuals.[5] This entire system of naming was at odds with the Somali patrilineal Muslim naming system which instead adopts a common patrilineal pattern by naming people with their <own name> their <father's name> their <grandfather's name>.

Alternatively, the matrilineal system tends to forget individual ancestors through the mechanism of hiding them within the name of their *kolwa*, i.e. the matrilineal group name. For the patrilineal Somalis this is inconceivable: clearly remembered patrilineal genealogies indicate the present social position of people in the community. In many instances, to be able to refer to a well-defined genealogy – possibly reaching as far back as to some Kuraishitic ancestors[6] – is a mark of nobility. Consequently, within the community of non-Somali ethnics in Somalia the exhibition of a long and clear patrilineal genealogy is considered a marker of freedom and, therefore, a sign of high social status. In the case of the Zigula in Somalia their matri-kin-based naming system had become an obstacle to being recognized as free people: not only did they have to face and counter the stereotype physiognomy of an 'ugly slave' (curly hair and large nose) but they also had to defend their own system of naming, which followed a different kinship criterion from the Somali one. Zigula and other non-Somali groups increasingly adopted the Somali-Muslim way of naming along the patriline, at least in public contexts, in order to avoid embarrassing questions.

For instance, in the 1950s the elders belonging to the *wachina m'vamira* (*m'vamira* people), a specific *kolwa* among the Zigula, decided to start calling themselves in the Somali Muslim fashion and to inherit the *kolwa* of the patrilineal line. The new choice met the standards required in Somalia for recognition as people of a certain status. This, of course, also entailed accepting some implications concerning preferential marriages. Not least it created some confusion among Zigula speakers who did not know precisely how the naming system was organized or the choice made by the *wachina m'vamira*. A few decades later, when asked how their naming system worked, a number of younger Zigula people faced some difficulties explaining it.

Finally, to close the circle of finding ways to show their status of free people, in the late 1980s most Somali Zigula traced their genealogies through mother or father lines to early ancestors, either to the chief Mkomwa Mwaligo, the son of Mwaligo Mazali who came originally from outside Somalia, or to his wife Hawa Chikula, who also arrived from East Africa.[7] This was meant to clarify the fact that their original ancestors had come from much further away than those towns in Somalia from which the escaped slaves came, i.e. Merka, Brava, etc. Despite appearances, this system expresses a desire to be legitimate not as belonging to another country, but as being free Somalis in their own right and to be so by reason of having conquered a territory in battle.

Boundaries in a trans-local context: Refugees in Kenya and Tanzania

Following the onset of the civil war in 1990 many Somali Zigula escaped to Kenya and Tanzania together with the largest flow of refugees from Somalia. The first stop of the forced migration was often the refugee camps of Dadaab, in north-eastern Kenya. The surge of the civil war pushed the Somali Zigula to reconsider their old idea of using their Zigula language as a 'passport' in case of emergency in order to enter Tanzania. They mixed with other trans-frontier travellers and crossed the Kenya-Tanzania border without being stopped. Those who proceeded from

Somalia directly to Tanzania did it in the hope that they could find better conditions in a country where they knew the language and where they had relatives, in the wider sense. During the initial stages of the flow of refugees from Somalia, and in 1994, the refugee camps along the Kenya-Somalia border were the closest shelter to escape from the war: people could reach them by car from the town of Kismaayo and some also tried their chance on foot. Yet, the edges of the camps were still a target for bandit raids aimed at stealing the refugees' provisions.[8] Some sexual abuses were perpetrated against refugee women who went to fetch water (Musse Fowzia 1993; UNHCR 1993c).[9]

On 6 June 1992 a group of 140 Zigula escaping from the atrocities of the civil war in Somalia reached Tanzania via Mombasa-Tanga and went to the government officers of the Tanga Region.[10] The group asked the Tanga authorities to recognize them as legitimately Tanzanian, arguing that the Somali Zigula were descendants of the inhabitants of the region. The institutional answer from the Tanzanian government was to set up a refugee settlement in Mkuiu, a former National Service Camp 20 kilometres northwest of the main town of the Handeni district where the Tanzanian Zigula language is spoken. In July of the same year another 200 joined their countrymen at the settlement. In mid-October 1994 the Somali Zigula refugee coordinator counted 1,121 individuals living in Mkuiu.[11] Later, in mid-January 1996, the same source counted 3,717 refugees in the settlement.[12]

The entire case presents interesting facets. The Somali Zigula argument that they should be recognized as Tanzanian since they are Zigula whose ancestors originally had left the Handeni territory could not be accepted as such in a modern nation. And yet, part of the Somali Zigula negotiations with the Tanzanian government dealt with the fact that, as well as speaking the same language, the Somali and the Tanzanian Zigula have the same origins in terms of matrilineal grouping, the *kolwa*. Sharing the same *kolwa* kin groupings means 'coming from the same place', 'originating from the same mother' (*tombo*, i.e. the same breast), and therefore being 'brothers and sisters'. Among the Somali Zigula the *kolwa* groups were exogamous. A man and a woman belonging to the same *kolwa* were considered as son and daughter of the same mother, and therefore brother and sister, and their descendants were considered as having been nursed at the same breast. Indeed, several *kolwa* are the same in Somalia and Tanzania[13] and some *mviko* traditional rituals, i.e. the *chisasa* and the *ukala*, are also the same,[14] as the Somali Zigula discovered on their arrival in Handeni. These intimate aspects of the Zigula culture are almost unknown to outsiders: their knowledge cannot but reveal familiarity and commonality. Therefore, the desire of the Somali Zigula to achieve equal status within modern Somalia through the preservation of their language and origins became a concrete, not an ideal passport to Tanzania and, more than anything else, was a crucial factor for integration during their life in exile.

Unsurprisingly, this familiarity with certain ritual structures and the fact that the Zigula language had been spoken in Somalia for centuries predisposed the local population of Handeni positively towards this particular kind of *wakimbizi* (i.e. refugees in Kiswahili). Only later, in 2005 did the Tanzanian government start to offer citizenship to this group of people. Despite the several hundred kilometres which separated the Somali and Tanzanian borders (Kenya is in-between), the spoken language and the ritual knowledge became a very important marker of distinction testifying to the 'origins' of the Somali Zigula.

The border context of the refugee camps and freedom

In March 1994, according to UNHCR reports, the Somali 'Bantu' in the three camps close to Dadaab, in northern Kenya, numbered 10,143 individuals (UNHCR, 1993a; 1993b; 1994). They claimed origins from East Africa as follows: 26 per cent Zigula; 6 per cent Zalamo; 20 per cent Ngindo; 17 per cent Yao; 8 per cent Makua; 13 per cent Nyasa.[15] The United Nations officers did not indicate the language they spoke, but probably the Makua, the Zalamo and some Nyasa spoke Kizigula as this was the conformation in Somalia where, moreover, those who spoke Kizigula were by and large considered Zigula.

The initial impact of the very fact of living in the camps was quite amazing as regards their self-confidence as a group. In the camps most workers were Kenyans, who spoke Kiswahili and were obviously considered Kenyan citizens in their own right. Suddenly, these Zigula who had never travelled outside Somalia experienced the difference of being considered human beings equal to others. At least two people I knew from Somalia and who I met during a short trip to the Dadaab camps in 1994 came to tell me that, in these Kenyan refugee camps, where people with curly hair and large noses are the majority among the officers, they felt like 'real people'. They were grateful for this because finally the Somalis were kept at bay since they were in a foreign country. In particular, the security and police officers were Kenyans and the Zigula felt they showed them compassion and were ready to defend them in case of need in a way that they had never experienced before.

It must be remembered that in Somalia the police, even before the recent war, were particularly abusive towards the descendants of ex-slaves. During the 1970s and 1980s, for instance, several families farming along the Juba River lost their farms through trials in which false witnesses had been called to testify that they were not the traditional owners of the land. Later, when they complained to the police, they were put in jail instead of being protected. The police defended the rich Somalis who took over the land. The victims were even forced to pay a fine to be released from prison. Thus they lost their farms, the money of the fines, and confidence in themselves and in the protection of the state institutions. A number of other farmers were forced to accept selling rights to their land in order to avoid going to prison and losing money in seeking release.[16]

This case parallels those reported for the Middle Juba, where since 1975 – the year of the promulgation of the Land Law – much cultivable land was titled to politically well-connected people other than the traditional holders (Abyan 1986; Besteman 1996: 41–5; Declich 1988a; 1988b; 2002: 92). In other words, the process of applying land title registration which followed the promulgation of the Land Law in 1975 fostered a concentration of the land in the hands of people coming from outside the area, to the disadvantage of the riverine local small farmer. Moreover, the taxation system used during the socialist period pushed households towards claiming only one plot of land even where, traditionally, they ploughed more than one (Declich 1986; Menkhaus 1996: 138; Menkhaus and Craven 1996). And many adult women produced personally controlled income by working on plots of their own which were also not formally claimed (Declich 1997a). The tax records therefore did not reflect the real distribution and use of cultivable land among the peasants in the Middle Juba.

In general, most of the Zigula had never experienced being treated as equals before leaving Somalia. Once they had this chance in the refugee camps bordering Somalia a number of new options became available to them. Some families decided not to go back to Somalia and to settle in an area in Kenya where people with their same *kolwa* origins lived. One such man was Mohamed, a Shanbara Ngindo man who lived in the Somali village of Mareerey before the war. Had it not been for the war, he would not have left Somalia to look for Ngindo people in Kenya. I remember what he used to say in 1986: 'We very much like to live where our elders have been buried. We have been here for a long time and we like to stay here. This is why I shall not go to Kenya.'

However, the experience of being considered as humans equal to others raised a number of new expectations and aspirations among the Zigula Somali refugees. The Somali Bantu identity that would never have served to achieve anything 'good' before could now be put forward to seek for better conditions of life and individual recognition and legitimacy. On these terms, life in the refugee camps of Dadaab, though hard and difficult, opened up a number of opportunities, including a number of new 'capabilities'[17] for those Somali Bantu who spent time there in exile. Crossing the boundaries, in this case, and living in a camp on the border has been an extremely important experience which has unlocked a range of options that people did not even imagine possible before. Alternatively, however, the concrete means to obtain the new imagined possibilities of well-being are not always at hand within the camp.

The Tanzanian pan-Zigula movement and its impact on Somali Zigula

The interconnections between Somali and Tanzanian Zigula, though very rare and scattered, date a long way back, possibly to the nineteenth century (Cassanelli 1982, 1987; Grottanelli 1953; Kersten 1871). Some known contacts between the Zigula of the Juba River and the coast of East Africa at the end of the nineteenth century are represented in one oral account, among others.[18] The story goes that the Somali Zigula chief Mkomwa Mwaligo had a wife by the name of Masunya who was a traditional birth attendant. She was once called by an Indian man from Kismaayo to attend the delivery of his wife. The child died because of its position in the womb but the man accused Masunya of its death. The case was brought to court in Zanzibar in the time of Sultan Said Baragash. The court decided in favour of the midwife. The elders who accompanied the woman returned from Zanzibar with mango seeds and other goods in addition to receiving information about the existence of German Tanganyika.

A number of British Army *askaris* had remained along the Juba River during World War II and they interchanged information with the Somali Zigula about the political transformations in East Africa. Apparently, following a number of contacts, at the end of the war the Somali Zigula were offered transport back to Tanzania in British boats. However, they refused. The Zigula in Somalia had family roots and were settled on the very fertile land along the Juba River. Their family networks, at that point, were far more extended in Somalia than in Tanganyika. They therefore did not see good reasons not to remain in the area they were living in although they were located at the margins of Somali society, both geographically and metaphorically. A man from the Somali village of Moofi went to Handeni in the years shortly before Somalia's independence in 1960, in search of political connections and information, but did not stay and came back to Somalia.[19]

In Tanganyika a pan-Zigula movement followed a number of crucial steps. In 1928 the journal *Mambo Leo* mentioned that some Zigula were living on the Island of Witu. Later, in the mid-1930s, the same journal published two articles discussing the case of a Somali Zigula man, Abdalla bin Simba. This Zigula who was born in Somalia got his passport from the Italian administration in Kismaayo in 1932 to go and visit his relatives in Lamu. He later went to Tanga and told the story of the Somali Zigula to Sulemani Kiro, an important notable Zigula, later also made a Member of the British Empire (MBE).[20] Abdalla bin Simba's story was then reported in writing by Bakari Bin Mdoe of Handeni. The story of the Zigula people's arrival in the town of Brava from the coast of Pangani after being deceived, captured as slaves, and then escaped from slavery, was then published and became known publicly in Tanganyika. This kind of article published in newspapers nourished the rise of a pan-Zigula identity in Tanganyika.

In the 1940s a number of young Zigula from Tanganyika who had been educated in missionary schools decided to launch a movement called *Moyo Wazigula na Ngulu* ('Heart of the Zigula and the Ngulu'), whose aim was to awaken the people's consciousness against colonialism.[21] They claimed the union of the Zigula and the Ngulu with the people of Korogwe and the Usambara mountains as well. Later some Tanganyika Zigula intellectuals started publishing a newsletter.[22] The objective of the journal was to publicize development projects and other activities in the Handeni District and at the same time educate people to read and write Kiswahili. It should be noted that at the time classes in schools were conducted in English and the aim of spreading literacy in Kiswahili was somehow rebellious against British cultural colonization. Moreover, those who had been educated in the Christian schools had been prevented from attending traditional youth initiations[23] and were, instead, offered the chance to join Boy Scout groups. It comes as no surprise that literacy in Kiswahili sounded to them like a modernizing factor which, however, maintained the African character they felt they were missing. And yet this group of intellectuals cherished the idea of the union of the Zigula residing in different parts of East Africa.[24] They constructed the idea that the Zigula consist of several branches living in different countries but are, in fact, one family. At one point the newsletter published some articles concerning the Somali Zigula.[25] The leaders' Christian education provided imaginative suggestions from the Bible: the Zigula scattered in different countries were compared to the Jews dispersed in the diaspora.[26]

Sporadic exchanges between the leadership of the Somali Zigula and the Zigula in Tanganyika occurred after Abdalla Bin Simba's initial visit to Tanga in 1932. The leaders of the group had come to know of the Somali Zigula who had visited Tanga in the 1930s and apparently, according to some elders, sought them out in Somalia and invited two of them as guests in Handeni,[27] where they arranged for them to meet some pupils from the Anglican village school of Kindeleko.

After independence a Swahilization process took place in Tanganyika and public education in the Swahili language became compulsory. The former students of the Anglican schools of Handeni, who then became active teachers in the local schools, were proud of their Zigulaness. Times had changed and they now felt that spreading Swahilization among the Zigula could encourage the disappearance of some of their core cultural meanings. Inspired by this feeling, a book of proverbs in Zigula was published by a teacher who was also an Anglican priest and had previously worked on the newsletter of the Zigula movement.[28] In 1979 a study on 'The impact of Kiswahili language on ethnic languages: a case study from Handeni district' was produced as an MA dissertation at the University of Dar-es-Salaam. In this context, for the Tanzanian Zigula the existence of relatives in Somalia was considered as strengthening their ethnic feelings in the young nation. For the Somali Zigula such a long-distance connection had different aspects: it was a confirmation of their territorial origins to be claimed in case of need, as well as an option of good sites for future migrations. The large majority of them, however, opted for staying in Somalia, at the borders, enjoying the fertile land of the Juba River and only claiming the unity when needed or indispensable.

Several interchanges at a high institutional level took place between Somalia and Tanganyika/Tanzania in the 1960s and 1970s. A Somali Zigula born in the village of Moofi worked during that period as a journalist for Radio Mogadishu and participated in several official delegations between Somalia and Tanzania. He spent one year working at the Somali embassy in Dar-es-Salaam and was part of the elite group of 'intellectuals' who favoured for several years exchanges between the two countries. It is remembered by people who were present (Mze Mkomwa Mwechiwa Yerow and Mze Awes Jama Msami, chief archivist of the Somali Ministry of Education)[29] that Julius Nyerere, who was President of the Tanganyika Africa National Union at the time, was invited with other African delegations for the celebration of the independence of Somalia (after 1 July 1960). On that occasion he was asked to give a speech at the University Institute in Mogadishu founded by the Italians (it became the Somali National University in 1970), which was the only public university in the entire country back then. Before this meeting he was invited by a group of Somali Zigula as a guest at the home of a Somali Zigula military police captain who had the most modern home of all.[30] The Somali Zigula gathered at the meeting gave details of their origins from the Handeni area and Nyerere suggested participating in the activities for the independence of Somalia as well as getting Zigula students into the University Institute. One of Nyerere's secretaries was a Tanganyikan Zigula and this helped the exchange of ideas between Nyerere's delegation and the local Zigula. In his speech at the University Institute, Nyerere pointed out the importance of equality among people which was one of the aims of African independence, and stated that he wished the Somali Zigula, too, could benefit from a newly independent Somalia.

Pan-Zigula ideals continued to inspire movements in Tanzania, gaining renewed strength from the arrival of the Somali refugees in the mid-1990s. Recently two books (Nkondokaya 2003, 2004) were written by the son of a former teacher at the school in Kindeleko village, who held in high esteem the leaders of the early *Moyo Wazigula na Ngulu* movement. These books express strong pan-Zigula ideals, and trace the origins of the Zigula to biblical sources. The Tanzanian author claims common origins for Somali and Tanzanian Zigula, putting forward a number of different hypotheses concerning the origins of this entire linguistic group in Africa.

For the Somali Zigula, the creation of a written tradition about their origins was already a concern in the 1960s and '70s. A number of young Somali Zigula had been educated in Christian missionary schools and clearly understood the importance of possessing a written history. Several Zigula people living in villages such as Mugambo and Moofi in Somalia started collecting oral traditions from their elders. To my knowledge the only collective written work concerning Somali Zigula history was produced later, in 1999, during the civil war.[31] This work was partly realized under the umbrella of SAMO (Somali African Muki Organization) the political movement of the Somali agriculturalists which, among other things, fosters Zigula equal status with ethnic Somalis in Somalia. The manuscript is a vast cooperative work entirely in *Kizigula* which not only describes the origins of the Somali Zigula but also the history of the Lower Juba area during the last hundred and fifty years according to oral narratives. The second part of the document also reports the descent of the new leadership of the SAMO political movement. As previously, emphasis is placed on the Zigula's origins in Tanzania to testify legitimately to the free status of the Somali Zigula.

Due to the existing long-term cultural movement in Tanzania and the exchanges which occurred at a high institutional level between the Zigula leadership of both countries, it is clear that, when the Somali Zigula refugees arrived in Tanzania, they found a fertile cultural context to welcome their integration into that country. For some Tanzanian Zigula intellectuals their arrival was seen as a sign and public confirmation that the Zigula are a very large and important group spread over many parts of Africa. The influence of these intellectuals certainly facilitated the acceptance of the Somali Zigula refugees in the Handeni area and the entire process of their integration in Tanzania. Without family or sentimental motivations for claiming to belong to Handeni, the area is not particularly desirable: it has little fertile land, the rainfall is pretty unpredictable and the inhabitants therefore live a life of scarcity and are in permanent risk of drought crises.

On their side, the majority of the Somali Zigula chose to enjoy the privileges of this hospitality only following the persecution they were subjected to during the civil war. Had it not been for such an emergency, they would have stayed along the Juba, living separate from the Tanzanian Kizigula-speakers and using the argument of originating elsewhere to legitimize a higher position among the *jareer* within the Somali social stratification. Only a restricted number of mostly educated men decided to go and seek their chances in Tanzania when, in the 1970s, they experienced discrimination in accessing courses at the Somali National University (Declich 1997b).

Conclusion

Before the outbreak of the Somali civil war, the fact of having preserved their original Bantu language had the main implication of positioning the Somali Zigula group higher in the local social stratification as opposed to other alleged 'ex-slaves'. This helped the Zigula to establish boundaries between those whose ancestors never accepted their status as slaves and who actually escaped from slavery, and those whose ancestors were resigned to it. The latter were considered a less important category of people due to their scarce pride in their own group identity and minimal knowledge of their own ancestors, a viewpoint entailing an intrinsic assumption of the inferiority of slaves. However, for several decades the Zigula used this evidence to assert 'Somali-ness', in terms of belonging to the Somali nation, a country the Zigula had fought for before and after independence and where they would have liked to be recognized as equals. Based on such ideas of superiority, some Zigula men ended up in important positions in the Ministry of Education and in the army after independence and the military socialist revolution. The way the Zigula language has been maintained, as well as the way the patrilineal idiom has been embraced, shows clearly the embeddedness of the Somali Zigula in the power struggle over social stratification in Somalia which, apparently, they did not contest through direct opposition. The desire for inclusion and integration in the national boundaries of Somalia did not prevent them, however, from maintaining these internal boundaries which could provide an escape route to Tanzania in case of emergency. The Zigula language as well as certain kinship similarities became a tangible passport to a place safe from warfare.

For many Somali Zigula the stay in the refugee camps in both Tanzania and Kenya in the early 1990s opened up a number of different options. Achieving recognition among the Somali was no longer the only possibility for enjoying dignity in life and preserving their means of production. A certain 'ethnic freedom' was enjoyed in the camps. Zigula no longer needed to aspire to Somali-ness in order to be acceptable to their social/cultural environment. In this context boundaries were particularly useful for a twist in the identity perspective.

In Somalia the 'pure' Somalis – mostly members of nomadic clans – were considered the 'noble' people, whereas the Bantu-speakers were perceived as 'slaves'. Across the border, in Kenya, Somalis were a rather disregarded minority and were considered as *shifta*, i.e. bandits, who had been raiding this frontier area for decades. To sum up, people were enabled to play out the different aspects of their own identity by crossing borders, and this can be considered a positive aspect of living on this kind of frontier.

Once the Zigula had been pushed out of Somalia, the initial fact of having kept their language and of being able to speak Kizigula changed its meaning in the context of their exile in Tanzania. The wish of the Somali Zigula to be considered free met coincidentally with the claims of the past and with the modern local pan-Zigula movement. Since the Tanzanian Zigula are a large linguistic group in Tanzania, their interest lies, in part, in demonstrating the extent and the importance of the Zigula people not only in that country but all over East Africa. In this framework part of the Somali Zigula leadership/elite – being forced to settle in Tanzania – no longer need to fight for freedom, and their desire to participate in the power struggle has shifted towards supporting local negotiations among ethnicities in modern Tanzania. This does not prevent them, however, from seeking in Tanzania the enforcement of their new rights matured as refugees and, therefore, as people entitled to free education for their children and land to cultivate for subsistence, as well as food and food items offered by the aid agencies.

Strategies adopted in exile are complex and varied. Different personal choices can be involved which cannot be explored at length here.[32] It is important to notice, however, that not as many Somali Zigula as expected accepted Tanzanian citizenship when it was offered in 2005 by the government in Dar-es-Salaam. Some had already married and integrated with the families living around Handeni. A large number of those who had fallen ill, for instance, decided to go back and die in their home villages in Somalia. Those who most interest us are those who preferred to go back from Tanzania to the refugee camps in Kenya where they thought there were better opportunities for their future. Some of them thought that, being in Kenya, they could pursue their chance of the possibility of being resettled in the US, under the label of Somali Bantu. A large number moved from Chogo, the area allocated to the Somali Zigula for resettlement in Tanzania, to the Kenyan Kakuma refugee camp from where the first group of resettled people has left for the US. Some, however, had already made their choice for a number of other reasons, including that of living closer to their relatives who had remained behind in Somalia. Eventually, even fifteen years after the Somali Bantu were forced into exile, the frontier area of the refugee camps continues to attract people who believe that their main hopes lie in the continuously rising and shifting possibilities offered by the transitional context of the refugee camps.

Notes

1 This chapter is part of a larger study concerning the diaspora of the Bantu of the Juba River. It is based on several years of fieldwork carried out at different times. The initial research work in the field was carried out over two years between 1985 and 1988 along the Juba River in southern Somalia before the civil war and is the basis of my doctoral thesis. Thereafter, as people were forced flee from civil war, follow-up multi-sited fieldwork has been carried out since 1993. My research concentrated on different countries/locations where the Somali 'Bantu' from the Juba River had fled and been received as refugees, e.g., Kenya (the Dadaab refugee camps), Tanzania (refugee settlements at Mkuiu and Chogo as well as in Dar-es-Salaam), and the US (San Diego, California and Buffalo, New York). As some Kizigula-speakers were returning to their ancestors' land in the Handeni district of Tanzania, I could observe the way in which this 'historical' meeting between Zigula who had been 'separated' by slavery centuries ago took place. During the period of fieldwork since 1993, I managed to interview a number

of people whom I had known since the 1980s, and to follow their migratory path from Somalia to Dadaab, Mkuiu, Dar-es-Salaam and sometimes the USA. My work has been supported by various research funds over the years. I wish to thank the IFRA (French Institute for Research in Africa) of Nairobi, the post-doctoral scheme of the Istituto Universitario Orientale of Napoli, the World Bank, and the section of the University of Urbino COFIN. Research projects during the period 2002–6 have been financed by the Italian Ministry of Universities and Research.

2 Archivo Sterico del Ministero dell'Africa Italiana, Po. 55/6, Fasc. 42.

3 Ironically enough, those who designate themselves as Makua in Somalia nowadays speak the *zigula* language rather than the *mahaway* dialect, the *somali* or the *makua*.

4 Interviews with Juma Mganga Mwaleni, Mugambo (Somalia) 1988 and Mze Saladi Shebule, Dar-es-Salaam (Tanzania) 1994.

5 See for instance, Mze Zando who belonged to the Migwa *kolwa* and is almost always remembered as Mze Migwa (Declich 2000).

6 This means tracing back a genealogical tree up to the family of the Prophet Mohamed.

7 For this genealogical tree, see Declich (2002: 55).

8 Interviews with UNHCR officers and refugees in Dadaab camps (1994).

9 This was mentioned also in interviews with Zigula women in Dar-es-Salaam in 1996, and during collective interviews with some women in the Ifo refugee camp in 1994.

10 Tanganyika Christian Refugee Service, *Annual Report*, 1992, Lutheran World Federation, Tanzania and personal interviews with refugees, Mkuiu and Dar-es-Salaam 1994.

11 Omari Lugundi Muia, interview, 17 October 1994.

12 Omari Lugundi Muia, interview, 12 January 1996.

13 For instance the *m'baga, bena, bondo, chibindu, fimbo, handeni, m'honji, m'kumbi, lomwe, luhamba, miono, negero, m'panga, m'pembeni, samicri, m'sangazi, shangiro, m'vamira, mvuo, m'valeni, m'wenhumba, m'weruhanga, m'wesusa, m'wesuwa, m'wevuti* as mentioned in Grottanelli (1973).

14 The *mviko* in Gosha area of Somalia are ritual celebrations belonging to specific groups of people, usually sharing matrilineal ties, regarded as crucial to the fertility and the well-being of that group. The *chisasa* is one of the central celebrations of the Somali Zigula used to invoke the ancestors of an entire community. The *chisasa* performed by the Tanzanian Zigula is recognized by the Somali Zigula as being substantially the same as that they celebrated in Somalia. The *ukala* is a *mviko* performed by the men before they go hunting. In the Uzigua in Tanzania there are *ukala* celebrations whose songs are different from the Somali Zigula ones. Nevertheless, the Somali Zigula attending a *ukala* ceremony in Tanzania recognized it as the same kind of celebration. During fieldwork in Tanzania between 1993 and 1995 I participated together with Somali Zigula in both these *mviko* in Tanzania, during which I gathered the comments reported here. See also Grohs (1980).

15 Jacoub el Hillo, UNHCR Officer in Dar-es-Salaam, interview, 31 March 1994.

16 The source of this information is autobiographical material collected in the Lower Juba in 1988. Also Menkhaus presents some examples of the process in which smallholders were dispossessed of their land with no legitimate legal reasons (Menkhaus 1996: 134, 146–7).

17 This new trend of studies explores the potential of the apprehended or internalized 'capabilities' to achieve well-being and freedom to pursue well-being. See for this approach Sen (1994: 63–4; 1980; 1985a: 82; 1985b).

18 Mze Mkomwa Mwechiwa Yerow, interview, Dar-es-Salaam, 12 January 1996.

19 Mze Saladi Shebule, interview, Dar-es-Salaam, 31 October 1994.

20 Mze Muse Sulemani, Mze Hassani Kiro and Mze Reynolds Nkondokaya, interview, Kindeleko, 14 October 1994.

21 Father Zakayo Chabay, interview, Handeni, 28 October 1994.

22 Mze Mathiew Mgaza, co-editor of the newsletter, interview, 15 January 1996

23 Mze Reynold Nkondokaya, interview, Handeni, 1994.

24 Father Zakayo Chabay, interview, Handeni, November 1994.

25 Mze Mathiew Mgaza, co-editor of the newsletter, interview, 15 January 1996.

26 Father Zakayo Chabai, interview, Handeni, November 1994.

27 Mze Reynold Nkondokaya, Handeni, October 1994.

28 Compiled and published by Father Zakayo Chabai (1992).

29 Interview, Dar-es-Salaam, 13 January 1996 and Mogadishu, 1 August 1988, respectively.

30 Mze Mkomwa Mwechiwa Yerow, interview, Dar-es-Salaam, 13 January 1996.

31 Aweso Huseni Honero, Miyono Hasani Arbo Kazie, Huseini Mohamud Musa, Mwenkumbi Osmani Mhando Abhiro, Saladi Chivala Mhina, 'Zigula dya Kaidi Somaliya', Manuscript dated Mogadishu, 9 January 1999.

32 One essay concerning these issues entitled 'Seeking refuge and finding resettlement. The *diaspora* of the Somali "Bantu" of the Juba River: options and concerns' was presented in Helsinki at the 'Workshop of the Nordic Network: Diaspora and State Formation in the Horn of Africa' on 11–14 May 2006 and will be published in the subsequent proceedings. See also Declich (1997b).

References

Abyan, I.M. 1986. 'Development and Its Social Impact on the Local Communities in the Juba Valley'. in A. Puglielli (ed.), *Proceedings of the Third International Congress of Somali Studies*, Rome: Il Pensiero Scientifico Editore.

Archivo Storico del Ministero dell'Africa Italiana, Po. 55/6, Fasc. 42.

Aweso Huseni Honero, Miyono Hasani Arbo Kazie, Huseini Mohamud Musa, Mwenkumbi Osmani Mhando Abhiro and Saladi Chivala Mhina, 1999, *Zigula dya Kaidi Somaliya*, Mogadishu: Manuscript, January 1999.

Besteman, C. 1996. 'Local Land Use Strategies and Outsider Politics: Title Registration in the Middle Jubba Valley', in C. Besteman and L. Cassanelli (eds), *The Struggle for Land in Southern Somalia. The War behind the War*. London: Haan, pp. 29–46.

Cassanelli, L.V. 1982. *The Shaping of Somali Society. Reconstructing the History of a Pastoral People 1600-1900*. Philadelphia, PA: University of Pennsylvania Press.

—— 1987. 'Social Construction on the Somali Frontier: Bantu Former Slave Communities in the Nineteenth Century', in Igor Kopytoff (ed.) *The African Frontier: The Reproduction of Traditional African Societies*. Bloomington: Indiana University Press, pp. 216-238.

Crauford, C.H., 1897. 'Journeys in Wagosha and Beyond the Deshek Wamo'. *Geographical Journal* 6(57).

Declich, F. 1986. *Contributo allo studio sull'organizzazione femminile in rapporto alla divisione del lavoro tra i 'Goscia'. Tradizione e mutamento, il caso di Mareerey e zone limitrofe nel distretto di Gelib in Somalia*. Tesi di laurea in etnologia, Rome: Università di Roma 'La Sapienza', Facoltà di Lettere e Filosofia.

—— 1988a. Fieldnotes and interview in the Agricultural Office of Jilib.

—— 1988b. *Analisi di alcune storie di vita femminili raccolte tra gli Zigula somali* Tesi di perfezionamento in Metodologia della Ricerca Sociale, Rome: Università di Roma 'La Sapienza', Facoltà di Sociologia.

—— 1997a. 'Groups of Mutual Assistance: Masculine and Feminine Agricultural Work among Agriculturalists along the Juba River'. *Northeast African Studies* 4(3): 77-89.

—— 1997b. 'Migration, War and Adaptive Strategies: the Somali Zigula Migrants and Exiles in Tanzania'. Paper presented at the African Studies Centre, Evanston: Northwestern University, 27 February.

—— 2000. '"Gendered Narratives", History, and Identity: Two Centuries along the Juba River among the Zigula and Shanbara'. *History in Africa* 22: 93–122.

—— 2002. *I Bantu della Somalia. Etnogenesi e rituali mviko*. Milan: Franco Angeli.

Dundas, F.G. 1893. 'Expedition of the Rivers Tana and Juba'. *Scottish Geographical Magazine* 9(1): 13-126.

Epstein, A.L. 1983. *L'identità etnica. Tre studi sull'etnicità*. Turin: Loescher, orig. 1978, *Ethos and Identity. Three Studies in Ethnicity*. London: Tavistock Publications.

Father Zakayo Chabai 1992. *Simo, Njelo na ngano za kizigula*, Dar-es-Salaam: Printpak

Tanzania Limited.

Grohs, Elizabeth. 1980. *Kisazi, Referiten der Mädchen bei den Zigua und Ngulu Ost-Tanzanias*, Berlin: Dietrich Reimer Verlag.

Grottanelli, V.L. 1976. 'I Bantu del Giuba nelle tradizioni dei watzegua'. *Geographica Elvetica* 8: 249-260.

Horst, C. 2006. 'Buufis amongst Somalis in Dadaab: The transnational and historical logics behind resettlement dreams'. *Journal of Refugee Studies* 19(2): 143-157.

Kersten, O. (ed.) 1871. *Baron Claus von der Decken's Reisen in Ost-Afrika in den Jahren 1862 bis 1865*. Leipzig.

Menkhaus, K. 1996. 'From Feast to Famine: Land and the State in Somalia's Lower Jubba Valley', in C. Besteman and L. Cassanelli (eds.), *The Struggle for Land in Southern Somalia. The War behind the War*. London: Haan, pp. 133-154.

Menkhaus, K and K. Craven 1996. 'Land Alienation and the Imposition of State Farms in the Lower Jubba Valley', in C. Besteman and L. Cassanelli (eds.), *The Struggle for Land in Southern Somalia. The War behind the War*. London: Haan, pp. 155-178.

Musse, F. 1993. *Women Victims of Violence. Report on Refugee Camps in Kenya*. Nairobi: UNHCR.

Nkondokaya, V.G. 2003. *Makabila ya mkoa wa tangai kitabu cha pili. Asili ya waseuta yaani wazigua, wasambaa, wabondei, wakilindi na waluru*. Dar es Salaam: Chuo Kiku cha Dar es Salaam.

—— 2004. *Asili ya Waseuta. Yaani wazigua, wanguu, wasambaa, wabondei, wakilindi na waluvu*. Dar es Salaam: Peramiho Printing Press.

Perducchi, E. 1901. 'Statistica della Goscia, fatta sul luogo paese per paese'. October, Archivo Storico del Ministero dell'Africa Italiana, Pos. 68/2.

Sen, A.K. 1980. 'Equality of What?'. in Sterling McMurrin (ed.), *The Tanner Lectures on Human Values*. Salt Lake City, UT: University of Utah Press and Cambridge: Cambridge University Press, pp. 195-220.

—— 1985a. 'Well-being, Agency and Freedom: The Dewey Lectures 1984'. *Journal of Philosophy* 82(4): 169-221

—— 1985b. *Commodities and Capabilities*. Amsterdam: North-Holland.

—— 1994. *La diseguaglianza*. Bologna: Il Mulino.

UNHCR, 1993a. *Fact sheets*. Nairobi, 26 October.

—— 1993b. *Fact sheets*. Nairobi, 14 December.

—— 1993c. *Refugee Women Victims of Violence. A Special Project by UNHCR*. Nairobi: UNHCR, October.

—— 1994. *Fact sheets*. January.

Eleven

Conclusion
Putting back the Bigger Picture
CHRISTOPHER CLAPHAM

The detailed studies presented in this book have amply demonstrated that the state frontiers of the Horn, no matter how arbitrarily and indeed sometimes brutally they have been imposed, nonetheless provide a host of opportunities for the peoples who live on either side of them. Members of borderland communities travel one way or the other as smugglers or in order to swell the votes of their kinsfolk during elections on either side of the border. Guerrillas and clan-militias prepare for armed forays across frontiers in order to support their kin in power struggles against other groups, or weaken much hated authoritarian governments. Hoehne showed that in the contested borderlands between Somaliland and Puntland, Warsangeeli and Dhulbahante Somalis not only change allegiance between the two emerging state administrations, but may even turn up in high government office first on one side, then on the other – and, as Cedric Barnes makes clear, Somalis have been making use of these opportunities for a very long time. Refugees who cross the frontiers between Sudan and Ethiopia, Eritrea and Sudan, or Somalia and Kenya, find at least in their camps across the border conditions less intolerable than those they have felt obliged to leave behind, and gain some access to international humanitarian resources – even, in the case of the Somali/ Tanzanian Zigula, to a new national citizenship. The ubiquitous khat or *miraa* sneaks unstoppably across the borders that separate its producers from its consumers. Only the rigid highland frontier between Eritrea and Ethiopia, guarded by armies and landmines on either side, and until recently patrolled by United Nations peacekeeping forces, appears to correspond to the popular conception of a border as a barrier between peoples.

Much more often than commonly accepted, at least with regard to the Horn of Africa, borders appear to encourage more than they inhibit population movement, simply by creating different conditions on either side that foster the growth of not only 'arbitrage economies', but even – for voters, refugees, guerrillas and political entrepreneurs alike – 'arbitrage politics', which seeks to exploit the opportunities offered by divergent state systems.

This concluding discussion seeks to draw together some of the threads woven into the complex case studies already presented, and to use them to draw broader conclusions about the 'affordances' of state boundaries and borderlands in the Horn. In the process, it necessarily abandons the micro-level analysis consciously adopted in the earlier chapters, and – while continuing to emphasize the importance of the opportunities for local agency presented by boundaries – examines how these relate to macro-level processes of conflict and integration in this extremely distinctive part of Africa, and indeed to the relationship between the region and the globalized economy and political system of which it forms part.

One starting point for this quest lies in the recognition that 'borders' in the Horn are not only of recent, deliberate, or even human origin. This is an area obviously characterized by dramatic physical and ecological differences. Sometimes, as with the escarpment that marks the edge of the Great Rift, or the gorges that separate provinces in the Ethiopian and Eritrean highlands, these are indelibly imposed on the landscape, and on the consciousness of both indigenous inhabitants and external observers. Even where the gradations are more subtle, they nonetheless correspond to ecological zones, which permit different kinds of human settlement, promote different forms of indigenous economy, and are inhabited by peoples who distinguish themselves from their neighbours in terms of such markers as religion, language and ethnic consciousness. There is, in short, no Horn without borders, and no possibility of creating, even in the most idealized world, a seamless region whose peoples and ways of life merge imperceptibly into one another. Whatever the problems and opportunities created by state frontiers of the kind imposed since the late nineteenth century, these frontiers were imposed – sometimes broadly in corres-pondence with the ecological ones, much more often at variance from them – on peoples to whom the idea of a border was already thoroughly familiar.

Some of the cases with which we have been concerned in this book represent, in part at least, a modern form of cross-border transactions that derive as much from ecological as from political frontiers. This is most evidently the case with the Kenya-Somalia borderland examined by Lee Cassanelli, which of all the state frontiers examined in this book has generally been the least effectively policed, and the least affected, there-fore, by artificial differences between its two sides, of which local actors of one sort or another could take advantage. Though peace and prices in Kenya certainly make a difference, much of the trade in livestock and *miraa* across the frontier, and in animal and other products from the hinterland to the coast, little more than coincidentally crosses modern state boundaries, on one side of which there has in any event been no 'state' in any plausible sense of the word for nearly twenty years. Correspondingly, too, this zone provides a fertile seedbed for forms of economic management and integration that derive from local entrepreneurial flair and necessity, rather than from the kinds of state-directed economic 'development' that have generally had such a catastrophic impact on the region.

The Afar-Somali conflict zone assessed by Yasin Mohammed Yasin is likewise in essence an ancient form of conflict in the region, albeit now strongly influenced by modern boundaries and access to new resources derived from integration into the global system. It demonstrates the way in which the historic ebb and flow of expanding and retreating peoples across a fluid borderland has been affected by the imposition of the essentially stationary frontiers associated with the impact of 'modernity'. The frontier most immediately at stake is the internal division between Afar and Somali National Regional States, created only since 1991 by the system of ethnic federalism devised by the EPRDF regime in Ethiopia, and international boundaries come into play largely as a result of the resources which these provide for the rival nationalities engaged in intra-state conflict. Critical also to this case is the control over trade routes between the coast and the interior, which has provided a *leitmotiv* for regional politics since the earliest times, even though its importance has grown dramatically, both with the increasing integration of the region into the global economy, and with the imposition of state systems that – especially since Eritrean independence – have placed the coast and the interior under different and at times rival states.

The contrast between the most intense of these rivalries, that between Ethiopia and Eritrea, and the border between Kenya and Somalia, illustrates the extent to which the affordances of international frontiers depend on the interplay between the ways in which the differences between the states on either side of them actually matter, on the one hand, and the ways in which they can be subverted, on the other. The great majority of the opportunities examined in this book are created by this divergence. Where the border is virtually irrelevant, because there is no significant difference between conditions on either side, the opportunity to benefit from it disappears. Where it is so closely policed that interaction across it is virtually impossible, then the opportunities that it provides are in principle very great, but it is extremely difficult to profit from them. In the case of the Eritrea-Ethiopia frontier, the sole one in the region to which this applies, such opportunities appear to have accrued especially to the peacekeeping forces provided by the United Nations Mission to Eritrea and Ethiopia (UNMEE), whose members were accused, especially by the Eritrean government, of using their uniquely privileged position in relation to the border to smuggle people across it in one direction, and goods in the other. The key to borderland politics and economics, in short, is that all frontiers are partial frontiers, and it is by manipulating the particular differences to which each specific border gives rise that local entrepreneurs gain their opportunities for arbitrage.

The introductory chapter has already outlined some of the differences that matter most in this respect, including, for example, the degree of economic differentiation between states, the level of political marginalization between borderland peoples and central state governments, and the depth of political cleavages across frontiers. The opportunities for economic arbitrage are most clearly revealed by the three chapters – by Cassanelli, Fekadu and Wafula – that discuss Kenya's borderlands respectively with Somalia, Ethiopia and Uganda. Because it has had the most open and successful of the regional economies, while remaining politically on generally good terms with its neighbours, Kenya's role has been defined largely by its status as an economic hub, at least relatively unaffected by the intense political rivalries that have fractured the region as a whole. This has for the most part given the Kenyan state an interest in encouraging the flow of goods across its frontiers, especially when – as in the case of the Uganda frontier examined by Peter Wafula – conditions on the other side have made it advantageous to smuggle primary products into Kenya, and manufactured goods out of it.

Though Ethiopia's relations especially with its eastern neighbours, Eritrea, Djibouti and Somaliland, also have a significant economic element, this has been so overlaid by political issues as often to mask the economic factors involved. In the case of Eritrea and Ethiopia, especially, rivalries have been so intense that these have totally subordinated the opportunities for mutually beneficial economic relations, to the extent that the port of Assab in Eritrea has remained virtually closed for the last decade. Ethiopian resentment at what was perceived at least to be Eritrea's exploitation of its favoured position across Ethiopia's principal trade routes to the sea was indeed one factor that accounted for the bitterness of the war between them in 1998–2000.

War, obviously enough, creates the most extreme and often perverse affordances for borderland peoples, which are generally massively overlaid by the costs that it imposes on them. Wars in the Horn have generally been fought in the borderlands, and their consequences – the use of safe havens across the frontier, the arms trade, war profiteering, refugee flight, the destabilization of states by their neighbours – all illustrate the uses of frontiers for some actors, at no matter what cost to others. In a book devoted to exploring the opportunities provided by frontiers, it is understandable that war, though lurking in the background to many of the case studies, should not be their primary focus. In the case of other forms of political conflict, even those that sometimes erupt into violence, the trade-off between costs and benefits is rather more ambiguous; Hoehne shows, for example, how Harti borderlanders benefit but also suffer from their ambiguous position between Somaliland and Puntland. This book touches only incidentally on the dubious distinction that the Horn of Africa possesses as one of the main refugee-generating regions in the world, and on the long history of guerrilla insurgencies that have to a significant extent benefited from their ability to make use of borders – not only as refuges, but as conduits for humanitarian and military supplies, and the opportunities for maintaining diplomatic and publicity connections with the outside world. Though this neglect is more than adequately justified by the extensive literature already covering these subjects, it is at least open to question whether the eventual overthrow with the aid of borderland resources of regimes like that of Mengistu Haile-Maryam in Ethiopia eventually brought benefits to the peoples of the region sufficient to outweigh the suffering involved.

Critical for much of the politics of borderlands is the extremely rough-and-ready relationship between the position of the formal frontier and the territories associated with the various peoples who may live on either side of it, or both. Borders in the region run overwhelmingly through lowland areas, and have therefore for the most part had the greatest impact on pastoralist peoples. It is certainly no coincidence that the major exception to this rule, the highland border between Eritrea and Ethiopia created in its current form by Italian colonialism after 1890, has also been the most rigid and violent. Though pastoralist societies are characterized by endemic low-level violence, their low population density, high population mobility, and development of mechanisms for conflict management also help to keep this violence under control. Different lowland peoples may nonetheless stand to gain or lose from the particular relationships between frontiers and social groups resulting from the initially haphazard nature of the partition. Dereje Feyissa has shown how, in the Gambella salient of Ethiopian territory protruding into southern Sudan, the Nuer benefit from the fluidity of the border zone, whereas their rivals the Anywaa call for its rigidification. On the south-eastern borderlands of the Horn, correspondingly, the location of the formal frontiers helps to empower some Somali clan groups, and to disempower others. The boundaries of former British Somaliland, now resurrected as those of the still unrecognised Republic of Somaliland, help to define a state in which Isaaq Somalis possess an unshakeable demographic preponderance, a fact which at the same time generates instability especially in its eastern borderlands, where the same lines on the map divide the territories of the Warsangeeli and Dulbahante clans. The fact that Issa Somalis 'possess' a state in Djibouti, where they have achieved effective hegemony over the other indigenous group, the Afar, gives them a base from which to promote Issa interests in both Ethiopia and north-west Somaliland. In Ethiopia's Somali region, often referred to (especially by outsiders) as 'the Ogaden', boundaries likewise entrench Somalis of the Ogaden clan as the predominant force, against which other Somalis have to define their political stance. It is worth noting at this point that the nature of the Eritrea-Ethiopia border denies equivalent opportunities to the Kunama and the Irob, while, as Wolbert Smidt shows, the border has helped to define and reinforce the extremely complex and ambiguous relationships between Tigrinnya or Tegaru peoples, long closely linked to one another, speaking the same language and adhering to the same religion, on either side of it.

Both the boundary between Tigray and Eritrea, and that between

Somaliland and Somalia, were until 1991 no more than internal divisions within states, which although they originated from colonialism had been overlaid by the incorporation of Eritrea into Ethiopia, and the union of former British Somaliland with Somalia. Neither of which (even though the final status of Somaliland remains to be determined) survived the upheavals of later years. The Horn differs markedly from the rest of Africa, and much more closely resembles Europe, in the extent to which existing state frontiers can be challenged and changed. This gives a particular resonance to the one attempt that has been made in Africa, through the system of ethnic federalism introduced in Ethiopia after 1991, to reconstruct *internal* borders to correspond to the territories occupied by the various ethnic groups (or 'nationalities', the term derived from Soviet Marxism-Leninism that is normally used in Ethiopia). Since these are the only borders in the region that have explicitly been designed to reflect existing social divisions, rather than merely reflecting the arbitrary carve-up resulting from colonial (and also Ethiopian) conquest, they may well acquire a legitimacy denied to more arbitrary frontiers – in the process (as has happened in much of central Europe) forcibly separating people caught on the 'wrong' side of the border from resources on which they have long had claims.

That this division already creates its own affordances is made clear by Yasin's and Dereje's chapters, even though the Gambella case is anomalous in that this is one of the very few 'regional states' within federal Ethiopia that is defined by territory rather than ethnicity. Throughout Ethiopia's borderlands, from the Tigrinnya/Tegaru frontier through Afar and Somali territories to the Ethiopia-Kenya border and round to the frontier with Sudan, these internal boundaries affect relations between the peoples involved across the international frontier. In places, and notably in the Afar and Somali regions, they create at least the possibility that irredentist movements may seek to extend the principle that 'nationalities' are entitled to their own governments to their kinsfolk in other states. At the extreme, albeit an unlikely one, Ethiopia might follow the example of the former Soviet Union and Yugoslavia, in which administrative units that previously served as a basis for domestic government might fragment into separate independent states – a possibility explicitly allowed under the Ethiopian constitution – leading to a massive increase in the number and complexity of regional borders, each doubtless generating further affordances.

One striking feature of the borderland interactions examined in this book remains, nonetheless, their *instrumental* character. Wherever a border exists, opportunist entrepreneurs instantly seek to take advantage of it. But despite the utility of the border as an identity resource, as for example to those Anywaa who seek to present themselves as more Ethiopian than the Ethiopian state itself, it is difficult to discern any case in which borderland interactions create any shared identity or commitment that might acquire a legitimacy of its own, independent of the specific advantages that it

confers under the particular circumstances involved. To be sure, underlying social identities and cultural practices provide much of the currency
of borderland politics; but were the demographic situation of Anywaa and
Nuer in the Gambella salient to be reversed, for example, one could only
expect the Nuer to assume the postures currently associated with the
Anywaa, and vice-versa. Even where the border in its present form is
evidently disadvantageous to a particular group, as is most evidently the
case for the Afar, who are marginalized in all three of the states – Ethiopia,
Eritrea, and Djibouti – in which their people reside, it is difficult to discern
any substantial movement for Afar unity. Should the borders themselves
be moved, by some *deus ex machina* or stroke of the pen, then the cross-
border affordances that these papers have examples of would presumably
in each case simply be dissolved, and then reconstitute themselves along
the new frontier, wherever that happened to be placed. The one
borderland in which this does not appear to be the case is unsurprisingly
the Tigrinnya-Tegaru one, where, as Wolbert Smidt shows, differences
that in some degree go back into the pre-colonial past have been
reinforced by political conflict and divergent historical experiences, and
the linkages across the frontier are at the same time balanced by an
awareness of separation.

This in turn leads on to the most basic of the questions raised by this set
of studies. Do they really, as the introductory chapter suggests, demonstrate the 'positive' aspects of borders? Or are the interactions that we have
been examining merely compensatory mechanisms, devised in order to
rescue a few small consolation prizes from a territorial demarcation that is
on the whole deeply disadvantageous to most of those who are affected by
it? In the case of the economic resources created by the borderlands, the
answer is at least relatively clear. The interests of the vast majority of
producers and consumers in the region would generally best be served by
unrestricted trade, both within the region, and between it and the global
economy. The differences that cross-border trade seeks to arbitrage derive
from generally counter-productive attempts by governments to regulate
their domestic economies, which in turn enable smugglers to profit by
furnishing the benefits of the open market. Frontiers are evidently of
benefit to states, which seek to uphold them for precisely the reason that
smugglers subvert them – to extract resources from trade. But the
economic effects of this process are distorting, while the benefits of state
control for local populations are all too often chimerical. The disadvantages of misconceived state control are most intense on the Eritrea-
Ethiopia frontier, where it is extremely difficult for smugglers to operate at
all; but even where they are much more permeable, borders still impose
costs, which even the most efficient smuggling operations can only partly
diminish. Even where borderland communities themselves benefit from
the frontier, the costs frequently are disproportionately paid by peoples
further from the border. The basic economic argument for free trade
applies as much in the Horn as elsewhere.

The politics of borderlands, however, is much more problematic. There are, as has been argued, real boundaries in the Horn defined by ecological diversity and social difference, even though current political arrangements only very partially correspond to them. No attempt to impose any common political structure on the Horn has ever succeeded, and attempts even to maintain existing states have generally resulted in appalling levels of human suffering, as testified especially by the wars in Eritrea and southern Sudan, and the breakdown that accompanied the Siyad Barre regime's futile efforts to cling to a shell of statehood in Somalia. The region's dismal record as one of the world's major generators of refugees derives largely from levels of bad governance within states, against which the borders provide at least some safety net. The resulting political pressures have been overwhelmingly towards creating *more* boundaries in the region, whether by seeking to establish new sovereign states by splitting existing ones, as with the separation of Eritrea from Ethiopia and Somaliland from Somalia – and very possibly also southern Sudan from Sudan – or else by establishing new internal borders like those created by ethnic federalism in Ethiopia. It is hard to envisage this process of fragmentation being reversed, and the broad conclusion must be that borders in the Horn, while certainly not preventing conflict and often indeed helping to create it, are generally regarded in positive terms by those who have to live with them.

All the same, the emphasis in this book on the affordances created by the existing borders may well distract attention, not only from their negative impact on local populations, but also from alternative opportunities that are inhibited by the borders' existence. This is most evident in the Somali case, where border politics has operated very much in favour of interests defined by clan politics, and in opposition to any wider Somali identity. The one period in modern history when the whole Somali-inhabited area (apart from Djibouti) came under the control of a single power, in the aftermath of its conquest by British forces in 1941, is not now remembered as a time when Somalis were denied the opportunities presented by their former borders, but rather as one when the political arrangements encouraged the promotion of a sense of Somali unity, and led to the formation of a single nationalist party, the Somali Youth League, which provided the driving force for the subsequent programme of Somali unification. The attempt by the Union of Islamic Courts in 2006 to impose a common moral as well as political structure on a shattered Somali society, though certainly welcomed by many Somalis, rapidly foundered because it necessarily challenged the existing borders, and aroused the opposition of the United States (concerned primarily with the 'global war on terror'), of Ethiopia, and of locally-based Somali politicians who depended on a fragmented political order to maintain their own power; but the problems created for Somalis by the presence of borders, and the absence of political and moral order, remain as intense as ever. Though opportunities or affordances are certainly created by the existence of borders, alternative opportunities are likewise created by their absence or abolition. The Tigrinnya-Tegaru borderland provides another and very different case in which an alternative construction of borders could likewise have generated another and very possibly less damaging set of interactions.

For the peoples of the Horn, the borders are an inescapable fact of life. Borderlanders have seldom sought to change those borders, recognizing that they are in no position to do so, and that even the attempt would be extremely hazardous. Almost all of them far removed from centres of power, and obliged to make the best of the extremely fraught circumstances in which they seek to survive, they have instead accepted the borders, and responded to them with the resilience and ingenuity that the contributions to this book so strikingly and often movingly demonstrate. Whether, at the end of it all, their efforts really indicate the 'positive' aspects of the border, is a much more complex question.

Index

Index

Assab 85, 190
assimilation 16, 27, 29, 31
Astier Almedom 69
Aulad Ali 14
Aulihan sub-clan 143
Australia 34
Austria-Italy border 8
Awash Arba 91; river/valley 85, 86, 88, 90
Awdal region 85
Axmed 111-13

Babukusu 14, 151-5, 158-67 *passim*
Bach, D. 155, 161
Badime 69-71 *passim*, 79
Bagisu 14, 151-5, 158-67 *passim*
Baharasame sub-clan 110-11
Bahru Zewde 29, 30
Bale 87
banda 50
bandits 10, 56, 72, 133, 145, 146, 172, 175, 182
Bantu 17-18, 151; Somali *see* Zigula
Barnes, Chris 14-15, 88, 122-31, 187
Barre, Mohamed (Maxamed) Siyad 5, 16, 87, 88, 101-2, 111, 136-7, 142, 147, 194
Barth, Fredrick 10, 11, 56
Bassi, M. 46
Battera, F. 102
Baubock, R. 159
Baud, M. 1, 9, 12
Baydan, Bashiir Jaamac 113-14
belongingness 62, 66, 68, 70, 76-7, 79
Berbera 15, 100, 107, 134
Bereket Sim'on 77
Berhe Kahsay 72
Berlin (Congo) Conference 21
Besteman, C. 177
Bevin, Ernest 136
Bihidarays sub-clan 109
Bilen 64
Bo'ame declaration 112
Bonaya, Dr Godana 54, 55
Borama 128-30 *passim*
Borana 16, 45, 46, 48-56 *passim*; -Garri conflict 48; militia 54
borderlands/borderlanders 1, 2, 9-59, 97-9 *passim*, 103, 105, 112-17, 124-6, 133-67, 187-95 *passim; see also* opportunities
borderlessness 7-8, 188
borders 1-44, 68-79, 103-21, 133-55 *passim*, 160, 161, 166, 187-95 *see also individual entries*; 'bush' 115; colonial *see* colonialism; as constraints 1-8, 10, 11, 21, 22, 27; crossing 2, 8, 11, 12, 104-21, 133-55 *passim*, 159, 188; definition 1, 2; irrelevant 2, 4, 7-8, 189; strategic

significance 19, 22
boundaries, internal 37, 38, 68-79 *passim*, 137, 192, 194; international 8-11 *passim*, 17, 61-4, 116, 122, 133, 135, 152, 153, 155, 159, 166, 169-86 *passim*, 188
Britain 4-6 *passim*, 15, 27, 29-30, 37, 45, 53, 68, 99-101 *passim*, 106, 109, 115, 116, 122-31 *passim* 136, 138, 140, 156, 178, 194; Military Administration 123, 127, 130, 136, 140
British Somaliland 5, 14, 15, 87, 97-101 *passim*, 107, 122-31 *passim*, 191, 192; -Ethiopia border 14, 15, 122-31 *passim*; Monthly Intelligence Report 128; Protectorate Intelligence Report 130
brotherhood 75-7 *passim*
Burco 103-5 *passim*, 107
Buuhoodle 106, 113-15 *passim*, 117

Cabdi 105-9, 112, 113
Cabdillahi 113
Cabdiqani, *Garaad* 111, 112
Cabdiraxmaan, J. 102
calendars 46, 52n16, 55
Cali, *Garaad* 100, 119
Cali, *Suldaan* Yusuf 100
Cali Keenadiid, *Suldaan* Yusuf 100
camels 46, 50, 55, 137
Cassanelli, Lee 14, 99, 101, 133-50, 178, 188, 190
cattle 13, 31, 45, 139, 141-6 *passim*
Cayn region 113
Ceerigaabo 110
Chabal, P. 32
Chepkube 14, 163, 165
Christianity 65, 66
Cigaal, President Maxamed Ibraahim 108, 111, 112
Ciidanka Darawiishta 105, 108
Ciisa clan (see also Issa) 15, 19, 20, 85-94 *passim*, 102, 191
citizenship 9, 13, 15, 17, 33, 35, 39-40, 42, 50, 159, 183, 187
clans 50, 51, 98-9, 127, 130, 139, 141, 147, 191, 194 *see also individual entries*; conferences 102
Clapham, Christopher *ix, x*, 2, 12, 19, 156, 187-95
cleavage 19, 22, 78, 190
closure, border 8, 45, 53-4, 160
coffee 30, 164
cognitive differences 4, 20, 22
Collins, R. 27, 29, 38-9
colonialism 2-4 *passim*, 7, 16, 17, 19, 21, 29, 45, 70, 78, 97, 99-101, 106, 122-31,134, 135, 137-41, 144-7, 151-6 *passim*, 166,

Index

Index

Ityop'ya 66, 78
ivory 14, 29, 137, 138, 146
Iyob, Ruth 70

Jackson, R.H. 9
Jacquin-Berdal, D. 71
Jal, G. 28
James, Pastor 37
James, W. 47
jareer 17
Jeberti 65, 66
Jigjiga 127-30 *passim*
Jikaw 33
jobur 36
Johnson, D. 17, 29, 31
Juba river/valley 135-7 *passim*, 145, 169-70, 176-9 *passim*, 181
Jubaland 146; British 136, 138, 146

Kaahin, President Dahir Rayaale 103, 105, 109, 115, 116
Kakuma refugee camp 183
Kakwenzire, P. 126
Kapenguria 160
Kassam, A. 46, 55
Katzellenbogen, Simon 21
Kayier, Peter 40
Kearney, M. 2
Kelly, R. 29
Kemink, F. 75
Kenya 1, 2, 4, 6, 14, 16, 20, 42, 45, 46, 49, 51-4 *passim*, 56, 87-8, 93, 132-67 *passim*, 174, 176, 177, 182, 183, 188, 190; -Ethiopia border 15, 16, 48-59, 190, 192; Mau Mau rebellion 136; National Rainbow Coalition (NARCK) 54; Northern Frontier District 14, 135-8 *passim*, 140, 143, 144, 146, 147; Northern Peoples' United Association 51; -Somali border 14, 132-50, 187-90 *passim*; -Uganda border 14, 151-67 *passim*, 190; war with Somalia 2, 56, 87, with Uganda 6
Kenyatta, Jomo 155-7 *passim*, 160
kew 37, 38
kin/kinship 3, 31, 45-59, 76-7, 86, 92, 93, 145, 147, 159, 164, 169, 173-5 *passim*, 182, 187, 192
Kinissa 54
Kipande (Identity Card) 159
Kiro, Sulemani 178
Kismaayo 136-8 *passim*, 143, 144, 175; Port Project 137
Kiswahili 14, 18, 159, 166, 176, 179
Kizigula 170-2, 176, 181-3
Kittermaster, Harold 129-30

Kolia, S. 161, 164
Kolmodin, J.A. 73
Kolossov, V. 3, 7, 9, 16
kolwa 173-5 *passim*
Komo 32, 34
Krug, S. 72
Kunama 64, 191
Kurimoto, E. 31
Kymlicka, W. 39

Laascaanood 97, 103-15 *passim*
La Fontaine, J. 151
Laisamis 53
land 126-7, 160, 176-7, 183; grazing 86, 123, 126, 144
language 17-18, 46, 55, 65-7 *passim*, 69, 75-6, 151, 159, 169-76 *passim*, 181, 182, 188, 191
Lascelles 124
law 75; game/trophy 138; international 1, 21, 70; land 177
Legesse, A. 46
Lennon, John 60
Lewis, I.M. 4, 15, 85, 99, 101, 102, 126, 136
Liban, Ahmad 111
liberation movements/fronts 5, 6, 31, 50-3, 179
Libya-Egypt border 10, 14
licensing 138, 140; import 163
Lienhardt, G. 38
lineage system 29, 38, 76 *see also* descent
Little, P. 13-14, 134-5, 137, 144, 145, 147
livestock 13, 14, 50, 100, 133, 137-40, 142-7 *passim*, 188; Trans-JubaProject 137
Lwakhakha 14, 161, 163, 165

Mabuloko, chief 170-1
Machar, Riek 39
Magendo 14, 152, 161-7
Mahmoud, H.A. 2
Majangir 32, 34
Majeerteen 98, 100-2, 106-10 *passim*, 112, 114
Makila, F. 151
Makua 170-1, 176
Malaba 163, 165
Mambo Leo 178
Mamdani, M. 157
Mandera 46
Marcus, H.G. 122
Markakis, John *ix, x*, 2, 9, 15, 51, 89
markets 13, 144-8 *passim*
marginalization 2-3, 9, 14, 15, 17, 18, 21, 34, 40, 42, 99, 170, 190, 193
marriage 106, 114, 151, 171, 175; inter-ethnic 30-1

201

Index

Marsabit 45, 46, 52, 53
Mascarene Islands 143
Masunya 178
Matthies, V. 2, 5, 101
Maxamuud Garaad sub-clan 111
Mazrui, A.A. 156
Mburu, N. 136
McGrew, A. 8
Mdoe, Bakari Bin 178
Medhane, T. 31, 39
Meles Zenawi, President 77
Menelik II 99
Mengistu Haile-Maryam 191
Menkhaus, K. 17, 133, 137, 146, 177
Mereb, River 73, 75
Merera, G. 16
Meroni, *negus* 76
Meru 139-42 *passim*
Midgaan 172
migration/migrants 14, 27, 32-6 *passim*, 41, 65, 69, 86, 134, 143, 187
minorities 15, 18, 32, 34, 39, 43, 54
miraa (khat) 14, 133, 139-42, 145, 147, 187, 188
Mkuiu refugee camp 175
mobilization, kin 49, 50; political 13, 15, 19, 41, 43
Mogadishu 139, 142, 144, 145; University 180, 181
Mohamed Zubeir clan 143
Moofi 178, 180, 181
morality issues 162-3
Moyale 15, 45-53 *passim*
Moyo Wazigula na Ngulu 179, 180
Msami, Mze Awes Jama 180
Mugambo 171, 172, 181
multinational corporations 7, 158, 164
Munyanda, S. 164
Murunga, G.R. 134
Musse, Fowzia 175
Muuse, President Maxamuud Cadde 111
Mwaleni, Mze Juma Mganga 172
Mwaligo, Mkomwa 174, 178

9/11 6, 8
Nairobi 6, 140, 141; Eastleigh 142, 147
naming system/names 17-18, 63-7, 173-4; self-designation 63-7, 78
nation-building 153-4
nationalism 2, 4, 16, 19, 45, 51-3 *passim*, 87, 101, 114, 117, 154, 166
networks, credit 145; cross-border 14, 15, 41, 46, 49, 74, 162, 164; financial 133, 134; kin/friendship 30-1, 76-7, 92-4 *passim*, 145, 178; political 50; trade/ economic 14, 141, 142, 146, 162, 165,

166; social 15, 139
Newman, D. 7, 8
Ngindo 176, 177
NGOs 33, 99, 103, 114-15, 137
Ngulu 179
Nilotic groups 151
Nkondokaya, V.G. 180
nomads 2, 46, 104, 125, 182
North Horr 53
Nuer 15-17 *passim*, 19, 20, 27-44 *passim*, 191, 193; Jikany 27
Nugent, P. 1, 10-13 *passim*, 28, 43, 53, 154, 161, 162, 164
Nuur Axmed sub-clan 105, 109
Nyasa 176
Nyerere, Julius 156, 180
nyieya 38

OAU 115, 154-5, 160, 166
Oba, Gufu 45, 50, 51
Obote, Milton 155-7 *passim*
Ochwada, H. 156, 158, 165
O'Dowd, L. 11, 13
Ogadeen clan 100, 102, 191
Ogaden 5, 87, 101, 143, 144, 191; Ogaden war (1978-79) 5, 87, 101, 149
Ojo Olatunde, J.C.B. 153
Okoth, G.P. 153, 154, 160
'Oltre-Gruba' 135
Omot Agwa 38
Opamo Uchok 35
Opo 32, 34
opportunities 1, 9-13 *passim*, 20, 21, 27, 33-4, 69-70, 99, 133, 144, 146, 187-9 *passim*, 191, 192, 194-5
Oromia National Regional State 45-9 *passim*, 52-3, 55; -Somali conflict 47
Oromo 2, 16, 45-7 *passim*, 51, 52, 55, 56, 62, 65, 68, 135, 143; Liberation Front 16, 51-4 *passim*, 56; People's Democratic Organization 52
Oromo-ness 55
'outsiders' 33, 153
ownership 40, 48, 172-3

pan-Africanism 157; -East Africanism 158, 165; -Somalism 6, 87, 101; -Zigula 178-81
pastoralism 2, 4, 20, 38, 45, 48, 50, 86, 104, 125-7 *passim*, 135-6, 140, 143, 145, 191
pasture 86, 92, 100, 126
Pateman, R. 75
peace negotiations 102, 105; Somali Peace and Reconciliation Conference, 108
Pelkmans, M, 11

202

Index

Index

EASTERN AFRICAN STUDIES

These titles published in the United States and Canada by Ohio University Press

Revealing Prophets
Edited by DAVID M. ANDERSON
& DOUGLAS H. JOHNSON

*East African Expressions
of Christianity*
Edited by THOMAS SPEAR
& ISARIA N. KIMAMBO

The Poor Are Not Us
Edited by DAVID M. ANDERSON
& VIGDIS BROCH-DUE

Potent Brews
JUSTIN WILLIS

Swahili Origins
JAMES DE VERE ALLEN

Being Maasai
Edited by THOMAS SPEAR
& RICHARD WALLER

Jua Kali Kenya
KENNETH KING

Control & Crisis in Colonial Kenya
BRUCE BERMAN

Unhappy Valley
Book One: State & Class
Book Two: Violence
& Ethnicity
BRUCE BERMAN
& JOHN LONSDALE

Mau Mau from Below
GREET KERSHAW

*The Mau Mau War
in Perspective*
FRANK FUREDI

*Squatters & the Roots
of Mau Mau 1905–63*
TABITHA KANOGO

*Economic & Social Origins
of Mau Mau 1945–53*
DAVID W. THROUP

Multi-Party Politics in Kenya
DAVID W. THROUP
& CHARLES HORNSBY

Empire State-Building
JOANNA LEWIS

*Decolonization & Independence
in Kenya 1940–93*
Edited by B.A. OGOT
& WILLIAM R. OCHIENG'

Eroding the Commons
DAVID ANDERSON

Penetration & Protest in Tanzania
ISARIA N. KIMAMBO

Custodians of the Land
Edited by GREGORY MADDOX, JAMES
L. GIBLIN & ISARIA N. KIMAMBO

*Education in the Development
of Tanzania 1919–1990*
LENE BUCHERT

The Second Economy in Tanzania
T.L. MALIYAMKONO
& M.S.D. BAGACHWA

*Ecology Control & Economic Development
in East African History*
HELGE KJEKSHUS

Siaya
DAVID WILLIAM COHEN
& E.S. ATIENO ODHIAMBO

*Uganda Now • Changing Uganda
Developing Uganda • From Chaos to Order
Religion & Politics in East Africa*
Edited by HOLGER BERNT HANSEN
& MICHAEL TWADDLE

*Kakungulu & the Creation
of Uganda 1868–1928*
MICHAEL TWADDLE

Controlling Anger
SUZETTE HEALD

Kampala Women Getting By
SANDRA WALLMAN

Political Power in Pre-Colonial Buganda
RICHARD J. REID

Alice Lakwena & the Holy Spirits
HEIKE BEHREND

Slaves, Spices & Ivory in Zanzibar
ABDUL SHERIFF

Zanzibar Under Colonial Rule
Edited by ABDUL SHERIFF &
ED FERGUSON

*The History & Conservation of Zanzibar
Stone Town*
Edited by ABDUL SHERIFF

Pastimes & Politics
LAURA FAIR

*Ethnicity & Conflict in
the Horn of Africa*
Edited by KATSUYOSHI FUKUI
& JOHN MARKAKIS

*Conflict, Age & Power in
North East Africa*
Edited by EISEI KURIMOTO
& SIMON SIMONSE

*Property Rights & Political
Development in Ethiopia & Eritrea*
SANDRA FULLERTON JOIREMAN

Revolution & Religion in Ethiopia
ØYVIND M. EIDE

Brothers at War
TEKESTE NEGASH &
KJETIL TRONVOLL

From Guerrillas to Government
DAVID POOL

Mau Mau & Nationhood
Edited by E.S. ATIENO ODHIAMBO
& JOHN LONSDALE

*A History of Modern Ethiopia,
1855–1991*
(2nd edn) BAHRU ZEWDE
Pioneers of Change in Ethiopia
BAHRU ZEWDE

Remapping Ethiopia
Edited by W. JAMES, D. DONHAM,
E. KURIMOTO & A. TRIULZI

Southern Marches of Imperial Ethiopia
Edited by DONALD L. DONHAM
& WENDY JAMES

A Modern History of the Somali
(4th edn)
I.M. LEWIS

*Islands of Intensive Agriculture in
East Africa*
Edited by MATS WIDGREN
& JOHN E.G. SUTTON

Leaf of Allah
EZEKIEL GEBISSA

*Dhows & the Colonial Economy
of Zanzibar 1860–1970*
ERIK GILBERT

African Womanhood in Colonial Kenya
TABITHA KANOGO

African Underclass
ANDREW BURTON

In Search of a Nation
Edited by GREGORY H. MADDOX
& JAMES L. GIBLIN

A History of the Excluded
JAMES L. GIBLIN

Black Poachers, White Hunters
EDWARD I. STEINHART

Ethnic Federalism
DAVID TURTON

Crisis & Decline in Bunyoro
SHANE DOYLE

*Emancipation without Abolition in
German East Africa*
JAN-GEORG DEUTSCH

*Women, Work & Domestic
Virtue in Uganda 1900–2003*
GRACE BANTEBYA KYOMUHENDO &
MARJORIE KENISTON McINTOSH

Cultivating Success in Uganda
GRACE CARSWELL

*War in Pre-Colonial
Eastern Africa*
RICHARD REID

*Slavery in the Great Lakes Region
of East Africa*
Edited by HENRI MÉDARD &
SHANE DOYLE

The Benefits of Famine
DAVID KEEN